BORN INNOCENT

BY CREIGHTON BROWN BURNHAM

Made into a Really Major Motion Picture Starting Linda Blair

with ten screen shots from the movie

ISHI PRESS INTERNATIONAL

Born Innocent

by Creighton Brown Burnham

Made into a famous movie starring Linda Blair

with ten screen shots from the movie

First Published in 1958

Made into a motion picture in 1974

This Printing in December, 2012
by Ishi Press in New York and Tokyo
with a new introduction by Sam Sloan

ISBN 4-87187-613-6
978-4-87187-613-1

Ishi Press International
1664 Davidson Avenue, Suite 1B
Bronx NY 10453-7877
USA
samhsloan@gmail.com
1-917-507-7226
Printed in the United States of America

Born Innocent

by Creighton Brown Burnham

Made into a famous movie starring Linda Blair

Introduction by Sam Sloan

Born Innocent is a biographical account by the Superintendent of the Tecumseh Girls Reform School in Tecumseh, Oklahoma. It is now called the Central Oklahoma Juvenile Center. It used to be called Girls Town and various other names. It is an institution for disturbed teenaged girls. This place was recently in the news because of a violent outbreak similar to that depicted in the movie.

The book has only a small connection with the famous movie by the same name, expect that the credits in the movie say that it was suggested by the book. The book came out in 1958, the movie in 1974.

Outside of this book, there is little biographical information available about the author, except that she was born on January 19, 1885 and died in November 1966 in Oklahoma. Her parents were John F. Brown and Samantha Ann Baker.

The movie is considerably more famous than the book. The movie has caused tremendous outcries and court cases and has resulted in changes in the TV codes and obscenity laws.

The most horrific scene in the movie occurs when the 14-year-old protagonist played by famous actress Linda Blair arrives in the reform school for girls and is initiated by a lesbian gang rape in the shower where the handle of a toilet brush is pushed inside her vagina.

The public outcry occurred when this scene was shown on prime time TV. It was immediately pulled and has never been shown on TV again, not even on late night TV. Years later it was restored to the DVD version only.

Introduction by Sam Sloan

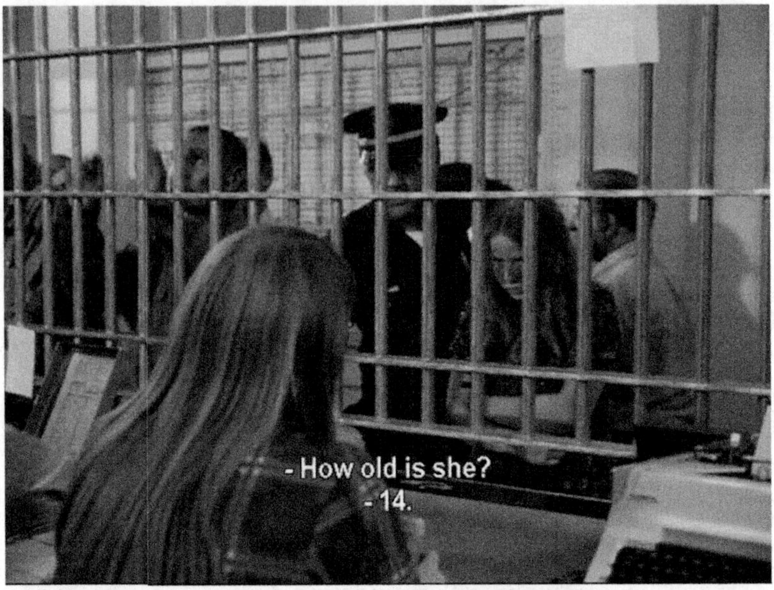

When brought into the prison system she is 14. The actress who played her really was 14 when this movie was made.

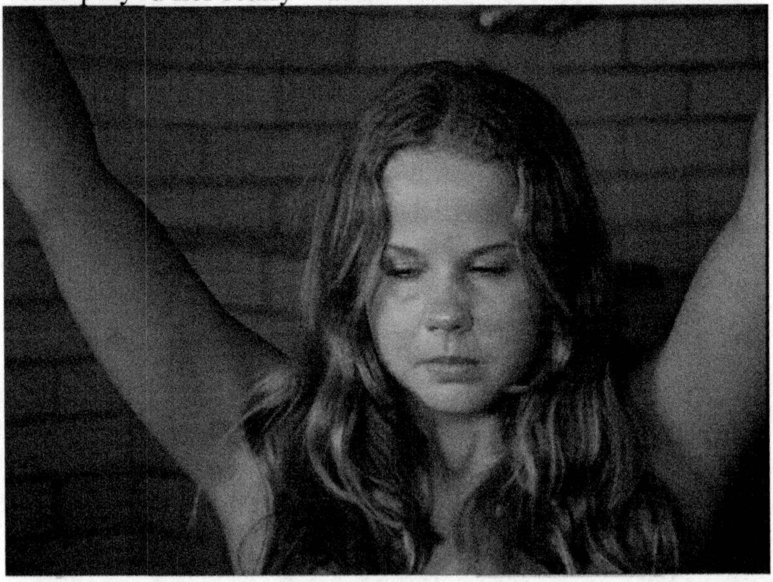

Linda Blair being strip searched while being brought into the Girls Reform School. It seems that the 14-year-old Linda really was naked for this scene. Nowadays they use body doubles.

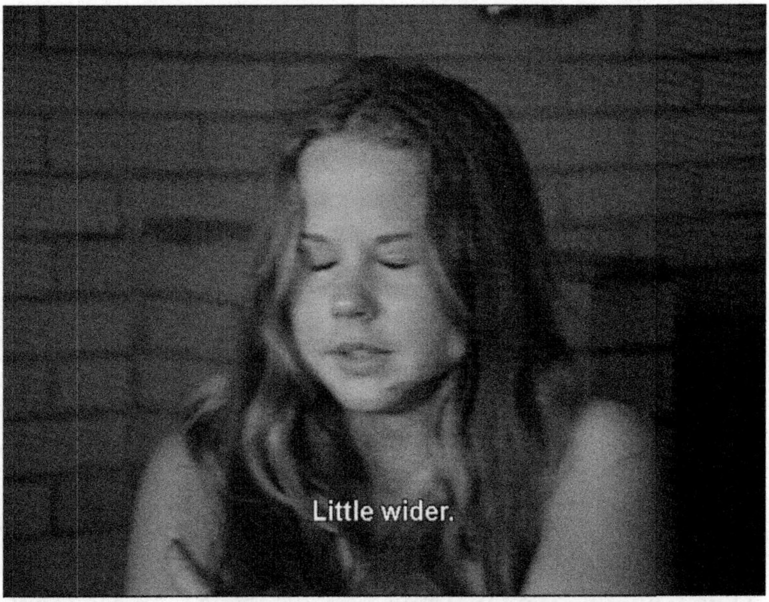

Linda is told to spread her legs "a little wider" while the prison official looks up her anus and vagina

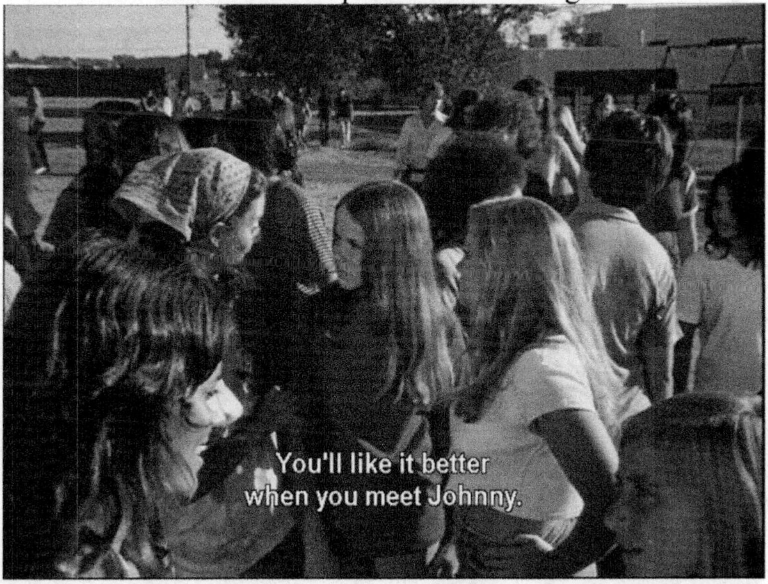

Linda is told, "You'll like it better when you meet Johnny". Then follows, "Yeah. He likes new girls". Turns out that "Johnny" is not a real human boy but is the toilet brush handle.

Introduction by Sam Sloan

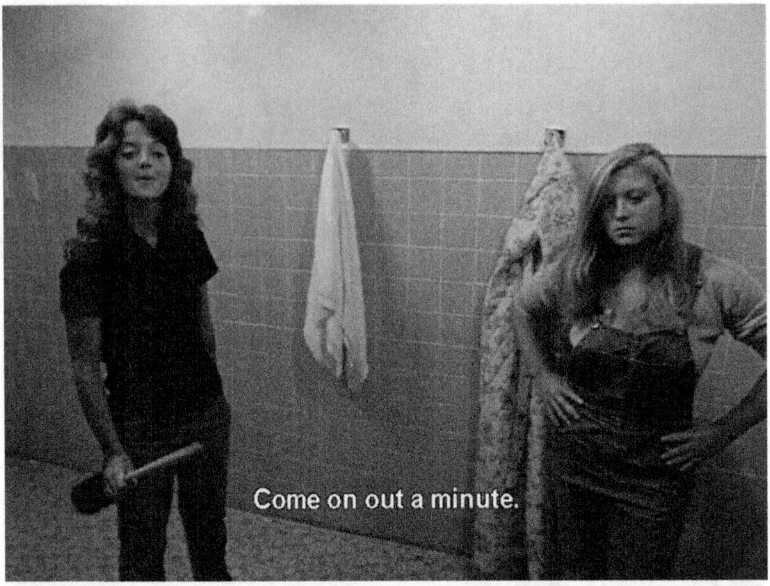

Denny holding the toilet brush handle waits with Moco for Linda to come out of the shower so she can jam the toilet brush handle into her vagina.

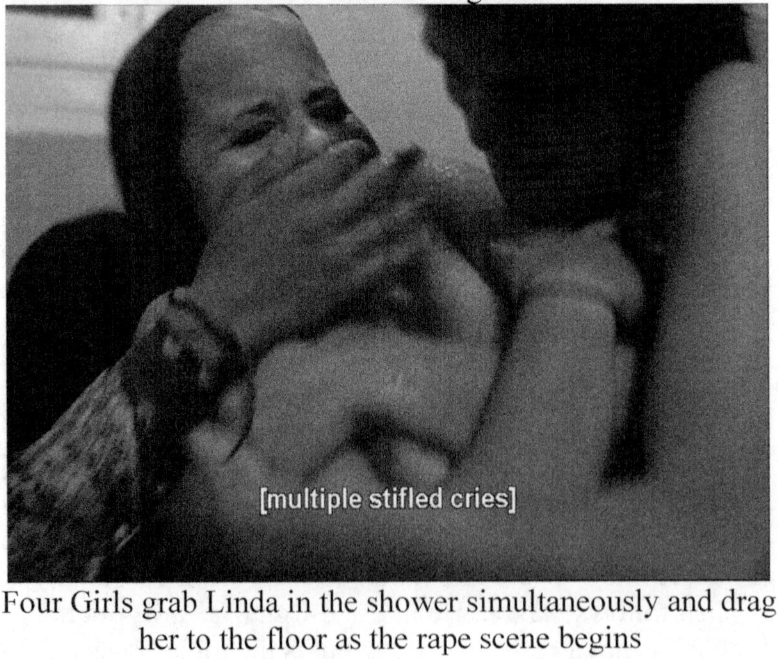

Four Girls grab Linda in the shower simultaneously and drag her to the floor as the rape scene begins

Introduction by Sam Sloan

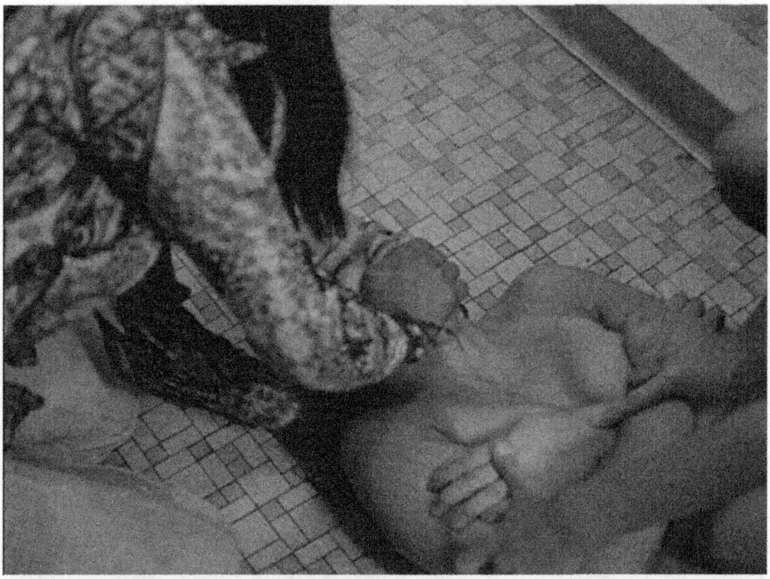

Here is Linda being held down while she is being raped. Yet, there is nothing obscene about this scene by modern standards.

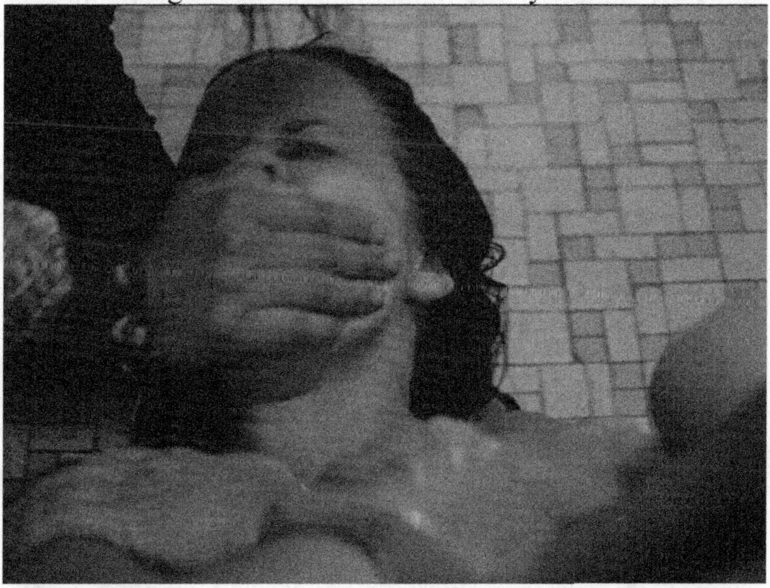

Here Linda is held and gagged while being raped

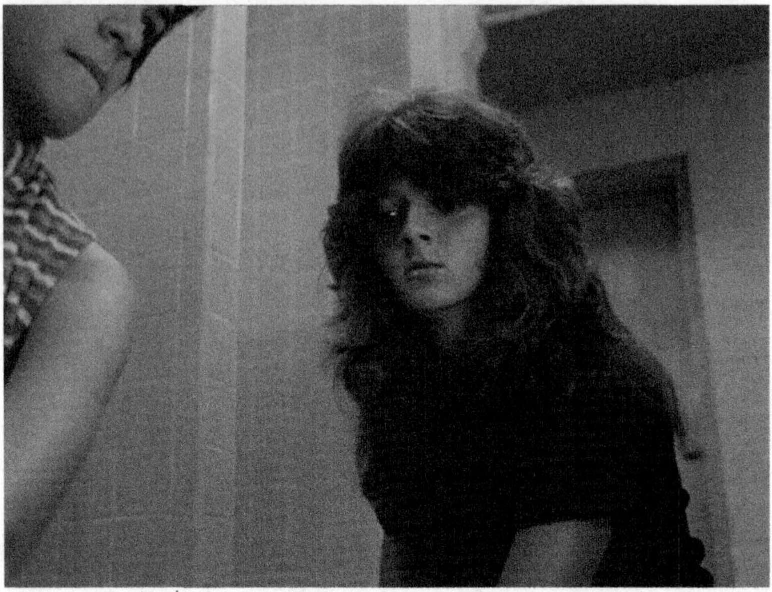

Here are the girls pushing the toilet brush handle inside her vagina. Again, there is nothing obscene about this picture. The scenes do not actually show anything. What is obscene is the context. You know from the dialog of the movie what is happening in the picture. Otherwise you would never know.

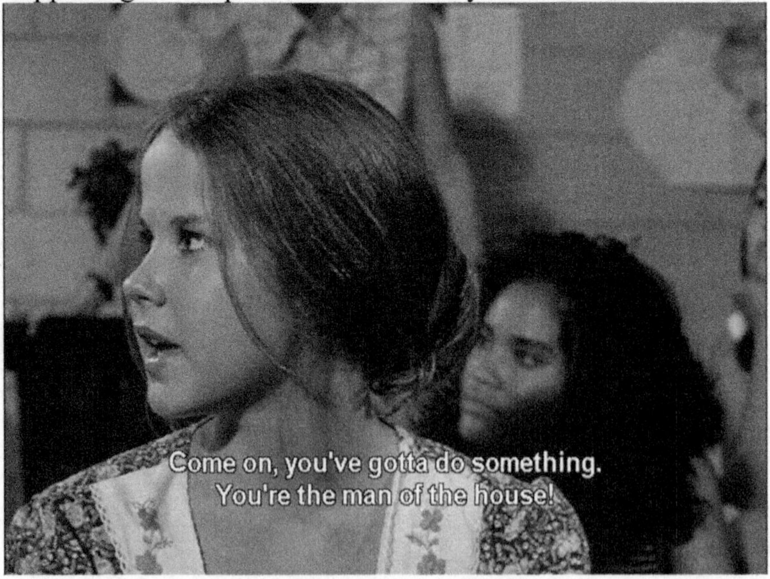

Introduction by Sam Sloan

Now the Rape is over and things are back to normal.
Linda sarcastically calls Moco "The Man of the House",
referring to the fact that Moco is a Lesbian bull dyke.

Almost everything about this scene pushes the edges of the obscenity laws. The girl being 14 and the real actress was also 14 is on the edges of the law. This movie could probably not be made nowadays. There are now laws against depicting underage children having sexual intercourse.

However, she is not really having sexual intercourse. She is merely having a toilet brush handle pushed inside her vagina. It can certainly be argued that having a toilet brush handle pushed inside your vagina does not depict sexual intercourse or indeed sex of any kind.

Sorry, guys! You will have to go elsewhere if you want to see a dirty movie.

Since then we have had the famous Lewinsky case where the President of the United States argued that the blow job that he received from Miss Lewinsky was not sexual intercourse. I happen to agree with the President. I think that a blow job is not sexual intercourse. However, a federal judge disagreed and ruled that it was sexual intercourse.

If a blow job is sexual intercourse, where do you draw the line? Is kissing sexual intercourse? Is a kiss on the cheek sexual intercourse. Is a hand shake sexual intercourse? According to my definition, sexual intercourse occurs when a penis is inside a vagina for reproductive purposes. If there is no penetration, there is no sex. When a condom is used, there is no sex. Otherwise, a doctor putting a thermometer inside a vagina is sexual intercourse.

Throughout the movie there are references to sexual type things, such as when the prison guard looks inside of Linda's vagina. Again, the movie does not actually show her looking. Rather, she tells Linda to spread apart a bit wider and then she comments "Girls sneak drugs in here any way they can, you know".

In the context you know that she has looked inside of Linda's anus and vagina even though the movie does not actually show it.

It must be hard to play a villain. Every thinking person knows that Linda Blair was not really possessed by the Devil. However, Nora Heflin who plays Moco, the main villain in the movie, probably has trouble convincing people that she is not really the hard-core lesbian bulldyke that she so effectively plays. Similarly the very pretty Janit Baldwin, who plays Denny, the lesbian who pushes the toilet brush handle into Linda's vagina, is probably not as evil in real life as she is depicted in the movie.

Some people get off too easy. The sentencing judge in the movie is just doing his job. However, we know that in real life some people who seek and get positions as juvenile court justices are actually evil monsters like Judge Lawrence Janow. These are people whom you would not want near your children, yet they have the power to commit criminal acts in the name of "justice".

Similar to the way that some gay men seek and obtain positions as Catholic priests because it places them in contact with young boys, some family court judges have a sadistic desire to destroy people's lives, and become judges for that reason.

I have personal experience because Charles Roberts kidnapped my daughter at age 8 and brought her to Virginia and my two sons, Michael and George, ages 7 and 5, were kidnapped by Rosemonde Pierre Louis and then transported from California to New York. These were obvious kidnappings, because

Introduction by Sam Sloan

Charles Roberts and Rosemonde Pierre Louis were not related in any way to my children and the children were carried across state lines. Yet they have never been prosecuted.

These kidnapers got away and none of these children were ever returned to their home states. Shamema never went back to New York. Michael and George never went back to California. The kidnappers have never been prosecuted and indeed Rosemonde Pierre-Louis was subsequently appointed Manhattan Deputy Borough President and is responsible for overseeing several of the borough's key initiatives. The lives of these children were messed up unalterably by these kidnappings. The kidnappers got away because they were personal friends of judges and influential politicians.

The problem nowadays is not abusive adults but abusive children. I know of one child who has had five adults arrested in separate incidents, even though the child has been diagnosed as schizophrenic. Nowadays, there is a "mandatory reporting" law. Every teacher and every nurse must pass a course in "mandatory reporting" in order to obtain employment. Nowadays, if a child comes to school with a scratch or an injury, the teacher may be required to report this to the law enforcement authorities and then the law enforcement authorities might be required to take action such as make arrest, even though they realize there is no basis to the claim.

The result will often be that parents are afraid to send their children to school.

Back in the old days, if a child misbehaved, the child would be spanked.

Nowadays, if a parent spanks a child, the parent is likely to be arrested.

Introduction by Sam Sloan

Parents have become afraid of their own children. The parents in the movie "**Born Innocent**" have assigned custody of the child to the state. Although the parents in this movie are bad, even good parents nowadays will give their children to the state because of the danger the uncontrollable child presents to the parents. We are not allowed to control our children any more.

Similarly, if a woman claims that she has been raped or even uses the word "rape" in any context, the police must make an arrest nowadays, even when it is obvious that the claim is false. This gives every woman in the world the power to have any man in the world arrested, even if the man can prove that he has never even met the woman.

The protagonist in "**Born Innocent**" whom I call Linda to avoid confusion, even though her screen name is Chris, is not a bad kid. She is a good kid with bad parents. However, her parents are far from the worst. Her father is temperamental and hits both his wife and his child. The mother does not know what to do about this and so she does nothing. The child understandably runs away. She has a brother, but the brother has a new wife and a newborn baby, so he cannot take care of her. Therefore, Linda must go to reform school.

Although Linda is not a bad kid, some of the other girls in reform school really are bad, especially the four lesbian girls who gang rape her with the toilet brush handle. After enduring the rape, Linda starts to become more like them. She sarcastically calls Moco "the man of the house", referring to her lesbianism.

We must feel sorry for poor Linda Blair for being forced to perform in this movie. Linda managed to get raped in almost every movie, except for The Exorcist, and, as a result, now the poor child is down to her last $16 million.

Introduction by Sam Sloan

There can be little doubt that most of the people who work in the courts and the juvenile justice system really do want to do the best they can for the kids. Many are religiously motivated. However, they also want to keep their jobs. Every person working in the system has to fear that a little mistake can cost them their job and their livelihood. For example, if there is a close question between letting a girl out or keeping her in reform school, probably the safest course is to keep her inside.

The judges are a different matter because they are immune from prosecution and cannot be fired. Nobody even dares to criticize them. Even politicians and presidents can say nothing negative about them, at least not in public. Again, in the Lewinsky Scandal there were many ridiculous decisions by judges. In any other so-called civilized country of the world, no such thing would have been allowed to happen. Here in the USA, our entire nation was held at bay for months and the end result was the president left office under a cloud and we got stuck with eight years of Bush.

Similarly, we have an absolute outright criminal, Judge Lawrence Janow, who was fond of having children kidnapped from other states and often did so. He is no longer a judge but he has never gone to prison where he belongs for his crimes. We just have to hope that he does not become a judge again. He surely would like to get his job back because nobody will hire him as a lawyer due to his notorious reputation. Even if not, we have to fear that somebody even worse than him might take his place.

Sam Sloan
Bronx New York
USA

December 23, 2012

This Was It!

**Tomorrow Morning at nine o'clock"
was only ten minutes away.**

Twenty hours ago I had been a contented vocal coach, complete with husband, home, college aged son, and cat. In less than a day, I'd acquired a new career, another way of life '. . . and two hundred seventy-six girls from the scrap heaps of society.

My home was up for sale . . .. my husband had offered to shift for himself until I got settled . . . my son was at school.

My car hummed down the long lonely road - a road which ended at an iron gate and an ironic sign: THE LANO OF BEGINNING AGAN." However, throughout the entire area, my destination was known simply as "The Reform School"

Everything had happened so fast in-the last few weeks. AII I remembered clearly was a voice of authority, "You'll start tomorrow morning at nine o'clock as superintendent at the State Industrial School for Delinquent Girls."

I slowed the car till it was merely creeping along. For the first time I fully realized that the next few years of my life belonged to two hundred seventy-six strangers.

"Girls – youngsters," I corrected myself. "All they need from me is a little help."

I stepped on the gas . . . now. speeding toward a full decade of daily crises.

Original Back Cover and Side Flaps

BORN INNOCENT
By CREIGHTON BROWN BURNHAM

A phone call in the night from the Governor-and within 24 hours Mrs. Burnham had left behind her life as a housewife and music teacher to super-intend nearly 300 defiant, desperate, misguided girls in the state industrial school.

Armed only with compassion, determination (and happily ignorant of what lay ahead) she was to live with crisis and danger for the next ten years. Her story is human drama at its most intense - of irresponsible adults and everyday mixed-up kids – all of then children who had been misguided and betrayed.

Among them were beautiful Vicky, a rebel with a high I. Q., who memorized Emily Post and the society pages of the newspaper and knew how to use them when she met the catch of the season. . . . . Ginger, the lovable firebrand, who arrived on her own and announced that she wanted to go to reform, and little Tootsie who preferred to swallowing buttons to serving them on – until she was given her first doll.

It is a story, too, of how an institution is run – of political pressure and public ignorance, of supervisors more delinquent than their charges, of staff rivalries and inadequate financies.

When Mrs. Burnham wanted to get attractive dresses for her girls and get rid of scratchy knee-length underwear and painful tourniquet-like stockings - she had to present her case to an all- male Board of Affairs. The chairman, who had no daughter of his own, was the first to explode when she presented the evidence: ". . . ! I don't blame them for being delinquent."

Original Back Cover and Side Flaps

Even the first mixed dance ever given at a girls reformatory became a subject of public controversy. But to girls who had never known social companionship with normal young men it was a revelation. One of them summed it up: "I had the best time last night I ever had in my life. And I didn't have a single thing to be ashamed of this morning."

It is a story of heartaches and wonderful triumphs. How did Mrs. Burnham handle such a job without experience? How did she deal simultaneously with political boards, epidemics of hysteria among the girls, supervisors who knew nothing about reform-but who knew the Senator personally? What has she to say about the problems of punishment and discipline in an institution?

Her story is unprecedented in its field - her theories are patterned after the master Christian: "Neither do I condemn thee. Go and sin no more."

". . a most important and significant addition to the study of the rapidly mounting problem of delinquency."

Raymond Gary
Governor of Oklahoma

To my dear friend

Elizabeth King Cowgill

with deep gratitude for her encouragement during the writing of this book.

If names of persons in this book bear any similarity to those of actual persons, the similarity is purely fortuitous.

1

This was it.

"Tomorrow morning at nine o'clock" was only ten minutes away.

Twenty hours ago I'd been a contented vocal coach, complete with husband, home, college-age son, and cat. In less than a day, I'd acquired a new career, another way of life . . . and two hundred seventy-six girls from the scrap heaps of society.

My home was up for sale . . . my husband had offered to shift for himself until I got settled . . . my son was at school . . . and I'd even been asked to leave my beloved cat behind.

Traffic was light and I had lots to think about. Without much help from me, my car hummed down the long lonely road—a road which ended at an iron gate and an ironic sign: "THE LAND OF BEGINNING AGAIN." However, in Tecumseh itself, and throughout that entire area of Oklahoma, my destination was known simply as "The Reform School."

A million questions churned in my mind, but first and fore-

most I had to figure out exactly how, where, when, and why I had become so involved. Everything had happened too fast in the last few weeks for any kind of reflection. About all I remembered clearly was the voice of my friend, a psychologist for the State. As usual, we were off on a favorite subject— The State Industrial School for Girls—and, as usual, I was airing my vehement, if untutored, views. He broke in.

"How would you like to be Superintendent?"

At first I thought he was rebuking me for running off at the mouth. When he repeated the question, of course I thought he was joking . . . even when he insisted that the Governor of Oklahoma, a mutual friend, would approve. I laughed off the suggestion, but he'd planted a seed that wanted to sprout.

After that, the memories run into and lap over each other like a too-wet water color. A rising intensity of interest . . . an accidental encounter with the Governor . . . many attempts to argue myself out of the arena . . . many efforts to "unsell" myself to the political powers . . . the secret, growing conviction that I could do the job . . . yesterday's introduction to the Board of Affairs . . . my numb acceptance of the commission . . . and another voice saying, "You start tomorrow morning at nine o'clock."

I slowed the car till it was merely creeping along. Every turn of the wheels put that much more distance between me and all that I loved. It was a disquieting thought. For the first time I fully realized that the next few years of my life belonged to two hundred seventy-six strangers.

"Girls—youngsters," I corrected myself. "All they need from me is a little help."

I stepped on the gas, happily unaware of the fact that I was now speeding toward a full decade of daily crisis with a grand total of fifteen hundred drunks, prostitutes, drug addicts, homosexuals, compulsive liars, thieves, homicidal psychotics, innocent victims of society, and plenty of just plain old-fashioned mixed-up kids.

This was it.

I drove through a wide gate, pulled up at a sign marked "Office," and turned off the ignition. Before me lay the institution my friend, the psychologist, had given such a big build-up. One hundred sixty acres of rolling pasture land and deep ravines. A high wire fence enclosing ten acres just inside the gate. On these ten acres, twenty-two square, one-story structures. The red-brick buildings rose from dead winter grass, their stark outlines grim against a dull slate sky.

No living thing was in sight.

As I climbed out of the car, I knew exactly how small David felt as he faced Goliath. My slingshot was zeal . . . my missiles were hope. I could only pray that the Lord would help me hit the mark.

I opened the office door and stood waiting. After a quick look around, the short plump woman inside continued to drag records out of a filing cabinet in the far corner of the room. Drawers banged and papers crackled under her hasty fingers.

I said, "Good morning," as pleasantly as I could to her belligerent back. "I'm the new Superintendent. May I come in?"

"Oh, you're here, are you?" The lady whirled around and files flew. "Well, let me tell you, I don't appreciate this one bit. They might have given me two weeks' notice at least. The first I knew, I heard it on the radio last night. They might have . . ."

The tirade that followed consigned the Governor, his aides, and me to a special sort of limbo. Though awed by the sheer non-stop energy of the woman, I managed to cut in. "Since you're busy here, I'll just get my things unpacked if you'll tell me where to go."

"You can't go to the apartment," she sputtered. "My things are still there."

I tried for a truce. "Well, then, if you'll let someone show me around, I'll take a look at the institution."

"Everybody's busy," she snapped. "If you want to see it, go look at it."

I went and I looked. But my eyes were still glazed and my ears still buzzed from that unexpected reception. An occasional employee wandered across my immediate line of vision, eyed me curiously, and scuttled away.

I drifted back to the office, hoping to find it ready for my occupancy. My predecessor was, as before, furiously tying up her left-over loose ends. I spoke from a safe distance. "Are my rooms ready yet? I'd like to move in."

"No," the lady said flatly. "I haven't vacated yet. I'm through here, though." She threw a ring of keys clear across the room. "I guess you'll be wanting these."

The keys had struck the side of my foot, scarring my shoe. I picked them up, not trusting myself to speak, and stepped aside as she swept through the door. Red-faced, in a nondescript crepe dress and with an outrageously scarlet and orange scarf tied gypsy fashion around her head, she was a ludicrous sight. Much to my surprise, I felt a quick surge of pity on the heels of laughter. All other considerations aside, she was an aging woman who had lost her job.

The peal of a bell halted her dramatic departure. This complication confused the lady to such an extent that she was almost polite to me. "That was the dinner bell," she called over her shoulder. "I guess you'd better come on."

We entered the dining hall together and took seats at the head of a long table reserved for teachers and office staff. The food was adequate and I was hungry, but my throat closed in the clammy atmosphere. The officers barely acknowledged my presence and lapsed into silence broken only by the sounds of eating.

As the meal moved to a close, the girls methodically sopped up their gravy with slices of whole-wheat bread and then sat back in their chairs, waiting to be dismissed. They seemed quiet and very well behaved. The retiring Superintendent waited until all attention was centered on her for the dismissal signal, and then rose tremblingly to her feet.

"My dear children and staff members," she quavered tearfully. "They're making me leave you. *This*," she jerked her head in my direction, "is your new Superintendent."

The group of girls facing me broke into horrendous groans that sounded more animal than human. With a twitch of fear, I remembered newspaper stories about certain uncontrollable delinquents—and here I was, surrounded by several hundred of them. Could this be the beginning of a mass uprising? A riot, maybe? In spite of the cold chill gripping me, I set my face in a smile. My nemesis spoke again.

"This meal is the very—the very last one," her voice broke pathetically, "that I'll ever—ever— Oh! I can't stand it! I can't stand it!" She burst into tears and ran from the room. One hand covered her streaming eyes as she waved farewell with the other.

As if on cue, every girl in the room exploded in a noisy upheaval of emotion. Guttural moans of grief burst from two hundred seventy-six young throats. I was too stunned to move.

I'd been mourning my own loss and feeling rather noble about my "sacrifice" on behalf of these youngsters. It hadn't occurred to me that the girls might not want what I hoped I had to offer. They'd obviously taken an instant and all-embracing dislike to me. I gazed in horror at a sea of faces screwed into contortions and grimaces of pain. They were quickly and surely working themselves into a wildly hysterical state.

"Somebody's got to stop this," I said to myself. Suddenly I realized the job was mine!

I glanced at my fellow-officers. They stared ahead—stolid as statues—but nervous fingers and tight-set mouth muscles gave them away. It was my move. What I did now would determine whether they followed me or fought me.

I felt the drama of the moment even as I despaired of averting disaster. The girls were already out of control. Probably nothing short of a strong-arm squad or a medical corps could calm them down. The small bell near my dinner plate looked about as useful to me as a Flit gun against a grizzly bear. Having nothing else, however, I tapped it. The howling stopped in mid-scream. The tears dried up like dew in the desert. I must have pushed the bell again because the girls obeyed the dismissal signal without a backward glance. The uproar had merely been a polite gesture of regret in honor of a departing official.

The wooden dining hall trembled rhythmically as the girls marched out in a straggly double line. As they filed by my table, I pasted the smile on again and tried to provoke some response. They reacted by turning their heads away and pulling up dress collars to hide their faces.

Only a few were curious enough to peek sly-eyed at me. I tried to believe that I saw some faint glints of approval, but the truth is, they expressed no emotion at all. The blankness terrified me more than their previous ravings.

That gloomy luncheon, climaxing a long morning of rebuffs, was one of the low spots of my life. Dozens of newly appointed State officials were settling into strange jobs, and I wondered if all of us were receiving the same sort of dubious welcome. I sincerely hoped that I was the exception.

Although my spirits were at half-mast, I still had some ballast aboard. After all, important and intelligent people had sent me to Tecumseh. If they believed I could do some good, I probably could! As my courage seeped back, my sympathy grew for the Superintendent I was dispossessing. I was taking over her apartment, her authority—her very place in the world.

Realizing this, it seemed that she should at least receive some token expression of gratitude. Surely there was some work she had done well. I immediately called a florist and had a dozen red roses sent to her room with my card. Sometime later I learned that they had arrived just as she was saying her final farewells—and advising her "honor" girls to ignore my leadership because I wore pendant earrings and so was bound to be a bad influence!

Four o'clock arrived before I was notified that the apartment was available. As I climbed into my car outside the office, a State car pulled up beside me. From her seat beside the driver, my ex-Superintendent friend waved imperiously for me to stop.

"Yes," I inquired courteously.

The lady never said a word. With my roses clutched to her breast, she gazed at me piercingly for a long long moment. Then, still silent, she motioned the driver to proceed. Thus the mantle of the chief settled on my shoulders. I hadn't expected it to be the mantle of Elijah, but I did wish it had borne less resemblance to a hair shirt.

The reception committee at my residence quarters consisted of one bulky and uncommunicative girl who was leaving as I entered. She pointed out my rooms with a stubby index finger, flung my luggage casually into a corner, and went away as quickly as she could. I stood alone in the middle of the living room and looked around at what I would now call home.

I saw two large rooms, two little ones, and a bath. My grand piano would fill one of the smaller rooms. The other was barely large enough to hold a bed. There were no closets. The good-sized living room opened into a charming sunroom. A wood-burning fireplace was set into one wall, and I was delighted to see that the other three walls consisted almost entirely of long wonderful windows. Then I pulled the drapes.

The east windows provided a close-up of the laundry and drying yard where shapeless blue garments flapped dejectedly in the breeze. The south windows overlooked the blank brick walls of the power house, a portion of the chicken runs, and some frame garages sadly in need of paint. The west windows commanded a view of the detention wing of the hospital and were almost within arm's reach of "Meditation"—a small building discreetly hidden behind a high lattice fence. In less euphemistic language, Meditation was a three-celled jail.

My living room opened off a large general staff reception room; six small cubicles and the one bath provided for the teachers were all in close proximity. Early mornings were punctuated by the slamming of bedroom doors and the bitter complaints of late risers who paced the communal hall, towels over arms, waiting for a turn at the sink and other facilities before the seven-thirty breakfast call.

Wide double doors made of mirror panes separated my living room from the main reception room. The first few times I passed them on the trip between my bedroom and bath, I scurried back with the alarmed sensation of having made a public appearance in my undies. Later, I grew to enjoy a brief but spirited dance of spring in front of those doors as a sort of antidote for the decorum demanded of me everywhere else in the institution.

The surprises weren't over. When I entered the dining room at supper time, I was greeted by applause as noisy and prolonged as the wailing which had marked the departure of the last lady in residence. The same girls who had sobbed the loudest farewells were now shrieking the warmest welcomes. I began to suspect that these pent-up, penned-in kids would seize any opportunity at all to relieve their feelings.

I was back in my office, complimenting myself on picking up so quickly, when my secretary, Miss Lulu, burst into the room. "Come quick! Mattie's on a rampage! It's awful!" she urged frantically. "She says she'll brain anyone that comes near her. She's got a hoe." Mattie had been pointed out to me as one of the shrillest screamers. Just more hysteria, I decided.

"For Heaven's sake, Mrs. Burnham, don't try to handle that girl alone." Mr. Carson, the Chief Clerk of the school, rushed in from his adjoining office. "She's a killer."

Those three words shattered my complacency into a million icy needles jabbing every nerve. Mr. Carson was *not* an hysterical type.

He continued. "I'll try to slip up behind her while you go toward her. But don't get too close," he warned again.

Automatically I headed for the center of the hubbub, behind the schoolhouse at the edge of the rose garden. A raging wild woman teetered back and forth across the border of a flower bed, her distended black eyes darting hatred in every direction. The freshly sharpened hoe in her hands cut through the air in long slashing swipes—vicious enough to kill.

"I hate you!" Mattie screamed at her cowering companions. "I hate this school and everyone in it. I hate God and Old Lady Burnham. I'm gonna smash the whole damn outfit!" She lunged a step forward and laughed crazily when a supervisor drew back in panic.

Twelve other girls stood paralyzed with fear. Mattie's voice rose to the breaking point, and I could see spittle on her lips. Then she spied me. "I hate you! Do you hear me? I hate you! I hate you! I hate you!" Her face was purpling.

"So you hate me, Mattie." I tried to speak calmly though I was scared to the marrow. This was a far cry from the uninhibited exhibition in the dining hall. Phony hysteria was one thing—homicidal mania another. I kept my distance.

"You hate me; that's your privilege." I was angling for time. "But I'll bet you don't know *why* you hate me. You don't even know me yet."

"I know you all right. You and God. You're like all the rest. God! God! God! I hate you all! I hate you all! I hate you all!" She kept repeating the four words like a pagan invocation—her throat so distended, I thought it would surely burst.

The girls behind me were beginning to whimper and I sensed the start of frenzy. Still, I couldn't turn my back on Mattie for an instant. The Chief Clerk, slowly inching up behind her, was almost within striking distance of the razor-edged hoe.

He plunged and pinioned her arms, but she used her teeth, her feet, and the top of her head as a battering-ram. Miss Lulu, the supervisor, and I rushed in to help. All four of us barely managed to subdue the berserk fifteen-year-old.

I had no choice but to put Mattie in Meditation. First we scoured the cell to make sure there were no nails, pins, sticks, or bits of glass anywhere around. I'd been briefed about this. These apparently harmless articles had often been used by inmates to cut their own veins or injure those who were trying to help them. Even bobby pins had to be removed from the girls' hair.

Such innocent things as china buttons could be dangerous too. Tramped underfoot, their broken edges could be employed to scrape loose the plaster and concrete around plumbing fixtures. Then the fun really started. Vitreous china toilet bowls would be torn from their moorings and beaten into pieces on the concrete floor. The jagged fragments were as dangerous as shrapnel when hurled at an attendant.

My psychologist friend had schooled me well in this area. When I first heard about such carryings-on, I assumed that the girls involved must be insane in the clinical sense. I learned that they were usually crazy-mad, but not really crazy. The lack of discipline during childhood had been carried over and intensified in adolescence. Their rage was no greater than that of a spoiled child who lies down to kick and scream and butt his head against the floor in infantile rebellion, but their physical ability to express their rebellion had reached adult—and more dangerous—proportions.

If Mattie was not a maniac, however, she certainly gave a grand imitation of one. Having been deprived of potential weapons, she howled bitter curses at God and man . . . and at me in particular. We stationed an attendant in the runway of Meditation to see that she didn't injure herself. The picture is indelibly stamped on my memory: a square muscular girl kicking the floor, cursing obscenely and beating the doors and walls with furious bleeding fists while a middle-aged matron sat outside the door, nibbling prunes and knitting as placidly as if she were rocking away on her own front porch.

Miss Lulu, Mr. Carson, and I paused just outside Meditation to rub bruises and regain our composure. Lulu's face was drained to a tired gray and the Chief Clerk's mouth was a tight line. I smiled blankly, merely to prove that I could, but I was conscious of trembling hands and shaky knees.

We hurried back to the rose garden to see if the trouble was all over. I knew—academically at least—that outbursts like Mattie's always left an aftermath of insubordination. Other incorrigibles plucked up courage to try out their own brands of anarchy. Border-line morons admiringly tried to imitate the rebels; it took the kind of excitement they stirred up to penetrate the dull, dim minds. Realizing that their own safety depended on restoring quick peace, supervisors always pitched in to rechannel energies and control fresh outbursts before they became contagious.

We found that the girls had been set to work weeding the roses as soon as Mattie left, but their sullenness was a sign of unrest. Unrest, in this group, was explosive. I saw that the group supervisor was keeping a sharp eye on a girl who was called Pinky because of the peculiar shade of her hair. She must have been sixteen years old, but her bone-thin, immature figure made her seem younger.

Pinky was complaining tearfully that "Mattie didn't mean no harm. Why was everybody so mean to Mattie?" The whining was having a bad effect on the others. It might incite some of the less stable ones to violence. I signaled for Lulu and Mr. Carson to lead Pinky away while I tried to quiet the rest.

I praised the girls for their self-control during Mattie's tantrum. As a reward, I sent for some ice cream. With Mattie and Pinky gone, tension gradually relaxed. Girls who might have rioted a moment before began to brag about their own superior sense and to wonder aloud how anyone could be as silly as Mattie.

With harmony restored, I went to see about Pinky. She and Miss Lulu were in my office while Mr. Carson stood guard outside the door. Curious inmates and employees found flimsy excuses to hang around the office, hoping to overhear some gossip for the grapevine. Pinky was shrilly defending her "pal" and refused to quiet down as long as she could be the center of attention. The only solution was to get her out of the spotlight. That meant Meditation for her too.

Back we trudged to put Pinky in the third cell-like room, with a vacant cubicle between her and Mattie. Above one girl's yelling and another one's crying, I explained that as soon as they could talk calmly, we'd sit down and iron out their problems. With never an upward glance, the matron in the runway continued to rock, nibble, and knit.

Mattie and Pinky kept up their caterwauling until well after midnight, but their voices grew huskier and there were longer intervals between their outbursts. At last they flickered out entirely and the girls were asleep.

As I collapsed into my own strange bed, I sent my mind back—was it only forty-five miles and twenty-four hours? Already I felt a million light-years away from the life "outside."

I wasn't the same person who had passed the State Capitol yesterday and glanced up at the wing housing the Governor's office. "That's my boss," I had thought proudly, and right there on the street I breathed a prayer that I might be worthy of his trust in me.

"I'll give the girls love," I said to myself. "I'll make them happy. Happy people are generally good people. Evil is just an attempt to escape misery." I sincerely believed that all young girls preferred to be virtuous and honorable, and that those who had somehow strayed would welcome my efforts to set them straight again. My plans were radiantly simple and allowed no leeway for complications arising out of political expediency, uninformed or misinformed public opinion, financial and legal wrangles, internal jealousies, or the unpredictable reactions of immature and vicious or badly warped minds.

Minus foresight, I couldn't know . . . but I was beginning to suspect. I stretched restlessly under the bedsheets; even the bed wasn't receiving me well. Or perhaps sleep couldn't creep past my sharp and whirling thoughts.

Was it Victor Hugo who'd said, "A leader is merely a man whose hour has struck"? I couldn't guarantee the accuracy of the quotation, but suddenly I understood its import. Times were coming when I would feel that not only had my hour struck . . . it had knocked me for a loop!

2

THE SECOND MORNING DAWNED ON A DESK PILED HIGH WITH mail. Most of the letters were routine enough for me to handle with ease, but others brought up questions for which neither Miss Lulu nor I had answers. I plowed on, putting aside anything I'd have to check against the book of regulations. As soon as possible, I intended to memorize the rules.

A county judge came up with the first puzzler. He'd promised a set of parents that they might call on daughter Nettie the following Sunday and take her home. Did the county judge have the right to reach into the school and release a girl who was a ward of the State? I rubbed a troubled brow—a gesture that was already a part of my new personality.

Surely parole procedure should rest with the institution, especially since school sentences were indeterminate. Was there a Parole Board to govern such matters or were they left to the discretion of the Superintendent? What kind of girl was Nettie anyway? Did she deserve dismissal? One question set off a score of others. I'd need a *detailed* guide book to get this untangled.

A mother threw me the next curve. "Please give my girl the enclosed fifty cents to buy cigarettes. She is used to smoking and gets nervous without it." I hadn't seen anyone smoking, either girls or officers, so I assumed there must be a regulation against it. I'd have to look that up too.

A Texas sheriff requested that we send for two runaway girls he had caught and was holding. That seemed simple enough, but some inner caution prompted me to lay that letter aside as well. At that point I decided that my wisest course would be to admit my ignorance. I rang for Miss Lulu.

That gallant soul had weathered the storms of institutional life for eight long years. Now she was sad of face and angular of body, and the victim of so many responsibilities and inhibitions that it was hard for her to indulge in the bits of foolishness and laughter with which the rest of the world eased emotional strain. In spite of the inhibitions—or maybe because of them—she was already a rock in the whirling rapids around me.

I'd been told about Miss Lulu's loyalty. She might disapprove of new procedures but, like a good soldier, she'd carry them out faithfully, rejoicing when they worked and withholding criticism when they failed.

I looked up as she entered the room. "Miss Lulu, may I have the book of rules?"

"Book of rules?" Her eyebrows lifted. "What book of rules?"

"Whatever you use as a procedural guide," I insisted. "Your codebook or regulation manual—whatever you call it."

"We don't have anything like that. It's all up to the Superintendent."

It was my turn to look blank. "How do you know how to operate? Every organization, even a bridge club, has *some* sort of by-laws."

"Maybe you can find what you want in the Oklahoma Statutes," she suggested. "I'll get them and let you see."

"Okay." What else could I say? The statutes would at least provide me with an over-all picture. Maybe then I could find my own way out of the maze.

I set the stage for a long session by drawing two chairs up to the desk and pulling the blind over the door glass. The closed blind meant "Do Not Disturb." Miss Lulu brought in a fat uninviting volume, bound in buff leatherette. I eyed the date line and exclaimed, "Oh, that's too old. Let's get a later copy."

Miss Lulu was miffed. "If there were a later copy, I'd have brought it. They're only printed every ten years."

We were off to a grand start. To help matters along, the hundreds of tissue-thin, close-packed pages were unnumbered. Cryptic-looking two-story ess signs preceding each law were the only approach to guidance or decoration in the entire book. I leafed through the dry pages and a shimmer of fine dust floated into the air. A page-by-page search finally unearthed a section succinctly called, "INSTITUTIONS." We settled in for long and careful study.

In toto, "INSTITUTIONS" contained two columns, embracing eleven statutes pertaining to delinquent girls. The first one had been written in 1909, when the State was barely two years old. It was a sort of afterthought to the thirty laws already enacted for delinquent boys, and provided that delinquent girls be received into the boys' training school on equal terms until such a practice should be, "in the opinion of the Board of Control, dangerous to the discipline of the school and harmful to the purposes thereof."

Evidently the girls were docile lambs for eight years. Then they must have kicked up a ruckus for, in a spate of lawmaking, the legislators ousted them from the boys' school and established a separate institution for them. The activity subsided again for thirty years—except for one glorious interlude in 1927, when the Superintendent's salary was upped to almost a living wage.

The first regulation enacted for the girls' school provided that it be located at some "convenient, accessible, and suitable place." Miss Lulu and I stared at each other in wordless astonishment.

Our location was accessible all right. But convenient? Suitable? For whom? Those who lived within the law or those who broke it? Certainly our labyrinth of ravines was suitable—for runaway girls. In one sprint they could reach the deep gullies surrounding our flimsy fence, and then pick a hiding place from among hundreds. Those ditches were Heaven-sent for girls intent on escape, but for law-enforcing agents they were a nightmarish maze that changed with every frost, thaw, and rainfall. In this one area, at least, I was completely informed.

Our rough acres had always attracted outlaws. When I was a kid, oldsters had kept me wide-eyed with tales of the gangsters who hid out in these gaps and fissures. Fortified with red-eye and brandishing pistols, they'd made periodic raids on the frontier town of Shawnee, just "down the road a piece" from Tecumseh. In those days the clatter of horses' hooves was enough to send law-abiding citizens scurrying for shelter . . . and they didn't emerge, if they were smart, until they heard hoofbeats heading out again.

With less faith now, Miss Lulu and I turned to the next regulation, providing for the training of institutionalized girls. It quite simply demanded that they be given a "thorough training in ALL branches of industrial education and domestic science." No provision was made for any of the equipment required for the "thorough training in ALL branches," nor were "ALL" the branches enumerated anywhere in the ruling.

Miss Lulu looked at me and dropped her eyes. For all I know, I may have been frothing at the mouth. Unexperienced as I was, I realized that a handful of teachers, one cook stove, six balky typewriters, ten foot-treadle sewing machines, and a batch of battered milk buckets didn't add up to a well-rounded industrial education for two hundred and seventy-six young girls.

But—darkness before light.

"Here's something!" Miss Lulu and I saw it at the same instant: "DUTIES OF SUPERINTENDENT—RULES AND REGULATIONS." Eight lines constituted the entire statute, including all figures, references, thereofs, and aforesaids.

I learned that as Superintendent I was expected to "define the duties of officers and employees and determine their salaries." I was to receive every girl committed and provide her with "food, clothing, and training, sustain her health and well being," and dismiss her whenever I felt that such dismissal was "neither incompatible with the welfare of society nor detrimental to her own good."

I was commanded to make voluminous reports of financial receipts and disbursements and to estimate, biennially, anticipated expenses for buildings, machinery, and maintenance. I was to set forth in detail an account of the reception, health, treatment, training, and dismissal of every girl and to compile a mass of information about the individual members of the school staff, their duties, and salaries.

No wonder no civil service test had ever been set up for this position! It would have had to encompass every subject from accounting to engineering, with side trips into soothsaying and abnormal psychology.

"But the book doesn't say a thing about smoking," I wailed.

"Or anything else we need to know." Miss Lulu frowned thoughtfully. "Well, I guess it's all up to you."

My heart took another quick trip to the pit of my stomach. The way affairs were going, it might take up permanent residence there any day now. I rose and snapped up the door blind. The conference was over almost before it had begun.

"We don't have any road maps, Miss Lulu, but we'll get there, one way or another." And where was "there"? I asked myself in the same breath. However, my glib—if innocuous—line seemed to reassure her. She gathered up her paper and pencils; I laid the book of statutes ceremoniously on her arm. "Guard it well!" I raised an admonitory finger. "Some day we may need it to prop up a wobbly table." Miss Lulu rewarded me with a weak smile.

A minute later I was alone with the troublesome letters and the files of the girls involved. I picked up the first with the fervent prayer that plain old common sense would suggest a solution. I stopped with my hand in mid-air. My appointment as Superintendent was doing *some* good. I was certainly praying more these days than ever before!

Nettie's file contained a story to shock anyone with even a vestigial sense of sin. She was fourteen years old at the time of admittance, the second of seven children in a family that lived in the slummiest section of its town in unimaginable squalor.

Her father had left no slimy stone unturned in his efforts to make a dishonest living. Working was for "jerks." Bootlegging and petty thievery were his main sources of income, but he was suspected of other and more unsavory activities.

Eventually the father noticed that Nettie was developing—as girls will—into an attractive young woman. With the proper handling, he decided that she could become a financial asset. He managed her like an ambitious agent, making "dates" for her with any man who had enough money to pay for the privilege. Nettie was instructed to "do as you're told." One thing she'd learned at an early age was not to cross papa. He got "mad." The girl had seen enough scars on her mother's body to know what "mad" meant.

One of the men Nettie "dated" was the middle-aged kingpin of the local underworld. He decided to marry the child, but since she was a minor, it was necessary to have the father's consent. Reluctant to lose a source of such easy income, the father stalled until a substantial cash settlement persuaded him to change his mind.

In her husband's home, Nettie had comforts that she'd never known existed. Her husband, however, was cut from the same cloth as her father and soon indicated that he expected her to earn back the money he'd laid out for her. In doing so, she landed in a police line-up and had then been sent to us for correction. Her husband and her father were united in one effort these days. They wanted Nettie out. After all, her talents were just wasting away with us.

Curious to know Nettie's own reaction to the career planned for her, I called her into the office. She was an amiable dish-water blonde of moderate intelligence. If she'd ever had a will of her own, it had dried up from disuse.

"Nettie," I finally steered the conversation to the subject I had in mind, "when you leave here, where do you want to go?"

"Oh, I don't know. Back home, I guess," she was cheerfully matter of fact.

"To your husband or your parents?" I persisted.

"My husband," Nettie covered a yawn with a polite hand. "My parents can't support me."

Obviously she thought of the school's correctional guidance program as a dream-like interruption of real life . . . the only life she'd ever experienced. The idea that she might support herself hadn't yet taken root. We needed more time—much more time.

I dismissed Nettie and immediately began checking with friends and acquaintances in strategic positions all over the State. I knew that they could supply me in minutes with more information than I could obtain in a month "through channels."

I found that Nettie's husband controlled the underworld votes in his area. Those votes were needed by a local candidate who found himself slipping politically. He'd made a contract with Nettie's husband, stipulating that he'd have her released from the school in exchange for the underworld votes at the polls.

Unaware of this pact and mired down by troubles of his own, the judge made only a cursory study of Nettie's case. He'd listened to the politician's plea that it was a first offense and that her husband had promised to keep her in line if she were allowed to return home. The result was a hasty decision authorizing Nettie's release.

I wrote a firm letter to the judge, setting forth facts I had learned and refusing to dismiss Nettie unless the reports were disproved or a more wholesome atmosphere than that of her husband's home could be found for her. The parole order was promptly withdrawn and the decision left to me. Thus I proved that the school had final jurisdiction over its girls.

With that problem started toward solution, I took up the matter of the mother who wished us to buy cigarettes for her daughter.

"Miss Lulu," I asked, as I spread the letter on the desk before me, "is there any rule here against girls smoking?"

"No, no rule," she shook her head. "We've just never let them."

"Moral grounds or what?" I watched her neck stiffen righteously.

"Mainly because we don't believe in it," she stated primly.

I don't believe in minors smoking either, but I felt we needed a better reason than my own personal prejudice. I tried to analyze the problem. Any privilege allowed one girl must be allowed all, or we'd have a mutiny for sure. Obviously our smaller girls were too young to smoke, even though they didn't think so. At home they'd puffed on the butts left lying around by their elders. I could think of a great many pleasanter things for them to do here.

I had to think of the fire hazard too. Cotton clothing, mattresses, bedding, drapes, a sewing room full of highly inflammable material, and a dairy barn stacked with hay offered too many attractive targets for careless—or vindictive—smokers.

Besides, who'd pay for the cigarettes? Few of the girls had any personal funds. The State would have to buy the smokes. Most of our citizens were strained to the breaking point to pay taxes. Surely they'd rather have their hard-earned money spent for meat and milk, or even candy for the youngsters if, by some miracle, there should ever be an excess of cash. So I wrote "No" to Lavita's mother, and marveled at her solicitude in such a minor area and her incredible indifference in so much greater matters.

The problem of the two runaways in Texas seemed easiest of all. They were ours. We wanted them. Texas didn't. All I had to do was wire the sheriff that we'd send a car with two officers to gather up our wandering girls.

A small nagging doubt persisted, but I rang for Miss Lulu and asked her to figure up the expenses involved. She looked dubious and I soon discovered why. A few judicious phone calls on my part and the original problem was buried under a flood of "ifs," "ands," and "buts."

First, did a semi-penal institution have the right to ask another state to extradite an escaped inmate, or should the matter rest in the hands of the Governor? Was a committed delinquent minor who had run away a child or an escaped criminal? Was it legal to spend State funds outside its own borders—even to return its own wards—when no provision had been made for such an emergency?

If spending money outside of State borders for the return of escapees was illegal, I hoped the girls would never find it out.

We were practically on a main highway. All they'd have to do would be to thumb a ride across the State line and they'd be free.

And what about girls whose only chance of success lay in being sent as far as possible from old environments? I discovered that not a nickel was provided for interstate transportation. For that matter, there wasn't any fund set up for travel within the State either, yet nobody wished to set a paroled girl down outside the gate and forget about her. Without funds, transportation, or a home to go to, what would become of her?

On this, my second day at the school, I still thought in terms of quick, business-like decisions—but Miss Lulu knew better. Her dubious look should have prepared me. The question wasn't answered the same day it was asked—or even the same year. Succeeding legislatures tossed it about . . . the epitome of political football. I never did find out where my would-be "Texans" wound up.

Later—more than a year later—the same situation was to crop up again in the case of Elma. By then I had enough gumption stored up to go right ahead on my own hook. Miss Lulu was still dubious.

Elma was an overdeveloped fourteen-year-old who "fell" from a town of about eight thousand inhabitants. Many of the laborers employed by local industry were drifters who frequented the slum district that was Elma's only playground. By the time she was in her teens, she could have taught Sadie Thompson a few tricks.

Eventually an alert probation officer found the girl living in a squalid hut near the river with an elderly man of weirdly mixed ancestry. She cooked his meals, such as they were, and supplied his amatory requirements. In return, she was free to share his food and shelter. Her clothes were fished out of ash cans or stolen from clotheslines.

The probation officer took Elma back to her shiftless parents and ordered them to watch over her and see that she attended school. Always without funds and with a large brood of younger children to support, the parents had been delighted when Elma took over her own maintenance. As soon as the officer left, they expressed their resentment at her return so forcefully that Elma was back in the old man's hut that same evening. Next time she was caught out, the officer recommended that the court commit her to Tecumseh.

The probation officer brought her to us himself, and explained in acute embarrassment that the linen duster she was wearing belonged to him. I wondered at his red-faced mumbling until Elma blithely peeled off the thin coat.

Her only garment was a backless dress made of an old and loosely woven sugar sack. The halter-necked bib front barely covered her, and the piece of rope cinched around the waist emphasized all that was barely covered. Obviously she wore no undergarments. Frayed cloth sandals were tied to her feet with rag strings.

Serenely oblivious of her nearly nude condition, Elma received my slightly strained greeting with a friendly smile. She had no idea why the kindly officer had required her to wear his nice clean coat.

Elma was a moderately attractive, good-natured girl with an intelligence quotient of 93—ten points above the school average. She hadn't meant to be "bad" and hadn't thought of her behavior as anything but natural. She had needed food for her healthy, growing young body and she had used the only means at her disposal to get it. For her, the matter was merely one of survival.

New "first-hand" clothes and good food amazed and delighted her, but she really went into ecstasies over the piano. To her it was a magnet, a thing of unbelievable witchery. The music lessons were simply an attempt to make her happy, but much to our surprise, she exhibited a genuine talent and had become a very capable performer by the time she approached her eighteenth birthday.

That date would mark the legal age limit for our school, and we were in a quandary. She had to go—but where to send her? It was sheer idiocy even to think of returning the pleasant, well-groomed musician she had become to the gross, sordid environment she had outgrown. We searched her records for the names of distant relatives and wrote avalanches of letters investigating their respectability.

Elma was more than cooperative. The very idea of going home made her actively ill. I didn't dare mention the possibility if I expected to see her at the supper table. As we drew closer to the fatal birthday, we located an aunt who lived halfway across the country, but whose worthiness was guaranteed by officials in her locality. We made immediate preparations for the journey, and Elma was about equally divided between sadness at leaving her many friends and exuberant joy at finding a place for herself. Then the question of using State funds for out-of-State travel cropped up again.

Elma's ticket would cost thirty-nine dollars. Was it legal for us to spend the money for travel beyond State borders? I insisted that returning Elma to her former home would result in her drifting back to old habits, thus negating all we'd done. Another lapse could cost the State a hundred times the price of a ticket.

Auditors and officials admitted the truth of my reasoning but they bogged down on the technicalities involved. One obscure girl clogged the State's legal machinery as effectively as a gnat in the gas line of an expensive limousine. Nothing moved . . . including Elma.

The officials had some real basis for their concern. They were seasoned politicians who had weathered many a local squall and State-wide storm. Every man of them knew that though a cause might be a worthy one, a single small deviation from the actual letter of the law could lay them open to attack from future opponents. A determined enemy could twist even so tiny a matter as this into a thundering denunciation of waste, corruption, and flagrant misuse of State funds.

So—while the officials of a great State haggled over whether or not they would spend thirty-nine dollars to complete the rehabilitation of a ward—we at the school chipped in and bought Elma's ticket. She boarded the train, smiling through her tears, and clutching an enormous box of lunch, contributed by the cook.

But as I sat at my desk that second day, Elma was still far in the future. The courage to blaze new trails was just barely beginning to foment in me. The knowledge that I literally held lives in my hands caused a throbbing shiver to run down my spine. Reeling head . . . plunging heart . . . shivering spine. Superintendent or case history, I asked myself wryly?

The luncheon bell rang and I realized that my day had just gotten off to a running start!

3

New situations kept cropping up thick and fast. Days and weeks began to lose their separate identities and mesh, one into another, with no sharp lines of demarcation. I felt less and less like a raw probationer, especially as I soon learned that other people handling delinquent girls got into the same sort of swivets and cold sweats.

One day, when I'd been in office less than two weeks, a neighboring judge called me. "I have a girl here," he explained over the phone, "who's done some pretty peculiar things." He related a long string of offenses. "Would you prefer to have her committed for a definite period of time or until she's eighteen? Or perhaps you'd like to suggest the term yourself?"

I side-stepped the question. "Whatever you do will be all right with me, judge." In my book a judge was a superior being in the intellect department. "I'll be glad to cooperate in anything you think best."

"Oh—ah—yes—thank you," he tossed the problem back to

me. "But we want to complete the matter in the way that will enable you to do the best job possible."

This "Alphonse and Gaston" routine could have continued for a week, so I decided to break down and confess. "I'm ashamed to admit it," I told the judge, "but I just don't know what to tell you. I'm so new at this job that I haven't even learned the language yet. Please decide for me and do whatever you think is right."

He chuckled and then roared. "Now *I'll* confess," I heard him say. "I'm as new as you are, and this is my first delinquent child case. I thought maybe *you'd* had enough experience to advise *me*."

The halt leading the blind!

I gained much through contacts with judges and ministers and other dignitaries of the neighboring towns. Sometimes they furnished me with a much needed laugh. One of these was provided by Dr. John Raley, president of a flourishing denominational school in Shawnee.

He called one day to extend greetings from his very large school to my small one. He accepted our invitation to lunch and afterwards made a short speech. His polish and eloquence had all of us sitting up a little straighter and I found myself trotting out my longest words to match his learned vocabulary.

After lunch, our visitor and I went on an inspection tour of all our departments. It was a long, hot journey under a blazing sun, and it was hard for me to stay serenely formal while mopping perspiration from my dripping brow. But the good Doctor remained a ramrod of dignity.

Of course we inspected the chapel whose narrow lawn adjoined the pig pens. A garbage wagon had just passed by and dropped a tin bucket containing some dregs of syrup. Sniffing the spilled sweetness, a young shoat had struggled through the fence for a treat and had poked his snout so far into the bucket he had caught its rim behind his ears where it held tight.

My guest and I arrived just as the terrified pig was struggling frantically to free himself from his tin prison. Unhesitatingly, Dr. Raley peeled off his coat and his dignity. He handed me the coat to hold while he went to the rescue of the small porker.

To the pig, who couldn't see a thing, the noise of Dr. Raley's fingers against the bucket must have sounded like the rumble of doom. With a frightened squeal he broke loose. Round and round went the pig, blindly bumping his bucket into trees and fence posts while Dr. Raley lunged after him.

At last, Dr. Raley won. He caught the pig and while it squealed and struggled, he eased the bucket off its head. He boosted the little animal back into its pen and turned to me for his coat.

There was little resemblance to the immaculate dignitary of a few moments before. Dr. Raley's hair stood in seven directions. His tie was under one ear, his collar and cuffs wilted and his face scarlet and streaked with perspiration.

I tried to keep a straight face but it was too much. Suddenly I howled and Dr. Raley joined in my glee. That hearty laugh cemented a friendship which has proved lasting. Certainly, his genuine compassion for one of the lowliest of creatures enlisted me as one of his staunch supporters.

I was a rank amateur in a good many areas, but I felt a great security in my staff. In the first glow of optimism, I expected that they—all more experienced than I—would deliver me from the worst dilemmas. Good old team spirit! Everybody pulling together for the common weal. I wasn't aware, as yet, that while most pulled, some pushed . . . and a few others burrowed from beneath.

But already I knew that Miss Lulu was solidly behind me,

and other faces were gradually coming into sharper focus. I could sort out the six day matrons from the six night matrons and even take a chance on attaching the right names to the right frames. The six part-time substitutes remained fuzzy for quite a while, but the seven schoolteachers were unmistakably individual the moment I met them. By the end of the third day, I'd stopped confusing the librarian with the laundress and the sewing teacher with the serving instructor. When I had the cook and the dean of the commercial department down pat, I'd run through the complete distaff side of our staff.

In this world of women and girls, my five males looked as odd and out of place as pumpkins in a petunia patch. The school farmer had the only direct contact with our girls—and he always kept a cow or two between them. The maintenance man patched, mowed, painted; and the engineer coaxed the power plant along. I learned to know the night watchman quite well; most deviltry was hatched and executed under cover of darkness. Since the Chief Clerk had saved my skin the very first day, I was inclined to regard him highly—and I never had cause to alter my opinion.

Naturally some personalities appealed to me more than others, but I thought I could learn to like all of my people quite well. Except one.

There was certainly nothing sinister about Leila Wiles except, perhaps, her eyes. As a matter of fact, they were the only memorable features of an otherwise eminently forgettable face. A pale, glassy blue, they had the kind of lidless reptilian look I loathe. I was annoyed at myself for the instant feeling of revulsion. It was an accident of pigmentation, I told myself sternly, not an indication of character. We had no time or room for unreasoning prejudice, so I decided to make an all-out effort to like Leila—whether I liked it or not.

A very little investigation proved that she was a valuable asset to the school. As a senior matron who doubled as vocational coach, she'd been a favorite with the girls at Tecumseh for more than seven years. I forced myself to list all her fine qualities. She was intelligent, sincerely interested in her work, and almost obsessively immaculate about her person. Her voice was low and cultivated, free of any regional twang or slur. Even though she worked daily with wet wicker, heavy clay, sharp tools, and other handicraft and hobby materials, her fingernails were always mandarin-length and exquisitely lacquered.

And—as long as I had gone this far—I also had to admit that her hair was "coiffed" whereas mine was combed; and her waist was twenty-three inches whereas mine was—well, obviously I was all wet. She sounded good, she looked good; ergo: she *was* good. Against all this weight in the scale, I could produce only a vestigial instinct and a very personal antipathy toward her particular type of bleached-out blue eyes. But, biased as it might be, I determined to keep a wary eye of my own on this veritable paragon of virtue.

However, things popped too fast for me to brood over the possibility of *future* problems. There was generally one in my lap and one waiting in the anteroom at any given moment. If we couldn't dredge them up fast enough on the campus, the phone could always be counted on to ring one in from the outside. Miss Lulu lived in dread of long-distance phone calls. I began to understand why on the day I innocently picked up a call from a member of the Board of Affairs.

"There's a Mrs. Lobban on her way down there to see you about getting a job," he said hesitatingly. "Guess you'd better put her to work. She's a very good friend of Senator Sprong."

"Do you want her to replace someone who's here now?" I asked.

"Oh, no, just put her to work anywhere at all," was his casual reply.

"I'll have to fire someone if I do," I objected. "The budget can't stand another person on the payroll, and I haven't been here long enough to know who can be spared. Can't Mrs. Lobban wait a while?"

His voice was apologetic—but insistent. "I'm afraid not. The Senator is a powerful man and we need his support on some important matters. We want to keep him feeling real friendly, Mrs. Burnham. I guess you'll have to find a place for her."

"All right," I agreed reluctantly, "but will this sort of thing happen very often? I don't see how I'll ever get the job done unless I can choose qualified people."

"We'll give you a free hand as often as we can," he promised, "but there'll be times when we can't. This is one of them. That's why I called you on it. She'll be there with a letter of introduction any minute now."

I hung up and tried to re-interest myself in the case history I'd been reading. No use. The girl inmates were supposed to be my first concern, but staff problems were taking more and more of my time. Mrs. Lobban wasn't my first hurdle by any means.

Before I was fully unpacked, I'd had to cope—somehow—with a staff member who regularly stole school property. The signs pointed to compulsive thievery, not thievery for profit. Obviously there was something basically awry in her thinking, and she was certainly no fit guide for young girls. However, like most of our staffers, she was a political appointee whose sponsor happened to be an exceptionally powerful person in the State. I realized that an outright accusation would set the scene for a mighty battle, and that countless of our girls would be casualties. Our entire training program would be disrupted, for culprit and sponsor would jointly see to it that the school was subjected to "investigation" and attack. I'd seen the same thing happen before.

On the other hand, I couldn't allow the woman to continue

her depredations . . . especially since all the girls knew of her activities and were beginning to work up admiration for an "operator" who was "putting something over" on the authorities. And, though it was a secondary reason, the school couldn't afford to lose as much as a spool of thread.

Most of the pilfering had taken place in the sewing room, so I alerted that instructor to my plan. Whenever she missed any item after daily inventory, she was to report to me—and we'd both prepare for action. When the light-fingered staffer was at supper or otherwise engaged, the sewing room instructor and I would conduct a retaliatory raid on her room, confiscating all that had been stolen!

After a few such forays, the woman caught on, but she couldn't very well complain. To do so would have tipped off her own transgressions and branded her, officially, as a petty thief. Our method proved effective; shortly after our fifth raid, she requested a transfer to another institution where, presumably, she expected the pickings to be easier . . . or the Superintendent less squeamish.

My office door opened and snapped me back to the present. It wasn't Mrs. Lobban yet—just Miss Lulu with a pregnancy problem. Annadee was approaching her time and we still didn't know what to do with her. We'd had plenty of expectant mothers at Tecumseh, but the girls had always been returned to relatives for care during confinement. There were no friends or relatives to help this youngster. For several years she'd been farmed out to agencies and strangers, and now nobody wanted her.

The school program was far too strenuous for a girl in the last months of pregnancy. I'd also been told that an expectant mother was an object of cruelty and ridicule on the part of the other inmates. The baby was entitled to some consideration too. I'd never willingly consent to the birth of an infant in a correctional school. And even if I agreed, it was against the law for us to receive anyone not committed by court order. Time was a'wasting, and Mother Nature wouldn't worry about a little thing like legality. I wondered who'd be called on the carpet if the baby decided to arrive ahead of schedule, while the mother was still with us.

The school was utterly unprepared to care for maternity cases; we didn't have anything resembling a nipple or a diaper pin on the premises. Miss Lulu said, "She's in her seventh month," with a quaver in her voice, and I started some frantic telephoning. Finally, after canvassing the larger towns in the area, I located a hospital with a heart and a ward that wasn't too crowded. It agreed to minister to this girl, and any others we might come up with, during confinement. I snapped up the offer and postponed thinking about the infant until he or she should arrive on the scene.

As I was winding up my notes on this case history, Miss Lulu scuttled into the office with her eyes saucer-wide. "There's a lady waiting to see you. She said the Board of Affairs sent her."

"That must be Senator Sprong's appointee," I observed as I rose to walk into the anteroom and extend a welcome.

Miss Lulu trailed out behind me, but I didn't understand her odd actions until I saw Mrs. Lobban myself. Unbelievingly I gazed at the ponderous bulk overflowing her chair in all directions. Fat cheeks and a triple chin submerged her features until they looked like thumb punches in a highly painted mass of dough. The squat neck was lost in mammoth shoulders, and they, in turn, were half-hidden by an uncontrollable cascade of what had to be hair. It grew out of her scalp string-straight and hoary white, then halfway down wound in frantic frizzled wisps of gold. Elephantine limbs ended in feet which had originally been designed for an undersized dwarf.

Needing time to gather my wits about me, I read and reread

Mrs. Lobban's letter of introduction. Superimposed on the letterhead, I saw pictures painted by my shock-stimulated imagination: this grotesque creature wobbling through the miles and miles of walking incidental to each day's duties . . . hoisting and clawing herself over high wire fences in pursuit of agile teen-age runaways . . . eating our budget to rack and ruin in a week!

An idea occurred to me, and I lowered the letter to look at Mrs. Lobban again. I couldn't avoid engaging this impossible lady, but she could refuse to accept the position. Maybe it would discourage her to get a really detailed, step-by-step rundown of her duties. It was worth a try—and if it worked, Senator Sprong wouldn't be able to say a word.

"Oh, yes, Mrs. Lobban," I began brightly. "You're Senator Sprong's friend, aren't you?"

"Yes'm," she nodded economically. "I done a lot to he'p him get elected."

With that English, I thought, she certainly can't expect to be a teacher!

"We're very glad to have you here," I smiled, remembering instructions from headquarters. "We think a lot of Senator Sprong and welcome any friend of his."

I then launched into a description of a matron's duties. I stressed the great amount of walking and explained volubly that we worked twelve hours a day and were subject to emergency calls at any hour of the night. I spoke of our meager salaries and compared them unfavorably with those offered by other institutions. I outlined the extra duties—the housekeeping and sorting and mending—that kept us constantly on the jump. When I finished, I was ready to pack up and leave myself.

Mrs. Lobban absorbed it all and chewed it over. I leaned forward in my chair, the better to hear her horrified "No!" But Mrs. Lobban was made of sterner stuff. She was eager to begin, she said. She declared herself competent to do everything I'd described. All she needed—my marrow froze—was a free hand.

"That's fine," I answered numbly, but a second-line attack had already suggested itself. "As long as you're going to be one of us, you'll probably want to inspect the premises. Excuse me while I see if my secretary is able to take you around."

I shut the door between Mrs. Lobban and me before I leaned over Miss Lulu's desk.

"Miss Lulu!" I whispered desperately. "You've got to help me out! Take that woman over every foot of the grounds. The pasture . . . the okra fields . . . the recreation area. From one end to the other. Double back and forth if you have to. Walk her down to a nubbin!"

Lulu looked wan but game. She was about to open the door when I caught her arm. "Wait a minute! We need insurance with this one. While you're walking, keep up a running conversation. Tell her everything awful the girls ever did . . . every glaring detail!"

Lulu's eyes began to gleam. "I won't have to embroider the truth, you know. Did I ever tell you about the time the kitchen girls cut up cockroaches in the meat loaf so everyone would get good and sick?"

"Wonderful!" I cried. "That's the kind of thing we're after. Come on now and I'll introduce you."

Mrs. Lobban acknowledged Miss Lulu with a lackadaisical "pleased ta meetcha." We both averted our eyes as she lurched and heaved out of her chair and wobbled through the door.

It was difficult to concentrate on my work while they were taking the Grand Tour, but I tried. They hadn't been heard from an hour later, so I gave myself a short break. I leaned back, intending to relax, rest my eyes, and search my memory for something pleasant. As usual, I didn't get farther back than my first days at Tecumseh . . . and another snafu on staff.

Even then, I realized that my superior officers wouldn't always be able to side-step pressures imposed on them. I knew—academically at least—that a system of give-and-take was necessary between departments just as it is between members of a family. Decisions were made on the basis of satisfying the biggest need, and anyone anywhere in the political arena had to accept that fact as a fact of life.

Because of just such a case, I'd fallen heir to an employee who was, in her way, as impossible as Mrs. Lobban. She'd also been announced by a Board member, but this one called to say that a new employee had just been engaged for me and was already on her way to the school to take up her duties.

"Oh, no!" I wailed into the receiver. "Must I take her?"

"You've *got* her," was his succinct answer. "She has a mighty strong backer."

"What can she do? How much shall I pay her—and with what?" I was mentally reviewing our anemic budget and our need for specialized instructors.

"Do? Why—I don't know—" He was clearly out of his depth.

"Is she musical?" I was desperate for a good piano teacher. "Can she play the piano? Sing?"

"No, I don't think so. But don't worry," his voice brightened. "You'll only have to pay her fifty dollars a month and you won't have to keep her long. Maybe not over six or eight weeks."

"Why such a short time?" I objected. "If I have to go to the trouble of breaking her in, I won't want to give her up as soon as she begins to learn the ropes."

"I don't think you'll want to keep her very long," the voice was unhappy again. "You see, she's not very well. She won't be there long."

Now I was *really* wrought up! "Not well?" I thundered at

the poor man. "We aren't prepared to look after sick people. Somebody will have to fetch and carry for her all day. She'll be more trouble than the girls. What's wrong with her anyway?"

"Wrong? Oh . . ." the voice trailed into silence. Then my informant picked up enough courage to continue. "Why—uh—I guess—well, I guess—yes, I guess you could say she's a little bit pregnant."

The young woman came, gaily frank about her condition. She could hardly have been otherwise, since it was highly evident to the most myopic eye. She wanted us to call her "Miss Alice," although there was a glib, if sketchy, story about a secret marriage and a deserting husband. She explained that she merely wanted to earn a little money to apply on her hospital bill when the time arrived for her confinement.

Since Miss Alice had no training of any sort, I asked her to supervise the playground. Her duties consisted of settling any disputes that arose among the girls, and keeping them from going A.W.O.L.

She promptly began to break more rules than the worst of our girls. For one thing, she ignored the school's strictest admonition, forbidding embraces between officers and girls. Many of our inmates slipped far too easily from emotional to physical attachments. Then too, such embraces placed a matron or staff member at the mercy of any girl who had violence and escape in mind. Even forgetting these considerations, we'd found that familiarity of this sort reduced the stature and dignity of the adult concerned . . . and our girls needed women they could look up to.

About the third day Miss Alice was with us, I saw her strolling down a play-area path, completely smothered in the arms of four girls. I hurried toward the group with the intention of calling her aside and reminding her of the rule. When I heard one of the giggling hangers-on call her "Alice," I changed my mind and beckoned to the girl instead.

"You must say 'Miss Alice' not just 'Alice' when you address your supervisor," I said firmly. "Miss Alice is in a position of authority and is entitled to your respect. Please remember to put 'Miss' before her name after this."

The girl stared at me boldly and put a question I couldn't answer. "Why must I show her any respect? She's no better than any of us. She's done the same kind of things we have."

Our worldly-wise youngsters weren't easily fooled. With uncanny accuracy they could always separate the sheep from the goats. Having Miss Alice around—a living example of "getting away with it"—wasn't helping anyone's moral fiber. Fortunately the school bored her and she soon decided that she'd earned enough for immediate expenses.

But swapping her for Mrs. Lobban would merely be exchanging one large juicy lemon for another. And speak of the devil! I heard her wheezing down the path before she came into sight. Miss Lulu was loping happily along, with Mrs. Lobban gingerly setting each foot in front of her as if on coals of fire. I later learned that she'd called it a day right after the ravines and just before the chicken runs, but faithful Miss Lulu was still droning terrible tales into her ears as they turned into the office.

Mrs. Lobban sank into a chair with a pneumatic squash and gasped for breath like a blowfish.

"When will you be down here to join us?" I prodded anxiously.

"I don't rightly know," she panted angrily. "I don't rightly know if I'm a'comin' a'tall. I'm a'goin' to talk to Senator Sprong. It's right nice here but there's a lot to be done. I can see there's a powerful lot—an' I kin tell you what this place needs."

"Tell me, Mrs. Lobban," I encouraged her. "I'll be so glad to get some constructive criticism."

"What this place needs . . ." she paused and stabbed me with a venomous stare, ". . . what this place needs," she repeated with great deliberateness, "is a good Christian woman at the head of it!"

That parting shot came so unexpectedly that I never knew whether we said good-by or not. All I could remember was a vision of the good lady wedging herself into a small protesting car and driving off in a cloud of dust. Presumably she was on her way to acquaint Senator Sprong with our shortcomings.

Miss Lulu and I bowed formally to each other, and then the laughter we'd bottled up all day exploded in noisy torrents. Nothing more was ever heard of the large-economy-size Mrs. Lobban.

4

It's lucky I had one good guffaw to sustain me through the following day. The morning began on a grim note that grew worse as the hours passed.

As usual, I was in my office, studying files and making decisions based on the information I dug out of them, plus my own observations and officers' reports. Pinky and Mattie were currently occupying my attention.

It was clear that Pinky was a weakling who'd drifted without volition into drunkenness and prostitution. Mattie's file indicated a more forceful character. Among other lurid episodes, she'd attempted to murder her mother with a butcher knife. I didn't require any more proof that Mattie would bear watching. Nevertheless, more proof—on the hoof, so to speak—arrived at my door as I was closing the folder.

The disheveled creature who entered my office was almost unrecognizable. The attendant pushed her forward until I could see through the matted hair and past the layers of dirt. It was Mattie—looking as if she'd just escaped a hogwallow. My first impulse was to send her straight to the bathtub, but the matron must have read my mind.

"She messed herself up some, Ma'am. Better take a good look at her legs." The woman stopped talking and pressed her lips tightly together.

I turned to Mattie. "All right, let's see them," I ordered.

With amused insolence she snatched up her skirts, revealing angry-looking scratches from ankles to thighs.

"Pinky's like that too," the attendant volunteered.

I sent her to collect Pinky, and then looked more closely at the abrasions Mattie was flaunting. They weren't random scratches, I saw, but deliberate tracings of names, initials, and designs. On investigating, we found that both girls were "decorated" from head to foot. Every part of their anatomy within reach bore some scribble or other.

Pinky kept up a silly giggle, but Mattie turned sullen and uncommunicative until the doctor arrived and pointed out the grave danger of blood poisoning. Then she confessed that the scratches had been made with a brass safety pin she'd managed to smuggle into Meditation. No amount of questioning could make her reveal where she'd had the pin hidden, but the rest of the story was easily extracted.

After the first few hours of confinement, when supervision had relaxed a little, Mattie got the project going by tracing Pinky's initials; then she fastened the pin in the end of her towel and threw it down the hall toward the third cubicle. Pinky tossed her blanket out over the towel and snaked it within reach. The pin passed back and forth until both girls were thoroughly scrolled.

Mattie, having worked herself into noisy hysteria by this time, ripped and tore at her dress and rolled wildly on the floor of her cell. Pinky, of course, followed suit, and the matron finally lumbered out of her chair to take a look.

While I was trying to make some sense of this senseless behavior, a student nurse named Jennie plucked at my sleeve and motioned me around a corner.

"I guess you don't understand." Her serious brown eyes searched my face and I could see a tide of embarrassment wash over her own.

Homosexuality! Obviously that's what Jennie meant. So far I hadn't met the problem face to face, but I was suddenly sure she'd called it right. I thought of the two girls, one dark, strong, domineering—and the other pale, yielding, and giggly. Had they found some sort of satisfaction in mutually accomplished idiocy?

It seemed like rank insanity, but I'd been meeting up with lots of insanity lately. I decided to play it safe and get an expert opinion. As soon as the girls were thoroughly cleansed, I had them bundled into a car, along with a guard to maintain an alert while I drove. We headed for the nearest mental hospital and arrived at dusk.

Sensing an emergency, one of the head doctors left a family dinner to speak with me and examine my scratched-up, patched-up pair. When he saw them, he stopped talking. Sometime later, Dr. Hathcart called me into his office; the girls were in an anteroom, he assured me, with my guard still in attendance. He went on to say that he was acquainted with this type of phenomenon, but that Pinky and Mattie represented one of the most extreme cases he'd ever seen. Would I allow him to keep the girls for a period of observation?

My face must have given me away for he pulled his chair closer and patted my hand. "Don't be too shocked, Mrs. Burnham. Undoubtedly you'll find more such cases as you go along, and you'll need your wits about you. You'll have to keep on the look-out every single hour you're at the institution."

"But what do I do when I find them, doctor? I don't know

how to handle anything like this." For once I wasn't ashamed to admit my ignorance. I needed all the help I could get.

I listened in growing apprehension, however, as Dr. Hathcart made an admission of his own. So far, he said, medical science had no sure cure for homosexuality, and controlling it would be entirely up to me. "Catch it early and treat each case according to its individual aspects," was all the advice he could give. I found it a little too nebulous to lean on.

"You must remember," he said in parting, "that the segregation of either sex is abnormal and breeds problems of this sort . . . especially when you're working with a collection of youngsters already overly concerned with sex."

Remember? I couldn't forget if I tried. I was a "normal" grown woman with no particular personality problems, and even I could see the strangeness, the lack, in these lives lived almost exclusively with only one sex. How could we expect girls to adjust to a two-sex society when we segregated them at the exact time they most needed to integrate? I'd often spoken out for a co-ed correctional school, but of course Dr. Hathcart couldn't know that.

In about four weeks, he returned my girls, along with a detailed diagnosis. It boiled down to the conclusion that Pinky was no real danger to herself or others, but there was a possibility that Mattie might become completely psychopathic. She was highly emotional and her ultimate mental health would depend on the way she was handled during the remainder of her adolescence.

The diagnosis added another obligation to the ones already aging me. Now, in addition to my duties of guiding, educating, and providing physical care for my girls, I was expected to take full responsibility for their mental welfare. Since I had no choice in the matter, I set about learning as much abnormal psychology as I could from books. The publishing industry got considerably more of my money that year than the dress designers.

When Mattie and Pinky returned from the hospital, I detained them at the office for an interview. If I had to make their mental gears mesh, I wanted to know as much as possible about the way all their wheels went round. I talked with Pinky first, since she presented fewer complexities; she would always drift with any current that caught her up. Mattie was the self-starter.

Pinky left and Mattie entered the office with uncharacteristic hesitancy.

"Hello." I made a point of reaching out and shaking her hand. "We're glad to have you back. Are you feeling better?"

"I'm glad to be back too." After a perceptible pause, Mattie had thrust out her hand to meet mine. "But I never was sick, really."

"I don't think you were either," I laughed, "but you sure put on a pretty good act." She grinned back at me—sheepishly and just for a second—but I felt a thrill of achievement. A month ago she might have thrown something.

"Sit down, Mattie." I pushed a chair toward her and she perched warily on the edge of it.

"Aren't you going to scold me?"

"Should I?" I countered.

"Well, I was pretty mean, I guess. I swore at you and did some other things that weren't real nice."

Now *there* was the understatement of the age! But I controlled the urge to say so. "That's true," I said instead. "Still, I think you've suffered enough for it."

"Nobody's done nothing to me. How do you figure I suffered?" Mattie's surprise was genuine.

I spoke slowly now, knowing that this was my chance to get through to the girl. "You were foolish, and because of that foolishness, you've lost a whole month out of your life. Time is the one thing you can't ever earn back no matter how much you want to. That's enough punishment for anyone, isn't it?"

"I didn't figure it that way." Mattie's face looked suddenly gaunt. I decided to drive my points home before the barriers flew up again.

"You forgot, Mattie, that everything we do has a consequence." She was listening, but "consequence" was too much for her; I broke it down. "A follow-up," I explained. "If we plant weeds, we get weeds; but if we plant roses, why we get roses. We have the privilege of choosing.

"Of course it's been said better," I admitted. "Someone once said, 'As a man thinketh, so is he,' but the best is, 'He that soweth the wind shall reap the whirlwind.' But that's the Bible, isn't it? And you're the girl who hates God."

She stiffened and cried out, "No! No, I don't!" then sank back, pulling herself away from her own outburst. In a calmer voice, she said, "I don't mind when you do the Bible like that, but I don't want to hear it my mother's way. I don't hate God, honest I don't. But I don't believe He's like my mother thinks he is. I'd hate that kind of God for sure!"

" 'God is love,' " I quoted. "Don't you believe that?"

The somber eyes flashed. "Not my mother's God! Everything bad I ever went through happened because her God was so hard. She was all the time singing hymns real loud and shouting, 'Bless God, hallelujah!' " Mattie's face twisted into an ugly grimace. ". . . especially when she wanted Him to 'strike down a sinner' like she was always praying."

I waited. I knew Mattie wouldn't stop now. The accumulated pressure of years was pushing the words out.

"I remember when I was just a little tiny girl," she began again. "Sometimes I'd stop a while on the way home from school to play with the other kids. She'd come out after me and grab me so I'd be black-and-blue . . . then she'd make me get down on my knees and pray God to forgive me for being so 'wicked.'

"Then one day I was really late getting home. I didn't mean to . . . I wasn't 'defying' her like she said . . . but we were playing hop-scotch and having fun, so it got dark before I noticed." Mattie hunched forward and laid shaking hands on the desk.

"My mother was on the sidewalk, watching for me. As soon as she saw me, she started to yell, 'Oh, God, forgive this evil girl. Oh, God, don't let her live in sin and lose her soul in Hell!' All the kids were listening."

Mattie's knuckles turned white as she pressed forward in passionate despair. "She wouldn't listen. She'd never listen. She said I did things I never even thought of. Then she called in some friends of hers and they got down on their knees around me and prayed and called out, 'Lord, forgive this sinful child. Lord, save her soul from damnation—bless the Lord!' I hated them, Mrs. Burnham, I hated them!" Her fists beat a tattoo of agony on the desk. Pity—and shame—closed my throat, but I nodded my head and she continued.

"My mother held me so I couldn't get away. I had to listen to them say terrible things—awful things they had in their own dirty minds. They all sang a hymn over me and I thought if God was fair, He'd strike them dead. Then they let me go to bed but I couldn't sleep. I just lay there, hating my mother and wondering how I could get even with her."

The pause this time was much longer. Mattie looked at me, weighed me—and finally went on. "You won't believe this, Mrs. Burnham," she began, "because I did it and I hardly believe it myself. But it happened all right," she assured me bleakly. I knew what was coming; it was all in the case history.

"The next morning my mother went out to feed the chickens.

She didn't give me supper the night before and she didn't give me breakfast, but she never missed feeding the chickens. I saw the butcher knife on the table and right away I knew what to do . . . like someone behind me, pushing. I grabbed that knife and started after her. I remember I kept screaming, 'You won't call me wicked any more.' She ran away from me and started to yell for help. Not to God, though—not this time. Someone grabbed me and got the knife. They took me to jail and the judge said I was an unnatural daughter and sent me here," she finished simply.

The story was ended; maybe now a new Mattie could begin. In telling me, she'd revived the old angers and injustices—whipped herself into the old rages—but at least the emotions were finally out in the open. Now that I knew where the trouble lay, perhaps I could pour in enough understanding to neutralize the poison. The case history, I remembered, had merely said, "Attempted to murder her mother."

I pulled my chair closer and touched her hand—lightly, tentatively. "Try to put it behind you, Mattie. I won't tell you to forget it because I know you can't—but you can push it back so you don't have to look at it. Hate takes up too much room," I told her. "It can crowd out all the good things if you let it. It's up to you."

She didn't answer immediately, and I was glad. A decision needs time—thought. At last she spoke. "Okay. Things couldn't be any worse, so I'll try it your way for a while."

"Not *my* way, Mattie." I threw the decision right back to her. "It's got to be what *you* want or it's no good at all."

I held my breath for what seemed a year. She looked straight at me, burningly, then slowly nodded her head. I'd won. We'd both won.

Mattie left and I sat behind my desk, drained, depleted of all energy and ambition. A throbbing pain moved in to fill the void. It started behind my eyes and was pounding at the confines of my skull before I could stumble, half-blind, to my room to relax. For the first time since I arrived at the school, I decided that I'd collapse into bed immediately after "Lights Out."

A hot bath gave some relief, but the nerves at the base of my neck were still knotted; I knew sleep would be some time coming, if it came at all. And I was the Mrs. B. who bragged about being able to sleep on a bed of hot rocks if I had to! Or *was* I the same Mrs. B.? I certainly had broadened, shriveled, soared, sunk, laughed, and cried enough to effect a transformation of some sort. I wasn't at all sure that I wanted to change. Over the years most of us, whether we admit it or not, become fond of our own quirks and tolerant of our own faces. Of course I'd always admired ascetic and aesthetic types, with pale luminous faces, ennobled by spiritual suffering or artistic striving. I felt wan . . . maybe I was luminous too?

The mirror threw back the same old hearty, healthy features I'd always had. Even with a head full of hornets and every nerve end crawling with ants, I'd never excite any sympathy. I sighed —but it was a resigned sigh. No one had ever been able to tell whether I was sick or well, calm or quaking, from what was going on around my eyes, nose, and mouth. Someone had once said that I'd look blandly confident with my neck in a noose and my heels on a rolling log. Probably that was why I'd been picked for this job. They must have figured that nothing would faze me.

On an impulse, I pulled out a handful of newspaper pictures I hadn't had time to paste up anywhere. The captions read: "New Superintendent Appointed to Tecumseh." I remembered grinning until my mouth almost buttoned in the back, excited as a kid, when the photographers flashed their bulbs—but sure enough, the pictures showed me with a happily matter-of-fact expression. A just-another-job kind of calm acceptance. Nothing could have been farther from the truth!

The clippings evoked all the memories that had eluded me till now. The very beginning came clear . . . the conversation that had eventually landed me in this morass of self-analysis. Could my psychologist friend have been fooled too? Did he think of me as a woman full of strong convictions, completely devoid of self-doubt? Well, I *did* have the convictions, but I'd certainly expressed the doubts.

When it had finally filtered through that he was serious about the possibility of my becoming Superintendent, I'd looked at him incredulously and asked, "Why me?"

He returned my stare thoughtfully. "I've been discussing the correctional school with the Governor. We're both disturbed about the condition of the girls. He asked me to keep an eye out for the right person to go in and take over."

"That certainly doesn't mean *me*," I laughed.

"But it does," my friend stared me down, "it most certainly does. The Governor and I agree that you're the best person we could possibly find for the job."

I shook my head vehemently and began to back away. "I guess you didn't look hard enough. I don't know the first thing about that sort of work. What could I do for those kids?" I thought I had him there, but it was just the opening he wanted.

He leaned forward, spoke earnestly. "They need you. You never saw kids that needed you so much. They're so forlorn—and so defiant. They're mistaken about almost everything; somebody's got to straighten them out before we turn them loose. Creighton," his voice hardened, "did you ever see an eight-year-old with rope marks around her neck? Or a seventeen-year-old who honestly believes that everybody either steals or sleeps around for a living?"

"No," I jumped in. "And that's what I mean. I'd be all at

sea. There are plenty of women in Oklahoma who could do the job. Important women. Civic leaders, teachers, professional welfare workers. Lots of them have degrees in sociology. I'm a fine arts major, remember?" I thought of a clincher. "Anyway, you must need some kind of civil service rating and I'm not about to start taking tests."

"Got you there!" he grinned. "I can even quote from the statutes: 'Civil service status is not a requisite for employment in Oklahoma institutions.'" He turned serious again. "Selections are entirely in the Governor's hands. The responsibility is all his, and that's why he's so anxious to find exactly the right people. We've found that the old hidebound methods don't work . . . and a lot of the latest scientific theory just isn't practical except under lab conditions. That's why he's decided to give the Tecumseh appointment to someone with a fresh point of view and the ability to make her own on-the-spot decisions."

That didn't lessen my astonishment. "What does he know to make him pick *me?*" I repeated.

My friend lifted his hand and proceeded to count off on his fingers, ". . . you're an active member of the Chamber of Commerce . . . charter member of the Little Theatre . . . hard worker on the Red Cross and Community Fund Drives . . . served for years as a top officer of one of our most active civic clubs . . ." I felt like a piece of furniture up for auction. He kept enumerating my "sale" points.

". . . and I've reminded the Governor of your work with the Hospitality Club, the P. T. A., and the music groups. Didn't have to remind him about the way you campaigned for him. He knows how many speeches you made—good ones—every place from auditoriums to street corners. He remembers all right, but this isn't a reward he's offering. You really get around, lady, and that's the kind of person he wants in his organization."

Why try to deny it? The soft words were eating big holes in

my resistance to the idea. I countered—weakly. "But what if I don't click with the girls? How does he know they'll respond to me?"

"That's where I put in my oar," friend psychologist grinned smugly. "I told him that you teach your students a lot more than voice . . . that they confide things in you they wouldn't tell their own mothers. *And* that you've helped more than one out of a hot spot."

I looked at him sharply; he knew more than I'd suspected.

"Remember that cute little society fluff," he continued, "the one that got mixed up with the congressman? Whew! That little story could have wrecked two homes and blown an election sky-high. I never figured out how you took care of that particular mess. Whatever became of the girl?"

"She's happily married. Her family never found out . . . and I don't want them to," I emphasized—rather strongly. "Our esteemed legislator is being a model husband these days. It's all over, so let's forget it."

"There!" He jabbed his finger at me. "That's the attitude we're after. Understand it, forgive it, fix it, and forget it. Not a bad formula for the job." He sat back complacently and I had to laugh. I was hooked and I knew it.

My muscles had unkinked and sleep was really on its way. The trip back to the beginning had restored some of my derring-do. Before I dropped off, I repeated my own magic formula for the job. "If they think I can do it, who am I to argue?"

5

THE SPEED WITH WHICH ONE PROBLEM FOLLOWED ANOTHER SOON convinced me that superintending an institution for delinquents would leave me neither time nor strength for outside contacts or recreation. My associations would have to be confined largely to school personnel. I didn't consider that a hardship since I'd been briefed about some exceedingly interesting people on staff. However, though I saw them chatting and laughing in small groups, they scattered like polite but frightened quail at my approach.

It was baffling, to say the least. I'd make overtures . . . they'd smile courteously . . . then suddenly remember some duty at the other end of the school. I began to wonder if I offended in some way my best friends wouldn't mention. I was beginning to eye the mouthwash ads, when one of my staffers supplied the answer.

One day I met a group of employees and managed to scatter them in the record time of two minutes. One man remained behind. He was a professional educator with a courtly manner that had won me on our first meeting. By this time, though, I'd have been happy to talk with him if he'd had two heads and halitosis. To thank him for breaching the wall built up against me, I tried to be as entertaining as possible.

Immediately I began to chatter like a wallflower on her first date. Then I remembered that courses on "How to Be Popular" stress the importance of being a good listener. Without warning, I tossed the conversational ball over to my companion but he turned brick red, looked wild-eyed at me, and had to swallow twice before a word would come. Then it was a husky whisper, "Will you come with me where we can talk privately?"

"Certainly." I ground my own voice down to a whisper. For companionship at this point I'd have learned sign language. "Shall we go back to my office?"

"No, no," he shook a troubled head. "Come this way, please."

In absolute silence, he led me around the campus, past the power house, and out beyond the cow barn. He stopped, peered around as cautiously as an arch conspirator, and only then did I see that he was struggling hard for control of himself. Our rendezvous suddenly lost its comic aspect.

"I've been working here for three years," he said shakily, "and I don't want to leave. I'm asking you please to let me stay. I'll be just as loyal to you and your policies as a man can be—only please don't let them get rid of me."

I'd forgotten that a new administration always meant staff changes, but nevertheless his intensity amazed me. I exclaimed, "But you're capable of holding down a much better job than this."

"That's true," he nodded, "but it isn't the money with me. I can manage—but this—" he embraced the whole school in his gesture, "—this is my life. I'm needed." He turned away to regain his composure.

I was in even worse shape if possible. He *was* needed. He was a brilliant, dedicated man—exactly the kind of person I'd prayed for—and I couldn't help at all. I laid a hand on his arm and tried to summon up the right words. Before I could say anything, he spoke again. "Please forgive me for putting you in this position. It's politics and you're in exactly the same fix. We're all in the same boat."

All I could think of to say was, "Can you get to your sponsor?"

"If you advise it, I'll try," he agreed bleakly. We both knew there was no hope. He thanked me and started back to work with the sun sparkling on a head held gallantly high.

My heart ached for the man, even as my mind rebelled at the system. His successor might be an equally fine, competent person, who in turn would be shifted around on the political chessboard without regard for his personal sensibilities. It was all the ghastlier because the sponsor who controlled the fate of men such as these might be the worst of party hacks with hardly an eighth-grade education and less sense of civic responsibility than my delinquents.

I remembered one sponsor I'd recently seen. He'd been seated in his office with his hat on and his feet on the desk; a wet black cigar grew out of the side of his mouth. I must admit that he tried to be gracious but was uncertain of his ground when I failed to respond favorably to his offer of "a slug of Scotch." A week later his ax had fallen, separating one of our best supervisors from the school.

"To the victor belong the spoils."

A world of heartache attends every political turnover. Most of the workers are worthy people who need their jobs and try to render the best service of which they're capable. But rotation, i.e. paying off of past favors, is the essence of politics, and few appointees can hope for any sort of long-range security.

Suddenly I understood why my employees were wary of me.

I was new—an unknown political quantity. It was safer to stay away from me entirely than risk my disapproval. Perhaps I wouldn't like them, in which case I might ask to have them replaced. Without their jobs, how could they buy the medicines for an invalid husband, or meet the school expenses of a daughter, or provide all the other necessities somehow eked out of their meager salaries?

I was learning—learning all the time. Often I didn't like the lessons but they were a necessary part of the life I was now leading. As soon as I could, I called all the school employees in and gave it to them straight. My advice was, "See your sponsor. Be sure of his support." And then I told them their jobs were safe as far as I was concerned. The barometric pressure in the room immediately rose. Already I could see that some staffers were less competent than others, but I had hopes of improving the poor ones now that the pressure was off.

Scared educators! I could have cried. We desperately needed trained people with heart and strength enough to give a part of themselves away every day, and these poor souls were as hagridden in some respects as the ones they were supposed to rehabilitate. Well, they'd have to straighten out their own snags for the time being. I needed an hour to myself or I'd be no good to anyone at all.

I tried to relax, but I'd lost the knack. I could perform all the physical acts necessary—the lying down, stretching out, closing of eyes—but I couldn't remember how to throttle down my thinking. My mind took over and raced off on its own.

My employee problems? They were unique in a way, but I knew already that all heads of institutions worry about their officers. Not about them, per se, but their effect on the inmates. Sometimes administrative details make it difficult to remember that the girls, after all, are the reason for the surveys, the budgets, the schedules, the staff meetings, the committee reports, and the rest of the addenda. The addenda, I thought, that often obscures the main issue.

I'd been corresponding with other people in my position, all over the United States. They were as dedicated as I to the improvement of young offenders, but after reading their long detailed letters, I was more adrift than ever; we had no common meeting ground. The problem itself was affected by geography, density of population, the presence of foreign elements, segregation or the lack of it, local feeling, et al. Then there were the varying degrees of ability to contend with the differences of opinion among judges, parole officers, welfare workers, wardens, superintendents, and teachers and the prejudice of each in favor of his own diagnosis and treatment. It added up to chaos, with each of us picking his own dangerous way out of the dark.

Deliberately I tried to turn my thoughts elsewhere. The "hour to myself" was, as usual, turning into a one-woman forum. And, of course, that was the trouble. *Every* responsible adult in a community should be interested enough to argue the problem; then the results on community levels could be fed into a larger hopper—right up the line till we wound up with a well-integrated national program.

Wherever it's found, delinquency is always an eruption of diseased public morale. Trying to cure it by treating isolated groups was about as sensible as attempting to cure smallpox by drying up a few pustules and permitting the infection to remain. What's worse, most of us weren't even agreed on treatment of the local eruptions.

I was too wound up to stop now. Anyway, I'd needed an opportunity to put some of these thoughts firmly together for a good long time. All I'd experienced so far at the school served to confirm the ideas I'd had as a private citizen. Maybe some day, if I screamed long enough, I'd make my voice heard.

Take the argument being advanced these days in favor of substituting foster homes for institutional care. It's a fine solution for normal kids who've been orphaned or abandoned, but delinquent children need reconditioning, not merely a roof over their heads. Sick and damaged personalities require correction in a school designed for that purpose, just as sick bodies need the services of a hospital.

Much too often foster parents are forced into that role by economic pressure instead of by any understanding of the problems involved and any positive desire, or ability, to help. Watching every mouthful a girl eats and checking her off as a profit or loss can hardly contribute to her sense of well-being. On the other hand, an erring youngster can cause an unimaginable amount of trouble for a too-trusting foster family. And the free and easy regime of a private home offers too many opportunities for a maladjusted child to spread her sickness among schoolmates and other associates. Amorality can be as catching as a cold.

"Delinquency is the result of a broken home" is a glib cliché, but it's one of the few dogmatic statements I won't snap at—too viciously, at any rate. It's about 99.44 per cent true. But though a foster home may occasionally supply the home life a girl has missed, it isn't retroactive . . . it can rarely cope with the character traits which are already well established.

Institutional life, on the other hand, impresses a delinquent with the fact that her misdemeanors are unacceptable to society, and that she must make a real effort to adjust herself, to learn to live by the rules. Once her moral responsibility has been re-established—or implanted for the first time—she's ready for either a foster home or other adjustment to "outside" society.

Of course institutions aren't perfect either. All I had to do was open my eyes and look out over my own domain, and mine was a great deal better than most. We all shared at least one fault in common. In spite of recognizing that most delinquency results from a lack of normal home life, institutional architects keep designing for factory methods instead of individual care. Economy seems to be the prime objective . . .

On that thought I trailed off. I always got back to the beginning of the circle. Until the general public found out what false economy it was . . . I cut that off too. My hour of relaxation was up. The luncheon bell said so.

My mental monologues on "the over-all picture" were always interrupted by issues that required immediate attention rather than an act of Congress. Today I'd have to do something about the situation in the dining room.

All of us ate together in a long narrow building. The teachers occupied a table at the north side of the room, downwind from the girls seated at the long tables south. The trouble lay in the fact that the prevailing breeze in our area of Oklahoma blows south to north. The teachers complained that when a zephyr swept across the room, the odor from the girls who worked on the farm and at the barn was unbearable. In some cases instructors were too nauseated to eat. They'd been urging me to shift the seating arrangements so the fragrance floated off in another direction.

I thought there was a better solution, and I broached it at a staff meeting that afternoon. "Ladies," I announced, "I agree that you must have relief, but I believe we should clean up the girls rather than shift their seats." Somebody gasped. "Give me a few days to see what I can work out."

The teachers were dubious, but I began to make plans. As long as I was at it, I intended to start at the skin and work my way out. Cleanliness was first on the agenda, but then I meant to see why the girls were required to wear those abominable blue uniforms. They were at an age when they should have been intensely interested in clothes and personal grooming. Instead, every gathering was an offense to the eye and ear, as well as the olfactory sense. They clumped and thudded in ill-fitting boats of shoes. Greasy, shoulder-length hair hung in stringy wisps. Dandruff decorated all. Make-up was taboo. And those figures were the bitter end.

The female form may be divine, but not in wholesale numbers. Not when hundreds of unrestrained bosoms droop, shimmy, and dance; and hundreds of posteriors register every thumping step: left foot, quiver . . . right foot, bounce . . . left foot, quiver . . . There's more revulsion than charm in the sight of so much jellying flesh. I felt an acute need to stabilize and drape it properly.

My first step was to investigate bath facilities. Every residence cottage had a huge living room flanked on both sides by enormous dormitories. Back of each dormitory was a bathroom containing three tubs, three stools, and three wash basins. Most of the fifty girls in each cottage were averse to bathing at any time. When a matron finally laid down the law, everyone wanted to use the tubs just before retiring. With fifty girls, six tubs, and a half-hour for the whole process, this was obviously impossible.

The plumbing was old, the water trickled, and the girls dawdled. It took thirty minutes for a girl to fill her tub, scrub, and clean the tub for the next person. Allowing thirty minutes per bath added up to a total of four hours and ten minutes. With this in mind, we worked out a new timetable.

Midday bath hours were assigned to girls on morning schedules. Early morning hours were given to the schoolgirls; and evening hours were reserved for the farm, barn, and kitchen girls. Everybody was required to bathe every day and house mothers were instructed to enforce this order. There was lots of grumbling at first, but by the time they were soaped and scraped back into the white race, I could see spirits rising, and personalities blossoming.

Clothing was listed for the next inspection. The girls were wearing shapeless uniforms with round collars about three inches wide. When greeted on campus by anyone but a fellow-inmate, they'd turtle down into their dress necks as far as possible, pull the collar up over their faces, and scuttle by without replying. They'd been taught that they were too evil to speak to respectable people! A legacy from my predecessor. It took months of re-education to overcome their cringing.

All clothing was issued from the sewing room where bolts of grainy, unpleasant material rose in dull blue stacks. Other tiers contained harsh red sweaters, seemingly designed by someone who'd never seen a female figure. Boxes of shoes and piles of cotton stockings filled a small storage room. That was it.

Mrs. Rorem, the sewing room supervisor, was a lively little woman with snappy black eyes and quick gestures. She had to be brisk to keep our girls from running around naked. With the exception of sweaters and stockings, every garment worn by every inmate came out of her sewing room—made, often as not, by girls who'd never seen either a needle or underwear before.

With no other help than that of her young amateurs, Mrs. Rorem also hemmed all the table linens, bed linens, and towels for the school. And the curtains which came out of her department were decorated with bright, attractive designs of appliquéd linen. Nothing was bought ready-made but our blankets and quilts. We even had quilting frames, and some of the girls asked to learn the old art, but such tedious handwork couldn't begin to keep up with the school's demands.

In addition to making, remaking, and mending practically everything on the premises, Mrs. Rorem was also in charge of storing every item in the fabric line. At the beginning of each season, she issued the proper clothing and bedding, listing each article and requiring the receiving matron to sign the manifest. At the end of the season, all articles—and she meant *all*—were returned to Mrs. Rorem to be cleaned, labeled according to dormitory, and stored until the next time around. New garments were never given out until the remnants of the old ones were turned in to be washed and made into bundles of dusting cloths. I never found out what Mrs. Rorem did with the old dusting cloths.

Harassed matrons complained that they spent half their lives keeping tabs on every pair of stockings strewn around by irresponsible inmates. However, even with fifty girls to a cottage, they managed to keep an accurate check. Not one of them was willing to face an irate Mrs. Rorem with as much as a hand towel missing. But by hook or crook, at tally-time the sewing room always balanced.

Mrs. Rorem's job was as many faceted as an ant's eye and radiated in as many different directions. Somehow she'd been stuck with the fitting of shoes too. We had no foot-measuring equipment, which was probably just as well. At least we didn't know how *far* off we were. Our shoes came from the penitentiary which could furnish nothing but "C" widths in a limited number of sizes. Girls with long slender feet were just out of luck.

Pinched and aching feet made the girls shed their shoes at every possible opportunity. Padding around barefooted or in their stockings was responsible for stubbed toes, bruises, and stone cuts, so—the lesser of two evils—I ordered that shoes must be worn at all times. Quite often, though, I managed not to notice when some youngsters playing soft ball in a corner of the campus shed their miserable foot gear and wriggled tortured toes in the soft grass. Shoes were the first item on my list of evils to be corrected.

Next, I went through the dress lockers, making no particular effort to conceal my disapproval. I wondered if our overworked Mrs. Rorem would blow sky-high if I offered a suggestion. I decided to phrase it diplomatically, as a question. "Do we allow just one style and one color?" I asked. "The girls don't learn much about designing and cutting and fitting by making everything on one straight up and down pattern, do they?"

"They certainly don't!" Mrs. Rorem's black eyes flashed. "It's not my doing, but that's all there is. Blue for week days and white for Sundays. All just alike." She was just as bored as the girls!

Mrs. Rorem and I fingered the ugly dresses, sharing an acute distaste. "And if you think *that's* bad, Mrs. Burnham," the brisk little lady was eager to pour her troubles into a sympathetic ear, "how do you feel about *this?*" She laid out some weird-looking garments, whose functions I couldn't fathom for a moment.

The first proved to be a coarse muslin slip which hung straight from the shoulders like the Mother Hubbard of the missionaries. Scratchy muslin drawers, not panties, were gathered into folds at the waist by a half-inch tape drawn through a heavy hem. The legs, extending well below the knees, would have been more than adequate bolster slips. The finishing touch was supplied by cheap beige stockings with shapeless feet and tight hem tops.

Bare shanks were strictly against the rules, but the discomfort of those tourniquet-topped stockings forced the girls to risk rolling them down around their ankles. I discovered that anyone caught with her stockings at half-mast was required to sew the top hems to the end of the drawer legs so that the hose and bloomers became a permanent prison.

As the fabric in the drawers grew old and worn, active, sweaty young knees poked holes in it. Over and over, the holes were patched with strong new muslin until the drawer legs were about as pliable as sole leather. I shuddered, thinking of the tender flesh subjected to the constant rasping and grating of those dreadful garments.

"Well!" I finally exploded, "I'll bet I get something done about this! Let's plan some sensible clothes for these kids."

Mrs. Rorem gave a little war whoop of delight. We spent a happy morning choosing colors and styles that would be both pretty and practical. First, we decided to replace those behemoth drawers with feminine panties. Next, we planned an individual color for each cottage. Distinctive cottage colors would simplify laundry checking and make it easier to spot-check the more elusive girls.

The new clothes must be sturdy and laundry proof, but also attractive enough to stimulate some self-respect. We decided on Indian Head linens in green, yellow, pale pink, orchid, and rose.

Mrs. Rorem was ready to whip out her scissors and begin, but I realized that such a radical change would first have to win the approval of the Board of Affairs. They'd have to be sold on the necessity for the new system and then on the proposed system itself. Next, they'd have to let bids and allow time for them to be tabulated and approved. We'd have to wait for all that red tape to be unwound and wound up again before we could go to work. To rush matters as much as I could, I armed myself with a package containing a sample outfit, made my appointment, and burned up the forty-five miles between Tecumseh and the State Capitol.

All the members of the Board were mature married men and I knew that two of them had teen-age daughters. Presumably they had some knowledge of feminine apparel, even underwear.

"Gentlemen," I said as I untied my package, "have you any idea of the sort of clothes the girls at the State Industrial School are wearing?"

They looked at each other sheepishly and shook their heads.

"Then I'll show you," I answered, and I spread the garments on the Chairman's desk with a dramatic flourish. "Please tell me if you think these are an aid to reform. I don't mind telling you I'd be as mean as all get out if I had to wear such monstrosities."

The men stared speechlessly at the drawers I was waving to emphasize my point. The Chairman, who had no daughters, was the first to explode. "My God!" he sputtered. "I don't blame them for being delinquent."

That settled the matter. The vote was unanimous for color, fit, and fashion—or at least variety—in the girls' clothing. Bids were opened and in a few weeks we were ready to start sewing. We bought brassières and girdles, and purchased neat wool coats to replace the ravelly sweaters which we reserved for work schedules. Our next shoe order came from a regular manufacturer, and we had an experienced shoe man bring us some sizing equipment and teach Mrs. Rorem to use it.

Knowing that all political officers are targets for every kind of attack, I was grateful beyond words to the Board of Affairs. It would have been far easier, and safer, for them to have voted for the status quo. While they continued to differ on a good many issues, they presented a united front in the fight to dress these delinquent girls like girls, not faceless felons. And as long as they were doing it, they did it right! If I could squeeze it out of the clothing allowance, they even okayed ribbons and nylon and lace. This helpful attitude was true of a great many of my political contacts.

I'll never forget the two senators from different counties who served on the State's Budget Committee. They knew our school was far down the line on the dollars-and-cents agenda and that we had no pressure group of enthusiastic alumnae to lobby for us. Correctional school graduates don't usually advertise their alma mater. Those senators always remembered to put the brakes on State budget spending in time to save back enough for our needs. It's good to remember, when disillusion is about to set in, that politicians can be human enough to concern themselves about the color of a delinquent girl's dress.

The new clothes made such a tremendous difference in the general morale that even the instructors felt a lift. Butterfly colors flitting about the campus brightened up our landscape and outlook, and all of us unconsciously tried to live up to the new aura.

But before that happened, the psychology of color had been made vividly clear to me by one slatternly girl. "Mrs. Burnham," she inquired unhappily, "am I going to have a new pink dress?"

"You certainly are, my dear," I smiled at her. "You'll get it just as soon as it can be made."

"Do I have to have it?" she wailed.

"Don't you want it?" I could hardly believe that she was really objecting.

"No'm, I don't! I'll have to keep a pink dress clean!"

Unintentionally, that girl supplied one of my strongest arguments in favor of the new regime. Everyone else seemed delighted at the change. Daily baths had become so popular there were occasional fights for possession of the tubs. Neatly controlled figures and well-fitted shoes even improved posture to a visible degree. However, there was still something wrong with the picture.

In the dining room one day, looking at the girls en masse, I saw what we'd missed. Their hair, while clean, was still no crowning glory. I went into a huddle with the Budget Officer and after a few earnest conferences, we finally managed to squeeze out enough salary to hire a licensed teacher of cosmetology. Prettying up the inmates was only a tiny part of my argument. Here was another profession our girls could learn and use when they finally went "outside."

Our first student operators went at it with vim and vigor. They devoured the textbooks required by the State Cosmetology Board and earned practice credits by working on the other girls for as many hours as we'd allow. Imaginations ran rife and we had some fantastic assortments of curls and braids and towering pompadours, but at last the girls were on the way to good grooming from head to foot. The cosmetology instruction also included information on the care of the skin and nails, and I decided it was about time to remove the taboo on make-up too.

Startling effects were achieved in those first attempts at make-up. Eyebrows disappeared entirely or swept up and out in perpetual astonishment. Cheeks took on a tubercular glow. Lips burst into red Cupid's bows and stamped the napkins and pillow slips and almost threw the laundry supervisor into hysterics.

Clean odors of soap and body powder replaced old aromas. The teachers forgot about wanting to sit on the south side of the dining room and actually agreed to sponsor girls' tables in order to improve table manners and promote worth-while conversation. The metamorphosis took about three months, but it was certainly worth the effort. The State Cosmetology Board gave the beauty-parlor girls an examination every year and granted licenses to the graduates. Because of that department, many a girl is now self supporting and self-respecting who would otherwise have been a permanent liability to the public.

6

The days were filled to overflowing. New policies, new procedures, reports without end, perpetual inventory. And—wherever there was a chink—personal interviews with inmates and employees, tradesmen and court officers, educators and crackpots. I discovered that Tecumseh was a tourist attraction. To my everlasting horror, I found that there are members of the human race who enjoy gaping and gawking at wretched young girls.

Whenever I tried to draw a deep breath, the steam boiler broke down or somebody stole a ham out of the storeroom. An indispensable employee was called home because of dire emergency. The refrigerator got hot instead of cold, or the stove cold instead of hot. I cried in exasperation the day a valuable cow died, even after more tender loving care than would have been administered to any of the instructors.

Each night added its quota of trouble. The dark hours were appropriately named. Transportation officers always delivered newly committed girls at the most unpredictable and inconvenient times for tired teachers. Our weary officers dragged themselves out and up to sign papers and to receive, to disinfect, and to outfit an incoming girl and stow her away until the new day —generally an hour or so off.

The "how" remains a mystery to me, but I know without doubt that an appendix can tell time. Without fail, they flared up at the witching hour, just in time to wreck the night matrons' routine and, incidentally, set off any small-scale riots that were about to detonate in any case.

Runaway girls counted on escaping more easily if they could slip out in the middle of the night. A break for freedom was announced by the blood-curdling blast from the watchman's whistle which cut through the darkness like a shriek straight from the deepest hollow of Hell.

A motley crew of men and women, sketchily clad in whatever was closest to hand, scuttled out at the sound like grotesque gnomes. Curl papers and bathrobes, overalls and bedroom slippers crept through or vaulted the high barbed fence to join in a frantic search behind bushes and down deep ravines.

If no night emergency occurred, sheer boredom might prompt a group of girls to hit their night matron over the head with a sand-stuffed sock, confiscate her keys, and escape in a body. One stormy night four girls stripped themselves nude, thoroughly buttered their bodies, and wiggled through a single pane in the bathroom window.

The dark bred epidemics of hysteria. If one girl started to cry, a wave of shrieking and weeping would sweep over the entire room. Our more imaginative inmates pretended to see phantoms and hear chains clanking until they had their mates shaking with terror. The six matrons who stayed awake all night, every night, knitted or pieced quilts to keep their eyes open and their skulls unsplit. Every thirty minutes they made their rounds to see that everyone was in the cottage, each in her own bed and alone. With no equipment for self-protection except her own alertness, every night matron supervised fifty delinquents, each of whom had been too big a handful for a whole corps of officers in her committing county.

Perhaps it was just as well that most of our matrons were large, placid types without highly sensitive nervous systems. Anyone possessed of a vivid imagination would have quaked unceasingly from dusk to dawn in the realization that, alone and unarmed, she was the sole barrier between potential outlaws and their freedom.

I was learning how to evaluate my employees in terms of their jobs rather than on the scales of the social scene I'd left behind. In some of my people I eventually discovered a good deal of gold that didn't glitter. In the early days, I was shocked to my soles when a matron was assigned to me who knew no grammar, read her newspaper with noticeable hesitation, and flung "I seen" and "I done" around with reckless abandon. But the thing that outraged me most was her frequent use of "I taken."

I secretly decided to discharge her at the first opportunity. How could her girls learn to speak correctly if they had to listen to a woman who butchered the English language in every sentence she spoke?

To my surprise, the girls rallied to this ungrammatical matron with fanatical devotion. Double negatives or no, her cottage was the cleanest, her lockers the neatest, and her girls the most cheerful and cooperative of all. From my unlettered matron, I learned that syntax runs a lame second to a voice mellow with genuine sympathy. She would never have passed her civil service examination, but she had a quality of leadership no test could have discovered. I learned to overlook "I seen" and "I done," and even became calloused to "I taken." Probably my own English suffered because of this protective immunity, but there was adequate compensation in the lesson I learned.

I was also determined to get rid of a matron I caught whipping an inmate—but something stopped me from taking immediate action. In a month's time, and to my own amazement, I was having a girl cut her own switch so that *I* could teach her a much needed lesson in the only area that seemed at all impressionable.

Discipline is the topic uppermost in the minds of all correctional school officials. Everybody in the wide world has a fixed opinion on this one subject and almost everybody airs his views long and vociferously. People who have never been near a correctional school, and who don't have the faintest idea of the problems involved, clamor for laws relaxing the discipline that often means the difference between life and death.

Parents who have just spanked junior for tracking mud on the carpet mount soapboxes to speak against corporal punishment for delinquent girls, many of whom have spent years as thieves, prostitutes, or addicts, and who have committed crimes up to and including murder.

Without some form of discipline—discipline they fully understand, that is—a few such girls would soon disrupt any school. They resent the very idea of rehabilitation and, if they believe they can get away with it, will deliberately attempt bodily harm on anyone in authority. Almost any school can cite instances of instructors hospitalized because of handy milk bottles thrown at them or matrons beaten black and blue in organized riots. How can such violence be stemmed?

"Talk kindly to the youngsters. Help them understand their problems. Withdraw their privileges. In extreme cases, isolate them." So say the experts. I used to say the same things myself.

Matrons with throats already sore from sweet talk smile wanly when they hear this advice. They know that real incorrigibles erupt without reason, and that words would be as useful as so many snowdrops to subdue Vesuvius. The privileges allowed in an institution are such pale substitutes for the lurid pleasures the girls once pursued that they don't mind losing them.

As to isolation, there's no better culture for propagating crime than long periods of solitary confinement. With nothing to occupy her mind but her own boiling hatred, many a girl has used the lonely hours to plan highly detailed and deadly revenge on the rest of the world.

Of course, no form of imposed discipline can take the place of self-discipline. Every intelligent juvenile officer tries to teach her charges how to control their own impulses and so gradually establish a good behavior pattern. However, even the best of such officers must keep unruly students in line until at least a tiny seed of training has taken root.

A switching, administered not in anger but as *promised punishment*, is quickly over and has immediate results. Better yet, the culprit can be restored promptly to participation in her usual activities. Such punishment should always be administered in the presence of an appointed committee by someone other than the supervisor involved.

I found that the states which prohibit corporal punishment entirely were forcing their employees into duplicity and deceit. Since some serious infractions must be handled by physical reproof, supervised punishment, as practiced in private homes by wise parents, is surely more humane than illegal and uncontrolled cudgeling.

"We were just desperate after corporal punishment was discontinued," the superintendent of an eastern school once told me. "The girls knew we were helpless and they kicked up a ruckus every minute of the day and defied us to stop them. I was about to give up in despair when I happened to think of something even more effective than a switching . . . and absolutely within the law."

"What in the world was it?" I asked. "Show me. Some day I may need it too."

She led me into another room and up to a cabinet about the size of a phone booth. "See all those spray heads in the lining?" she asked as she ran her hand over the metal interior. "When we strip a girl and turn all those needle sprays of ice water on her, it isn't long before she's ready to cry quits and behave herself."

I wondered whether a doctor would think that needle spray less of a shock to a girl's nervous system than a simple switching. Officers feel the need for quick punishment and will always find substitutes when the law denies them the quickest and easiest system.

Severe infractions are not too frequent and usually affect a small percentage of the inmates, but they're too explosive to be ignored or brushed aside lightly. Even the most persistent incorrigibles tend to simmer down when they begin to understand that the school, like society, punishes its offenders.

Of course, each case is entirely different from all others. The thought of the licking is enough to deter some, while the one or two masochists a supervisor might encounter could probably be beaten half to death without making any impression at all. The great majority of all inmates will "test" to see if the whipping is an empty threat or a promise they can depend on. When they get what they ask for, I've seen the light of respect dawn in many an eye.

If I speak often of eyes, it's because they've always been my most reliable guide to the minds and hearts of my girls. I remember the day I walked into my office for an interview with a new inmate. I saw a stiffly erect, poker-faced girl of fifteen seated on a straight chair in the exact center of the room. Light freckles polka-dotted her thin nose and high cheek bones. Dingy hair, straining back into a tight bun, was topped by a small felt hat anchored by something other than pins, ribbons, or elastic.

The law of gravity, I decided. Faded green sleeves stopped short of Linda's wrists, and a skimpy skirt barely reached her bony young knees. Bare shanks ended in long angular feet pushing their way through the toes of soiled tennis shoes. But the amber-colored eyes staring at me were those of a trapped animal.

While I signed papers and listened to the usual sordid details, those imploring eyes followed my every move. Overcome by their insistent appeal, I decided to complete the details of Linda's reception myself instead of turning her over to an assistant. As soon as the sheriff had bowed himself out, I turned to say, "Now, Linda, you're my girl for a while. Let's get acquainted."

A pleased flicker lighted her eyes briefly, but there was no other response.

"Let's see what you've brought with you," I tried another gambit, but as I reached for the cardboard suitcase, Linda snatched it up from the floor, shoved it onto the seat, and defiantly sat down again.

"No," she objected, as it creaked vehemently. "That's mine."

"Yes, my dear, I know," I held out my hand persuasively, "but we have to list your personal things so we won't forget any of them when you're ready to go home. Things you won't need here will be locked up in the storeroom for safekeeping."

I kept my hand out, and eventually she slid off the squashed suitcase. We opened it together, so perhaps she was too occupied to see my dismay. All it contained was a can of snuff and a pair of very dirty rayon stockings.

"You won't be needing this again," I smiled as I dropped the snuff into the wastebasket. "Take the stockings with you but be sure to wash them right away."

In silence, Linda helped me write her name on some adhesive tape to paste over the lock on her suitcase. Then, with a longing backward glance at the wastebasket, she followed me out of the room to the hospital. I explained that some health tests would be made and that meanwhile she was to have a bath, a shampoo, and some fresh clean clothes. Linda never said a word. Her forlorn glance followed me as the nurse took her arm and hurriedly led her to the shower. The memory of those eyes came between me and my work all afternoon.

At supper time I watched for the hospital girls and could hardly believe what I saw. Scoured and combed, Linda's cocoon of misery had cracked open to reveal a definite promise of charm. Freshly shampooed hair fluffed around her face in curly tendrils of reddish-gold. Even in the shapeless blue hospital uniform, she moved with quick grace.

The wariness in her eyes wasn't entirely gone, but I could see a new, eager curiosity there, too. Perhaps she would respond to the training in music and dancing and art which I was then in the process of planning. At any rate, she held out more promise than I'd dared hope. I made a note to speak with the child before assigning her to a cottage.

My interview with Linda came sooner than I'd expected. That very night in fact. "Lights out" had sounded; the campus was in darkness and the girls in bed. From my window I saw the flash of the trouble light at the hospital and heard the quick footsteps of the night watchman running to answer it. In a moment he headed back toward my apartment; I was on the porch to meet him.

"It's that new girl," he explained rapidly. "She's gone. Can't find her anywhere."

My dreams for Linda suddenly blacked out. "When?" I demanded. "How did she get away?"

"I didn't wait to hear." He flashed his light on the path ahead of us. "You'll have to ask the nurse."

"She was in bed when I turned out the dormitory light at

nine o'clock," the nurse greeted us excitedly. "But she's gone. I put her in the third bed. All the other girls saw me do it. They'll tell you so. She was here at bedtime. I checked them again at ten o'clock. I always do, every hour, all night long. I checked and she was gone!" She kept babbling nervously as I pushed by her into the hospital. "I check them every night—right at ten o'clock —and every hour . . ."

"I'm sure you were doing your duty. Don't worry about it." I laid a quieting hand on her arm. I was still the "new" Super, and she still wasn't sure of her status. "Let's see what the other girls know about it."

I turned to the dormitory where a dozen girls, startled by the unexpected commotion, sat bolt upright in bed. Near the back of the room a very little girl called Tootsie was jumping up and down to attract our attention. She waved a frantic hand over her head and called to the nurse.

"Mis' Groves! Mis' Groves!" Tootsie shrilled. "I know somethin'! I know somethin'!"

"Be still, Tootsie. We're busy." Now that her own tension was relieved, Mrs. Groves was impatient.

"But I know where Linda's at, Mis' Groves. I seen her."

"Where?" everyone shouted at once. Tootsie triumphantly pointed a small finger toward the floor underneath the bed in the far corner. The nurse, the night watchman, and I dropped to our knees on the concrete floor and flashed a light under the farthest bed. There, rolled in her blanket, was Linda, peacefully sleeping with her head on her arm. Mrs. Groves crawled near enough to give the girl a vigorous shake.

"Wake up, Linda. Wake up!"

Linda's tawny eyes dragged open sleepily. "Huh? Huh? What's the matter?" Suddenly she was wide awake and wriggling out from under the bed in alarm, "Something wrong?"

"Nothing's wrong, Linda." I was sure the sleep and the alarm were genuine. I held out my hand to her, "Come with me. I'd like to talk to you."

Mrs. Groves eyed me accusingly; obviously she was all for a licking, not a tongue lashing. Nevertheless, she folded a robe around Linda's shoulders and cautioned her not to take cold. As we passed Tootsie's bed on the way out, I paused to say hello to the little girl. "It was nice of you to find Linda for us," I commended, "but I didn't even know you were in the hospital. Are you sick?"

"No'm, I ain't sick," Tootsie burst into tears. "I just don't like to sew on buttons."

"You don't like to sew on buttons?" I asked as I felt Tootsie's forehead to see if she was feverish. "Well, do you have to sew on buttons?"

"Yes'm," Tootsie wailed. "Mis' Rorem makes me. Mine were all off my dress an' my pants an' ever'thin'. I don't care —I pinned 'em. I can pin 'em easier than I can button 'em 'cause I'm used to pins." Tootsie's wail rose to a howl.

"But you did sew the buttons on when Mrs. Rorem asked you to, didn't you, Tootsie?"

"No'm," a guilty little voice answered.

"Why not, Tootsie?" I put my hand under her chin and raised her reluctant head.

"I swallered 'em."

I smothered a laugh. "Were they good? I never ate buttons. How many were there?"

"Eight," Tootsie's sobs turned to giggles. "Four big ones for my panty-waist and four for my dress."

"Then, what happened?"

"Well, then Minnie told Mis' Rorem on me an' Mis' Rorem said, 'Tootsie, did you swaller them buttons I give you?' an' I said 'Yes'm' an' she said, 'Oh my goodness, I wonder if they'll hurt you. Come quick, let's go to the hospital.' " Tootsie was relishing the limelight.

"So I come to the hospital with Mis' Rorem," Tootsie reported importantly, "an' Mis' Groves made me eat a whole lot of soft bread, without any milk, an' then she give me castor oil," Tootsie made a face and I glanced at Mrs. Groves for confirmation.

"I don't think the buttons will hurt her any—now," the nurse nodded significantly.

"And how did you happen to know where Linda was?" I stroked her hair lightly.

"Well, I had to go to the bathroom so quick I fell out of bed. That was when I seen Linda back in the corner on the floor." Tootsie's eyes were beginning to droop sleepily.

"How old are you, Tootsie?" I asked as I watched her bare feet swinging against the side of the bed.

"Eight. But I'll be nine in two more months!" she bragged.

Eight years old! I wondered what she'd done that could warrant sending her to a correctional school. "If you don't like to sew on buttons, I'll bet you like to make doll clothes, don't you?"

"Yes'm," Tootsie roused at the thought of dolls. "But I ain't got a doll 'cept the towel Mis' Rorem rolled up for me. She sewed a face on it but I ain't got no clothes for it yet."

"Tootsie," I promised, "you learn to sew on buttons, good, like Mrs. Rorem shows you, and I'll see if you can have a doll—a real one that opens and shuts its eyes—and some cloth to make its dresses."

Tootsie gasped. "I will, I will! I'll sew 'em on good! Can I have a doll for my birthday?"

"Sooner than that, maybe," I winked mysteriously. "You

show me the buttons when you have them sewed on and we'll see."

Tootsie grabbed my hand and held it to her cheek in ecstasy. Then she squirmed back into bed and was asleep before I could pull up her blanket.

Eight years old and in a "reform school"—and no doll! To my mile-long list of mental notes, I added another: find out about Tootsie. But right now I had Linda in tow. We walked back to my apartment through the weird patterns flashed on the path by the night watchman's light.

Linda's self-consciousness subsided as I settled her in an easy chair and asked about her coming to Tecumseh. We discussed affairs in her home town which I happened to know fairly well. When I felt that she was relaxed, I asked casually, "Linda, how did you happen to crawl out of bed to sleep on the floor?"

"I just don't like beds," Linda answered haltingly. "It was too soft. I felt—smothery."

"Smothery!" I laughed. "Was the cement floor more comfortable than the bed? You don't sleep on the floor at home, do you?"

"Yes'm." Nervous fingers picked at the seam in her bathrobe. "I haven't got a bed. I never sleep in one, so I just don't like 'em."

"Wasn't it cold in winter, Linda?" I asked as matter-of-factly as I could.

"Well, in winter we'd put down old clothes for a mattress, like. We kept warm enough," she explained defensively.

"Of course," I hoped my pity wasn't too obvious. "Did you have a large house?"

"Big enough for us," the amber eyes were reminiscent. "There were two rooms and nobody but Mother and me and my two brothers."

"And your daddy?" I prompted.

"No," Linda shook her head, "he wasn't there. I can't hardly remember him. The laws came and got him one day when he was drunk and he never came back." She was silent a moment and then her head went up proudly. "But my mother took care of us all right. She's a good woman, Mrs. Burnham. She washes and cleans house for people to make a livin' for us kids. She don't run around and get drunk like a lot of folks do.

"She don't have pretty clothes and shiny nails nor go places just for fun," Linda's championship grew with the recital. "She just works and works and gives everything to us."

I remembered Linda's meager belongings—a box of snuff and a pair of worn stockings. Her mother must surely be a wonderful woman to inspire such fierce loyalty in the face of so much privation.

"That's fine, Linda," I approved with a lump in my throat. "A good mother is the most wonderful thing in the world. The next best is a good child. Let's make your mother as proud of you as you are of her."

"How?" Linda asked quickly.

"We'll teach you all sorts of new things here," I promised. "Some of them will help you earn a good living, then you can make life a little easier for your mother. You'd like that, wouldn't you?"

"Sure would—and I'll try," Linda's eyes glowed. "What do I have to do?"

"First, go back and learn to sleep on a bed." I rose and gestured for her to come with me. "You'll like a bed when you get used to it. In a few days we'll talk about what you'd better study."

"Okay. I'll do whatever you say." Linda was out of her depth but she sensed friendliness. She gave me a long, straight look that wound up in a relieved grin. "I'm not afraid of you any more," she said shyly. "I guess I like you kinda like I like my mother."

"This job isn't going to be so difficult," I assured myself brashly. "All I have to do is study the girls and win their confidence. As soon as they're willing to cooperate, the problems will smooth out automatically."

I'm glad I can remember that period of smug satisfaction. It was so brief.

7

Complacency over my success with Linda was tempered with humility. I'd evidently been all wrong about Leila Wiles, and for a change I was honestly glad to admit an error. Life was going to be complex enough without more snarls on the staff level. As long as I was now in the business of rehabilitation, I decided to start with myself. Resolution: I will never judge so hastily and arbitrarily again—at least on the basis of odd blue eyes!

Viewing the facts without prejudice, Leila was a veritable gem. Those seemingly fragile bones, barely covered with blue-white flesh, must have had the strength and resiliency of good structural steel. Sometimes she'd be up before me in the morning and occasionally I'd see the lights still on in her room when I was ready to topple like an axed ox.

On her own, she thought up exciting things for the girls to do—projects which they enjoyed and which cost amazingly little money to put into operation. Her surprisingly long and painfully thin fingers could handle anything from a fine silk filament to a hammer and saw. After looking on one day while she transformed a bit of scrap leather and a length of clothesline into a tricky belt, I was even able to understand how she managed to look so chic on an institution salary.

I finished cataloguing Leila's virtues, and then—having rubbed salt well into my wounded ego—turned back to my triumph with Linda. Maybe the job wasn't going to be quite as tough as it first appeared. Actually all I had to do was catch the girl's point of view and I'd automatically arrive at the proper approach to her problem. Of course that meant learning her background by heart. First stop: the files.

Probably the hour just before half-past seven breakfast and the beginning of the day's bedlam would be my best bet. The idea of turning out every morning at six didn't exactly intrigue me, but if sparrow-like Leila could cope, well, I guessed it wouldn't kill me either.

At dawn the next day, I wasn't quite so sure. February in Oklahoma can feel like the lower depths of an efficient deepfreeze. Flinging back the covers took all the strength of character I could summon up, I wondered if I could rebuild a reserve every twenty-four hours from there on.

I ran all the way to the office; at a walk I sincerely believe my feet would have frozen to the ground. Naturally no heat was up at that hour in the office, so I wrapped myself in an old army blanket, ignored my slowing circulation, and started on the job.

The histories were as icy as the atmosphere. Probably the coldest, most unemotional document in existence is a social service file. With dispassionate candor it describes age, size, coloring, intelligence, physical defects, and other "pertinent information." It lists members of the family, size and source of income, criminal commitments, and known perversions with all the tender sentiment of a statistical report. It also catalogues undesirable associates and reviews events leading up to the current commitment.

Vella's file was the first I opened—but how did one correlate "Sex—female; Age—15; Height—5′2″; Weight—118 lbs.; I.Q.—99; General Description—red hair, brown eyes, irregular teeth," with a vivacious "bebopper" who laughed off syphilis and cried for two days when a pet terrapin died? The skin and bones were there all right, but I could see we'd have to search out the heart and soul for ourselves.

I needed more but I knew better than to sell the facts short. Every scrap of information fitted somewhere in the jigsaw puzzle of a personality. The knowledge that Vella's father was a drunken loafer, and her mother a sickly mouse without food enough for her six youngsters, certainly gave me a frame in which to work.

By banging a piano in a cheap dance hall, Vella had earned enough for the cokes and hot dogs and slabs of apple pie she regarded as food fit for the gods. She'd been hungry so long, it took weeks to fill her up. By then, she'd discovered even better ambrosia. Hamburgers and beer. High life. Eventually, of course, the men around the place took charge of the fresh "talent" and introduced her to a few new pleasures which paid off in cheap jewelry and bright dresses. In some ways Vella remained naïve; it never occurred to her to ask for money.

I turned to Leta's file in the hope that it would be pleasanter reading. It wasn't. Her mother had died when she was seven years old. The father had made a real effort to rear the youngster and her smaller brother, but his business kept him away from home many evenings. The children were decently fed but starved for companionship.

On her way to school, Leta passed the home of a friendly woman who sometimes invited her in and fed her candy. There were always other people around—some friendly women, but mostly men—and the child drank in the liveliness of the place. The women fussed over her, the first attention she'd had since her mother's death, and soon Leta was spending most of her time with these pleasant people.

The men weren't quite so pleasant. They petted her too, but it wasn't the same. In fact, their attentions made her cry. Still, they gave her presents and told her what a pretty little girl she was. It was better than being all alone at home. Leta had become a public character before her father had an inkling of anything wrong. He found out when he visited the establishment for his own entertainment one night and opened the wrong door. At the sight of his beloved daughter in such a place, the man went completely berserk. Furniture crumpled like match sticks before his furious onslaught. Terror-stricken women were cowering in the corners and men were trying to dodge his murderous lunges with a broken chair back when the police arrived. Of course, Leta was sent to us.

Beth's case was less grim. Her family was well known in Oklahoma. An uncle held an important State position which he filled with honor. Her father was a man of intelligence and culture, but extremely heavy drinking had made him a social outcast.

Shunned by his own family and avoided by his peers, Beth's father finally married a simple, quiet girl from a much lower economic and intellectual stratum of society. However, the mother's character was above reproach and she struggled to provide a wholesome home life. The father gave up entirely and devoted himself solely to keeping himself in a permanent stupor. Beth, a super-sensitive child, refused to associate with friends or relatives who knew, and discussed, her father's state. Instead, she turned to a group of hoodlums who couldn't care less about a drunk in the family—or a murderer for that matter.

Fortunately, her mother saw what was ahead and had sense enough to appeal to local officers for aid when Beth refused to listen. With tears of anguish, her mother sent her to us to keep her from drifting into, or seeking out, serious trouble.

Once at the school, Beth's innate refinement gradually came to the surface. Our psychologist soon straightened out her emotional involvement with her father's problem, and helped to re-establish her identity as a separate individual, responsible only for her own actions.

The office was warming up a little. I crawled out of my blanket cocoon and stretched aching muscles. I couldn't do much right now about the mental twinges. I'd long since lost my optimism. This job was going to be even tougher than I'd anticipated in my most morose moments. Our girls ran the gamut; I'd have to run it too.

Suse's report was next. Here it was again—liquor. A father whose drunken rages kept his family cowering in terror, and a mother who lived only to placate him. Suse was only six when her parents placed her in a children's home in another state. They told her she'd only have to stay two weeks while her mother went to the hospital for an operation.

Through her tears, Suse watched her parents drive back down the road and out of her life. After weeks of fruitless, forlorn waiting, she took things into her own hands and ran away to search for them. Any family was preferable to none. Even a beating was better than no attention at all.

Police found Suse wandering through the streets of a large city, but the children's home refused to take her back. She was sulky and vicious, they said. For lack of any other alternative, she was placed in temporary foster homes. In time, she wound up with an overly severe woman who tolerated no nonsense and exhibited no sympathy. Not even for an abandoned six-year-old.

During her years with this woman, Suse's alert mind absorbed much more than her foster mother realized. She noticed that her mother's name, signed to a slip of pink paper out of a small book, was worth money at the store. Since there was certainly magic in the signature, she practiced copying it.

One day, when Suse was barely eleven, she found the little book of pink papers and filled one of them in for twenty-five dollars. She traced the signature carefully and nearly burst with pride when the man at the store unquestioningly cashed the check. Just like Mother. Suse spent a wonderful afternoon buying all the things an eleven-year-old loves. She remembered Mother, too, with a pink and silver scarf.

When Suse's foster mother discovered the transaction, she exploded with rage. "Thief . . . bad blood . . . born criminal . . ." Those were a few of her more intelligible comments before Suse and the local board. "Forger!" she stabbed a finger at the frightened child's face. Suse had never even heard the word before. For everyone's sake, the board decided to send her to Tecumseh. The school was Suse's nineteenth home since the age of six.

At least there was some hope of rehabilitation for those four, but what could be done about a girl like Hallie?

Shoveling manure had no allure for town and city girls who'd never been near a cow before and hoped they never would again. The task had one value, however. It served as a punishment schedule for girls who had misbehaved. Hallie put in a lot of time shoveling.

One day, she was working near the incinerator while a clean-up crew burned piles of dry leaves. A stray kitten was attracted by the warmth and, on her way to the incinerator, stopped to rub gently against Hallie's ankle. With a raucous howl, the girl snatched up the ball of fuzz and tossed it straight into the flaming mouth of the incinerator.

The kitten managed to scramble out of the fire but her fur and most of her skin was singed off and her paws were live coals. Still shrieking, Hallie went after her with the shovel; but another girl knocked her aside; while a third, in tears, rushed the dying animal to the hospital. The kitten squalled in agony and, in tears, myself, I ordered it chloroformed. The whole school was stunned. Girls wept and threatened vengeance. I couldn't face Hallie; I was too shaken to question her sensibly or to dispense anything resembling justice.

When I calmed down and forced myself to see her, I found that she was totally unable to grasp the enormity of her deed. Hallie shrugged, "All that fuss about a lousy kitten." Even our psychologist was unable to reach her, although her I.Q. indicated that she was of normal intelligence and should be receptive to logic. However, no test but life itself has yet been devised to measure the emotional quotient of a deeply disturbed girl.

I'd been ruminating while the office grew warm and the school came to life for another day. The assembly bell rang and I put the files away. Such a small stack to contain such a staggering amount of tragedy!

As I left the office, all two hundred and seventy-six girls and matrons were standing in a wide circle, surrounding the flagpole in the center of the campus. A lump rose in my throat as these imperfect "rejects" solemnly swore allegiance to their land. Whatever their other faults, these girls of ours were learning something about love of country. At first most of them didn't understand what really constitutes good citizenship, but patriotism was becoming crystal-clear. In their lexicon, it meant being American—and proud of it. Once gained it was their only source of pride, their only sense of belonging. When all else failed, an appeal through the patriotism they were learning sometimes put across the concepts of participation and responsibility.

Breakfast followed flag salute, and I hurried to the dining hall; one of my supreme pleasures was watching the way those youngsters ate. Our food was exceptionally good, and they could have as much as they liked. I'd established only one strict rule. Anything taken on a plate had to be eaten. Occasionally a girl would pile up Alps of food out of sheer perverseness, but whatever was left, she got again for her next meal. Along about the third time a stewed tomato or a slice of meat loaf appeared on her plate, she generally decided to keep her deviltry out of the dining room.

Most of our girls simply didn't know how to eat when they arrived—and I'm not referring to table manners, though they were also on the negative side. I've seen a ten-year-old stare at a tomato wondering what it was and how to attack it. Some of our girls had never tasted butter in their entire lives. The majority of the older inmates had been living on hot dogs, cigarettes, and beer for years before they came to us. Fresh fruit and vegetables were just color pictures in fancy magazines. However, this is one area in which they all learned equally fast. Our only big food problem consisted of stretching our budget to match their capacity.

I'll never forget eight-year-old Louanne, who came to the school from the local "poor farm" where she'd lived with her mother. She arrived emaciated and empty clear down to her arches. When she was told to take as much food as she liked, she obviously thought we were teasing and her eyes filled with tears. I assured Louanne that she could pick what she pleased; she timidly took a small piece of meat and one potato, then paused. No one stopped her, so in faster and faster tempo, she piled on everything she could reach. When the plate held a towering pyramid of food, she lost faith again. Probably we were just waiting for her to finish before swiping it.

Louanne ducked under the table with the first full plate of

food she'd ever had in her life, and wolfed everything down as fast as she could cram it into her mouth. Of course, she upchucked all a moment later. The same thing happened several times before her wizened stomach grew accustomed to the new era.

In a month, Louanne gained so much weight that we had to issue a complete new wardrobe down to and including the socks. At last the day arrived on which she pushed her plate away with a blasé air and said, "Wish they'd have something good for a change." Our starveling had suddenly become a gourmet! We couldn't have been more delighted. We knew that at last she'd filled at least one gaping void in her life.

Peace reigned for at least an hour. I was on my way back to the office when I heard someone come dashing after me, calling, "Mrs. Burnham! Mrs. Burnham! Blanche has gone crazy!"

When I arrived at the cottage pointed out by the excited messenger, I found that Blanche had barricaded herself behind the door of the big bathroom. The door had no lock, but she held it shut with unbelievable strength. Neither promises nor any form of persuasion caused her to come out or even to stop screaming and cursing for a single second. At any attempt to open the door, she hurled one of the heavy china tooth mugs. One cottage-mate was already in the hospital. She'd forced the door, poked her head in, and promptly had a washboard broken over it.

"Don't you come near me," Blanche screamed. "Don't you dare come near me, you bastards. Stay away from me or I'll hit you with everything in here. I'll kill you!"

Matrons and inmates stood around in futile groups. Eight-year-old Evvie whimpered, "I wanna go to the toilet," and a couple of the girls giggled. Another mug crashed against the door panel and the giggling abruptly stopped. Blanche didn't stop yelling for a second; it sounded as if she were approaching a truly insane state.

After a hurried consultation, I decided that we'd better call on our Chief Clerk again. He was rapidly becoming our riot buster when only physical means would suffice. While a girl went to fetch him back, I found a thick quilted comforter which would muffle the impact of anything Blanche might throw.

The Chief Clerk arrived, seized the quilt, and forced the door; just about as quickly as that. Blanche came at him furiously with a mug in one hand and a sharpened toothbrush handle aimed at his eye in the other. He drove in, head down, and wrapped the quilt around her, pinning her arms to her sides. Conquered and helpless, Blanche dropped her weapons. Weak and spent with frenzy, the fierce creature of a few minutes before was now a limp bundle which shivered and twitched in Mr. Carson's arms.

While waiting for the hospital report, I checked Blanche's record. It was almost a classic case. She was the eldest of five children, with the gross and shiftless parents I'd learned to expect. They all lived in two rooms in the most sordid section of our largest city, where sex and liquor ran slightly ahead of eating and sleeping in popularity. The girls quite naturally fell into the "normal" habits of the neighborhood . . . or maybe the parents even pushed a little. I wouldn't have been surprised. In any event, they accepted money the daughters sometimes brought home without asking any embarrassing questions.

As I reached the end of the case history, the nurse called with the report. Blanche, it seemed, had graduated from drinking to smoking. Marijuana, that is. Her tantrum had been a withdrawal symptom. There was a possibility that she'd been on something stronger, but the nurse didn't feel herself qualified to make a final judgment.

We did what we could medically, but it wasn't enough. The

trouble went deeper than marijuana or any other drug. I knew. I'd heard a lost, different sort of panic in the girl's voice. As soon as Blanche was calm enough, I put my arm around the slight, still trembling child, and walked her down to the rose garden, away from curious onlookers.

We sat on a bench and allowed the bright wintry sunshine to sink in. I began to talk about casual, unimportant matters. Blanche's answers were hesitant at first, but gradually she relaxed. Finally, I felt it was safe to steer the conversation around to the recent riot.

"I just can't stand it sometimes," Blanche said with great intensity. "There are too many people. Voices all the time. They pound at me and I know I can't ever get away from them, even for a minute. It's enough to drive you crazy. I guess I did go kind of crazy." She leaned toward me and I saw that she was trembling more than before. "Can't you put me in a room by myself? Even if it's only for a little while? *Please!*"

I patted her shoulder to soothe her, feeling completely helpless even as I did so. It was like offering one crumb to a person dying of hunger. But what could I do? I tried to explain. "My dear, there isn't a single private room in this whole institution. The nearest thing to it is one of the cells in Meditation."

She jumped at the idea. "Let me sleep there, Mrs. Burnham. Please, please let me!"

She was begging for her sanity. My heart bled that her sanity should depend on a jail cell. But in this case, the cell was a refuge, a haven. Lacking all comforts, it yet contained the greatest luxury in the world. Privacy.

We gathered up a few of her personal belongings, picked a bouquet of winter greenery, and made the small room as inviting as we could. The sun still shone as Blanche slipped into her gown, stretched out on the bed—behind bars—with a happy sigh, and drifted into a sleep that lasted almost around the clock.

I looked down at her, filled with a turbulent mixture of compassion for her and anger at my inability to do more. Tomorrow, or the next day, she'd have to rejoin the others—twenty-four hours a day for years to come without a corner to call her own.

To be sure, some schools recognized this basic need, but a very small minority had physical plants which would permit any privacy. I'd made a point of corresponding with those educators wise enough to appreciate the privacy problem and fortunate enough to have some means of solving it. I was frankly envious when I heard what some superintendents were able to do. In one institution, when a newcomer's behavior improved to the point where such a move was justified, she was allowed to live in a private-room dormitory. Small bedrooms branched off each side of a long hall, and each girl fixed up her room to suit herself. The results were often amazing. Handmade bedspreads, ruffled curtains, embroidered dresser scarfs, and other artistic embellishments proved the girls' pride and interest in the project. As I say, I was frankly envious. What better way to prepare girls for real home life?

The girl who was tired or ill or who simply wished to be alone for a little while might retire to her own quarters until she desired companionship. She was free to study in her room or work at any approved hobby, but—most important—she maintained, or built up for the first time, a feeling of individuality.

The same plan also benefited the matrons. A lock on each door allowed an unruly girl to be separated from the group, reducing the danger of spreading dissension throughout an entire dormitory. In the case of large-scale rioting, a master switch locked every door and kept all the girls confined until they quieted down.

But if I yearned over that sort of system, I felt a positive *craving* for still another kind of operation. I had visited a school which housed its girls in groups of ten or twelve in home-like cottages under the supervision of a carefully selected resident couple who acted in *loco parentis* to the inmates. These girls cooked and sewed and washed and ironed just as they hoped to do some day in their own homes.

A keen spirit of competition existed among the cottage "families." Special privileges were awarded those who excelled in setting the best table for the least amount of money, or in designing and making the most attractive dresses, or even in keeping the cleanest cottage. The idea, of course, was to provide incentive and instill a feeling of being "special" in a sociably acceptable fashion. In some ways, the plan was a little like "keeping up with the Joneses," but so is life "outside." Those girls were following the pattern of the world in which they would live.

That same school had taken another forward step of which I heartily approved. Like all institutions for delinquent girls, they had to cope with many pregnant youngsters. A maternity hospital was established on the grounds, but under a name different from that of the school itself so that no stigma would attach to any baby born there.

After the birth of her baby, each mother was given a thorough course in child care . . . so thorough, in fact, that the new mother was qualified to hold a position as a practical baby nurse upon leaving the school. Meanwhile, the children's bureau and the welfare agencies in the area worked with the mother in an effort to devise a way for her to keep the infant. When that was impossible, they supervised its adoption.

Unfortunately, my investigation disclosed the fact that such practical and intelligent treatment of delinquent girls was the rare exception rather than the rule. Methods ranged downward from this standard to schools staffed by officers who believed that their jobs began and ended with custodial care. The minds and hearts of their charges remained unexplored territory; their physical bodies were all that mattered.

Blanche moved in her sleep, and jolted me out of my reverie. Her hand twitched even while she slept. With regular hours and plenty of good food, we'd probably repair most of the physical damage, and with her health improved, her nerves would undoubtedly quiet to some extent. But again I knew the frustrating feeling that it wouldn't be enough, especially since the possibilities existed to do so much more if only I had access to the proper equipment and personnel.

I took a last look at the small pale face, the deep shadowed eyes, before I turned to go.

And she was just one. Outside, on the campus, I saw scores of my excitable, strange, amoral, uninhibited, terrible, and lovable girls. Each was an individual problem, each was a potential volcano or slough of despair.

I stood watching for long and agonizing moments. Never had I felt so futile.

8

No sooner did we solve a problem concerning an inmate than another cropped up having to do with staff. Occasionally I felt like the Superintendent of a see-saw. At other times, I suspected that I had oracular powers or extra-sensory perception. Actually, though, anyone with a grain of a brain would have spotted Miss La Quelle as capital T—TROUBLE—as fast as I did.

In the first place she was too young and too irresponsible. She was also vain, selfish, quick tempered, and not too intelligent. I was not overly impressed with the young woman. Nevertheless, we had to take her. Miss La Quelle was the cousin of a powerful legislator who could, and would, have visited his wrath upon us if we refused his relative. Apparently his cousin's escapades were beginning to be embarrassing. Senator Inchling seemed to think our school might impose regulations which would limit her activities.

I put Miss La Quelle in charge of a cottage full of my oldest and most reliable girls. They needed less supervision than she did. While they ran the cottage, reports filtered back to me that Miss La Quelle was slipping out nights, leaving the girls alone. I didn't encourage "tattling," but when the school was buzzing with the story, I had to ask questions which—I hoped—would allow me to quell the rumor once and for all.

A half-dozen girls claimed they had seen the supervisor climb the high fence and run down the lane to join a man in a waiting car. Toward morning she'd return by the same route, staggering up the path and noticeably disheveled. By day, she sat in a big chair in the living room, pretending to watch over the cottage operation but actually catching up on her sleep.

Anyone who dared wake Miss La Quelle from her daytime nap was in for a vicious tongue lashing. Girls wandered in and out at their own discretion and the disciplinary problems which ensued had us tearing our hair. We couldn't question Miss La Quelle about her misdeeds until we found a staff member who was willing to substantiate the girls' stories. Inmate reports were plentiful but we couldn't accept them as evidence. Girls could be accused of unreliability or of "framing" a superior. Employees knew the situation but were reluctant to become involved. The matter finally came to a climax with a head-on clash between Miss La Quelle and Ollene.

Ollene was a beautiful girl, frisky as a park squirrel and just as elusive. She was gay and likable but wary of friendships with either officers or other inmates. In spite of her usual withdrawal from close contact, she had taken a serious interest in the school's newly formed drill team. I was delighted; it could well be the first step in her adjustment to a society based on integration.

A drill performance was scheduled to take place in the dining room one evening after dinner. Personally immaculate, Ollene took her drill suit of white slacks and scarlet coat to the laundry where she washed and starched each piece to a state of crisp splendor. She spread the treasured costume on her bed in precise alignment, ready to put on as soon as she returned from her afternoon schedule. But she reckoned without Miss La Quelle.

Miss La Quelle resented Ollene. Perhaps she was jealous of my obvious liking for the child. Possibly she envied the girl's almost classic beauty. In any case, she did what she could to make Ollene's life miserable in a hundred little ways. Her dislike grew into something close to hatred when Ollene simply ignored her mistreatment and kept her explosive temper under control.

The spotless costume so lovingly spread out must have tempted Miss La Quelle beyond endurance. Although it was too small for her in the bust and hips, she tugged it on and burlesqued Ollene's drill performance for the edification of the other girls in the cottage. They laughed but somehow it wasn't really very funny. Knowing Ollene, they sensed trouble coming.

It arrived right on schedule. Ollene halted at the door while her roommates scuttled back to the side lines and silently watched. Miss La Quelle stood in the center of the room, her arms still raised in a ridiculous gesture, the costume now soaked with perspiration and split across the hips.

"What do you think you're doing?" Ollene blazed. "Take that off this minute! It's mine!"

"Don't you dare speak to me like that!" Miss La Quelle flared back. "I'm a staff member, I'll have you know! Not a lousy delinquent!"

"You're not as fit to be a staff member as I am," Ollene shrieked furiously. "You run around and cheat people that trust you! I didn't ever do anything so low! You're a sneak! You're nothing but a low-down sneak! Now get out of that outfit!" She caught hold of a sleeve and held on tight. "This is mine! Get it off quick or by God, I'll tear you out of it!"

Miss La Quelle's right hand swung in a circle and connected with Ollene's cheek in a loud smack. The fight was on.

For a moment Ollene looked disbelievingly at the sleeve that had come off in her hand. Then she tossed it away, crouched and sprang like a wild cat. Girls backed against the walls, half-pleased and half-fearful as the two women punched and clawed and spit and kicked. A high heel raked Ollene's leg from knee to ankle, and blood spattered over the white ducks. Miss La Quelle made the mistake of stopping for a second and jeering. "*Now* look what you've done!" Ollene drove in with both fists and bloodied her nose. By this time both of them were bawling and put up only token protests when the girls moved in to stop the scrap. The whimpering matron tore off what was left of the drill costume and threw it in Ollene's face. She ducked into her room, bolted the door behind her, and immediately wrote me a commanding note. "Come at once! One of your pets has just beaten me up!"

I found Miss La Quelle lying on her bed with one eye looking like the aurora borealis and a cold pack across her swollen nose. She exhibited every scratch and bruise on her body but she seemed to be very vague about how the scrap started. All she knew, she declared heatedly, was that Ollene had attacked her.

"I hope you'll give that s.o.b. the beating of her life!" She half-ordered. "She ought to be whipped till she's raw. It's a fine thing when a lousy inmate can get away with assaulting an officer!"

"I'm terribly sorry this happened, Miss La Quelle." I've never made a more sincere statement. "I'll have the nurse take care of your injuries, and you can be sure I'll investigate Ollene's part in all this. She'll get exactly what's coming to her."

But Miss La Quelle wanted blood. "She'll lie out of it . . . you know damn well she'll lie till she's blue." My partner in rehabilitation raised herself on one elbow and pointed a vicious finger in my direction. "And *I* know that you'll believe her."

My own temper almost boiled over but I managed to say quietly, "I'll send the nurse over right away."

"I'm going to phone my cousin about this. He'll come down here and see that something's done to that hell-cat." Miss La Quelle's shrill warning followed me out the door.

I quizzed the girls individually and reconstructed the entire story. Faced with facts, Miss La Quelle backed down to the extent of muttering that she'd only meant to play a joke. For the time being, I let her go on about her business; my primary worry was Ollene. This episode could undo all the progress she'd made in many painful months.

"It's no use, Mrs. Burnham," Ollene declared bitterly. "She won't let me behave. I suppose maybe I shouldn't have fought her, but she had no business ruining my costume." Her eyes flashed resentfully. "And who knows, maybe it'll do her some good to find out she can't whop people and get away with it."

I couldn't very well punish Ollene when Miss La Quelle had started the trouble, but it was clearly impossible to keep the two of them in one cottage. Of necessity, therefore, I moved Ollene from the honor building to one of lower rating. She understood my awkward position and cooperated in this apparent fall from grace. Through no fault of her own, she was losing certain privileges for which she'd worked—but that wasn't enough to satisfy Miss La Quelle.

"Is that all you're going to do," she asked furiously, "just move her away from my cottage? Well! I bet *I* can get something more done!"

Two days later, on Sunday morning, I was called away from the breakfast table to greet an unexpected visitor. The air quivered with ill-suppressed animosity as the big black-haired man rose from behind my desk.

"Mrs. Burnham, sit down." Senator Inchling issued the order, and Mrs. Burnham meekly obeyed.

"My cousin is all scratched up and black and blue!" he announced, in tones portentous enough to herald doomsday. The senator mistook my hesitation for submission; he went on at length, louder with each elocutionary outburst.

"What sort of institution is this?" he demanded. "Inmates encouraged to vent their spleen on officials of our fair State . . . a member of the staff scorned and insulted—yes, insulted! —by the Superintendent . . . the facts twisted . . . the guilty protected . . ."

The blast went on and on. Miss La Quelle had said *this;* Miss La Quelle had sworn *that;* Miss La Quelle had reported *this;* Miss La Quelle had denied *that.*

He finally exhausted my last ounce of ladylike control. I've never done it since, but I exploded.

"Oh, pipe down about your Miss La Quelle!" I stood up. "Now *you* sit down, Senator Inchling . . . and not behind my desk either. Doesn't *anyone* in your family recognize the property rights of other people?"

He dropped into the nearest seat as if he'd been stoned.

"Senator," I began, warming to my subject as I progressed, "I have a job to do—a mighty important job. Incompetent employees hinder more than they help. Bad enough when they're hired by mistake or because we can't afford better . . . but what's worse," I continued—and I remember wondering how far my voice was carrying—"is when someone in your position takes advantage of that honorable position to foist off a floozy—yes, I said a floozy." He opened his mouth but only managed a strangulated moan. Anyway, I wasn't close to finished.

"Miss La Quelle's too young, too wild, and too maladjusted

herself to supervise others. If the girls show a lack of respect, it's because she's failed to earn their respect."

"But she's my . . ."

"Cousin," I finished for him. "But you know my character analysis is correct. You knew she wasn't qualified in any way when you sent her here." I drew myself up—impressively, I hoped—and finished in the most accusatory tones my diaphragm would furnish. "If she has ruined a young life, *you* are responsible in the eyes of the Lord!" It seemed a good place to stop.

Senator Inchling rose from his chair, hunted for the door with dazed eyes, and lumbered out in a deathly hush.

Had I been brave and stalwart, or just plain stupid? Time, I was afraid, would tell. I dropped to my chair and let my head fall on my crossed arms. What was more important, my job or my girls? Should I compromise? Allow my girls to see that rules applied to some people and not to others? How could I accomplish *anything* if I allowed a Miss La Quelle to tear down in one moment all we had built over a period of years?

The telephone rang, shaking me out of my reverie. I couldn't do anything more about Miss La Quelle, but other problems required my attention. Senator Inchling didn't exactly fade from mind, but his apoplectic image was overlaid by others.

Shortly afterward, Miss La Quelle received a long-distance phone call, followed by a registered letter. Livid with rage, she informed me that "an emergency at home" was forcing her to resign. She was forced all right. Evidently the Senator still had a shred of conscience, or a fear of the hereafter.

Poor Ollene was the real sufferer. The very sight of the drill team caused her to relive the incident all over again, so I tried desperately to engage her interest elsewhere. I thought I had succeeded when the art teacher showed me some excellent drawings Ollene had made.

The school department was closed for the summer, so when Ollene and Esther, another art student, asked if they might use a vacant room as a studio, I was delighted to put one at their disposal. The two girls set about cleaning and decorating their new quarters, so absorbed in the project that I thought it safe to let them work without a supervisor. We were shorthanded, as always.

One day I passed the girls as I was returning to my apartment. They were bound for the studio, staggering under a load of draperies, but they managed to wave at me. As I left my rooms about an hour later, I almost stumbled over a vase of flowers set just outside my door. A note was tied to the vase with a bit of Christmas ribbon.

"Good-by," it read. "We love you but we feel that we must go. Thanks for everything. Your girls, Ollene and Esther."

If they hadn't left the flowers, their absence might not have been noted till supper time. As it was, they hadn't had time to go far; searchers found them within the hour. One look and I knew lecturing would do no good. Parole had been within their grasp but they'd deliberately chosen the outlaw path to freedom instead. For the rest of their stay they were polite and pleasant but completely untrustworthy. Ollene, I knew, had been the ringleader. Rack up one more failure to our system of selecting officers.

Most of our employees were women, so naturally most of our trouble-makers were women too. But no member of the feminine sex ever caused quite the hubbub stirred up by one of the few men on the school staff.

Our male employees were screened with finicky care. With few exceptions, they stuck to their jobs and scrupulously avoided any sort of involvement. But keeping clear of trouble wasn't easy. The girls were both susceptible and aggressive.

They craved the admiration they were used to, and any man would do, no matter how old, ugly, or irresponsible.

Their hunger for masculine attention made imaginations work overtime. In their eagerness, they injected the most commonplace incidents with all sorts of romantic meaning. Most of them stopped with daydreaming but Brenda—who would have been called a "wench" in Will Shakespeare's day—was more ambitious. By starting a rumor that our unsuspecting farmer had a passion for her, she either hoped to plant the idea in the poor man's mind or simply increase her prestige with the other girls. The details of his "pursuit" grew more juicy with every passing hour.

I was furious! If ever there was a decent, quiet, *un*licentious man in the world, it was our George. In all the years he'd handled a crew of milking girls, this was the first breath of scandal that had ever touched him. I'd have backed George against Salome, Circe, and any of our current sirens.

I sent for Brenda and fixed her with my beadiest look. "What's this story you're spreading?" I asked bluntly.

"It's no story, Mrs. Burnham." Brenda lowered her eyes coyly. "He—he sends me—I guess we just can't help it." She smiled smugly. "He says I send him, too."

"Oh, come *on,* Brenda!" My bald disbelief wiped her smile off in a hurry. "Why did you pick *George*, of all people? He wouldn't look at one of you girls and you know it. What's behind all this?"

Brenda stammered and seemed to shrink. "I guess I could have been mistaken."

"I guess you could have been." I mimicked. "Now how did this nonsense start?"

"Well, I got a sliver in my hand off the cow stanchion. It hurt and I couldn't get it out. George heard my crying and he said, 'I'll get it out for you.'" Brenda paused, hoping I'd let her off with that.

"Go on," I ordered relentlessly.

"So he got out his knife and sterilized it with a match and picked the sliver out of my hand," she went on with a rush.

"And then, what?" My glare was sufficient goad.

"Then he sent me to the hospital to get the place painted with iodine. He was real concerned," she finished lamely.

"And for that kindness, you tried to ruin his reputation?"

"Oh, no, Mrs. Burnham!" Brenda sounded genuinely shocked. "I just wanted him to know I liked him." And now she sounded like a wistful kid, but a kid who knew from experience that men were interested in just one expression of gratitude. George had done her a favor and was entitled to a favor in return.

Of course there was more to it than that. Brenda, like all the other inmates, was man-starved—sexually, but also in every other area of life. And as a hungry person pretends that a handful of beans is a banquet, so did Brenda attempt to fill her romantic, parental, and social void with the most casual male kindness.

I ached for her; but how could I explain these "whys and wherefores" in any way she could possibly comprehend? All I could do now was rescue George.

Brenda was waiting to be dismissed. I forced sharpness into my voice and said, "You go straighten out this nonsense. Tell everyone you lied to that you were making up stories. And be quick! If I hear that fib one more time around the campus, you'll lose every one of your privileges for six months. You started it, now stop it!"

I couldn't tell you how she quashed it so quickly but that was the last I ever heard of the story. To the best of my knowledge, George never knew his name had been bandied about.

Though this presented a tough enough problem, it wasn't a patch on the trouble a man could cook up when he was really in there giving it the old college try. One middle-aged Lothario, inherited from the last regime, made my life miserable for months.

Scoby was far from a matinee idol and his personality was on a par with his appearance. In fact, he looked, smelled, and acted more like a molting camel than anything else. About all he had to recommend him was his indisputable masculinity. Despite the truly fantastic gaps in his charm, that sole attribute was enough to make him the love object of half the inmates.

Girls tried to switch their schedules so they might work up close to him. Time after time he was found in some situation just short of compromising, but he was too shrewd and slippery to be caught out in a really adulterous act. I warned him that he was under suspicion and marveled at the bland innocence of his denial.

I had to bide my time because Scoby was backed by a powerful legislator to whom he would have appealed any accusation without air-tight proof. If I struck too soon, the blow would boomerang. All I could do was watch and wait—and remind him from time to time that I was keeping my eyes open. I figured this would make him nervous enough to slip, or scared enough to stop. I soon found he had no intention of stopping. Once or twice I flushed Scoby and a girl from some shadowy situation, but they always had a plausible alibi prepared. The girls involved would smirk and titter to the point of insolence. Lover-boy had undoubtedly informed them that he had influence "upstairs." A couple of times I overheard him mention his friend, the legislator—as he intended I should. Eventually it was this very sense of security that made him overbold and proved his undoing.

For no reason anyone could understand, he began stalking a

colorless little wren named Nellie, who was vastly flattered by his obvious attention. The thought of resisting him never even entered her mind.

Nellie wasn't ready for parole, and even if she had been, I couldn't have sent her home; her family was at least as bad an influence as our Lothario. His pursuit was intense and determined, but still discreet enough to make absolute proof impossible. In desperation, I sent Nellie to a foster home several miles away where she was to help with the work. For several weeks I relaxed in the belief that I had outwitted the ardent pair.

One day I had business in the town where Nellie was staying, and I dropped by her foster home to see if everything was going well. The lady of the house reported that Nellie had just left to spend the weekend with her family.

"But that's why I sent her to you," I protested. "I thought I'd made it clear that she was to be kept away from her family. Has she gone there often?"

"Not till a few weeks ago," she answered defensively. "But what could I do when her uncle insisted on taking her? Now he comes for her every four or five days and she isn't much help when she gets back."

"*What* uncle?" I sputtered.

"The one that works at the school," she explained. "She had a letter from him yesterday. It's probably still in her room."

"Get it for me, please."

The woman hesitated.

"She's still under age and my ward," I reminded her, "so I have the right to inspect her mail. In fact, it's my duty."

The envelope bore no name or return address, and the letter was signed with a slightly nauseating nickname. The contents, however, were highly inflammable and the handwriting was unmistakably Scoby's.

I crammed the evidence into my purse and rushed to my

special adviser on the Board. He was a long-time friend of Scoby's sponsor and I couldn't be sure how he'd react to my news. Maybe I was treading on dangerous ground, but I had no choice. I handed him the envelope.

"If this is going to work a hardship on you, I apologize in advance," I began, "but this situation requires immediate action. I don't ordinarily approve of ultimatums, but either Scoby is removed from his happy hunting ground or I'll have to leave, myself. I won't stand around and watch what he's doing."

The Board member listened to my account and read the letter through several times. "He'll have to go," he agreed, "but you'd better see his sponsor, yourself. He may want to ask questions."

After nerving myself to the ordeal, I made an appointment to tell my story. The legislator showed no sign of surprise, nor did he question a single statement. Evidently the proclivities of his protégé were well known to him. Now that they were out in the open, however, he saw the wisdom of withdrawing his support. The fact that he was up for election may have influenced him, or it might have been the fear that the newspapers would somehow sniff out the story. He wanted to remain popular with the local press. Whatever it was, Scoby left us within a week. Unfortunately the gray streaks in my hair didn't depart with him.

Certainly that ranked high among my most nerve-wracking experiences. The job of maintaining a barrier between an amorous, amoral male and a group of only too willing young women is an ulcer-maker of the first order.

Once again I thought longingly of a co-ed correctional school with adequately trained instructors of both sexes. I felt sure that boys and girls who saw each other in the ordinary course of events wouldn't be so apt to build up explosive urges.

With proper guidance, I didn't see why they couldn't attend the same classes, eat in the same dining room, and occasionally enjoy a well-chaperoned party in a communal recreation room.

Some day I intended to do more than send memos about it.

9

WITH LOTHARIO DISPOSED OF, I LOOKED FORWARD—THOUGH WITH no great hope—to a short period of peace. Most of the staff was working out well, and surely even our most inventive inmates required occasional intervals during which to think up new deviltry.

After all this time, I still hadn't learned that a school for delinquent girls is forever fermenting. Sometimes no bubbles break the surface, but there's always a yeasty turbulence somewhere down in the depths. I was finding out that the time to worry is when things are going too smoothly, when troublemakers suddenly become too cooperative, when the noisiest cottage becomes too quiet. The vat is constantly simmering, and only long experience warns when the brew is about to boil over.

A Superintendent, I found, has to be part private-eye. Not a spy exactly, but rather more like a detective of the Sherlock Holmes school, for whom every insignificant detail, every slight deviation from the norm, is a crystal-clear clue to trouble afoot.

I noticed that several of the inmates had new and elaborate hairdos, but if I thought about it at all, I attributed them to friends in the cosmetology course. However, I did question Janice and Lil, two of my fifteen-year-olds, when I saw bloody strings looped through the lobes of their ears. Mrs. Wiles, they said, had pierced their ears. Wasn't it okay?

"Fine," I assured them. "It was very nice of Mrs. Wiles to help you out." It was, I told myself. She did a nasty little job on her own time, so see how wrong you were about her, Mrs. Burnham, you infallible character analyst!

Evidence of unusual doings was so thick around me, I'm surprised to this day that I missed seeing it for so long. Of course, some of it did filter through. In one week, two girls were caught smoking—which wasn't unusual in itself—but I remember noticing that the cigarettes had bright red tips and wondering why that fact nagged at me for hours. So much is glaringly obvious on looking back. The pale coral polish on another girl's bitten fingernails, an odd but familiar color. The sudden appearance of a good silk scarf around the neck of an inmate who'd never owned so much as an old red ribbon.

"How pretty!" I commented in passing, and Ardeena touched the scarf and looked guilty. Probably my imagination. She couldn't have swiped it or I'd have heard a hullabaloo. It *did* look familiar though.

Later that same day I saw the fabric again, this time in the form of a housecoat hanging on a hook in the bath Leila Wiles shared with the other instructors. I could see that the robe had been shortened considerably. Undoubtedly Leila had thrown away the excess material, and Ardeena had come upon it in the trash. Still, something bothered me. It wasn't like Leila to toss anything away, not if she could conceivably make use of it.

Had she made use of it? And the cigarettes. Leila's brand had bright red tips—and her fingers were always tipped with an unusual coral polish. The questions were piling up.

I closed the door of my office, told Miss Lulu not to disturb me for fifteen minutes, and listed all the seemingly unrelated and inconsequential details I'd noticed. I confessed to feeling like an utter idiot, but perhaps I was just too stubborn to stop.

The girls whose names I'd jotted down had at least one thing in common: each was a natural leader with a faithful following; whatever they thought or did would be slavishly imitated by better than half the school. I'd already seen sufficient evidence of that.

These very girls whose names I was now studying had been increasingly difficult for some time now—but so subtly, so covertly, that I couldn't ever put my finger on the exact trouble or mete out proper punishment. What can you do about a girl whose excessive politeness skirts mockery? And how do you handle a sassiness that hovers right on the line between high-spirits and hell-raising? And now I remembered the way groups of girls would *watch* me, turning when I passed, and then giggle softly together. Why?

The leaders who had gravitated away from me were now circling in Leila's orbit, aping her in every possible way. How did she wield such influence over the wild ones? Much as I disliked and—yes!—distrusted the woman, perhaps she had something I lacked. It wasn't a pleasant thought. I called in Miss Lulu, my unofficial eyes and ears, and we put our heads together. A week later, when we put our heads—and our observations—together again, I had the answer. We knew just exactly what it was that Leila Wiles was using.

Nail polish . . . cigarettes . . . chocolates . . . dabs of perfume . . . bits of pretty material . . . movie magazines . . . and little services, such as ear-piercing. In one word, bribery.

While I was angry enough at what I considered an underhanded way to win affection, Miss Lulu was literally red with rage. I wondered at the violence of her reaction.

"She's deliberately breaking our basic rule, Mrs. Burnham. It's not in any book, but she's been here long enough to know that 'if one gets, all get.' Once you start playing favorites in a place like this . . ."

Of course! Without knowing it, I'd always recognized that unwritten rule. Our girls had felt discrimination enough in the "outside" world. Here we saw to it that each received exactly the same treatment as all the others. Certain privileges could be earned—not given indiscriminately or solely at the discretion of an individual instructor. Leila, though, was not being at all indiscriminate. She was carefully distributing her favors among the most influential inmates, the ones who by their very nature would most resent my adherence to the policy of "equal portions of everything for all."

Miss Lulu broke into my thoughts. "I suppose you know she expected to get your job. It looks as if she's still after it."

I could see that a private army would be useful in overthrowing a regime. Mine, that is. Yes, Leila would have her loyal cohorts—loyal to the last chocolate bar—but that wasn't what was making me mad. And by now I was sitting there seething. Most of our girls were in trouble and in Tecumseh because already they thought they were "special" and not subject to the regulations that govern the rest of the human race. Here, where we were supposed to be helping them to adjust, an instructor was deliberately feeding already distorted and inflamed egos—egos which could some day suppurate and burst into any social disease from mayhem to murder. I could probably forgive her for trying to undermine me, but twisting these young minds into tools for her dirty work was too much. I sent a messenger to fetch Mrs. Wiles to the office.

While waiting, I made up my mind to a course of action. Leila, like everyone else around, was a political appointee. She couldn't be shed without a major struggle which would hinder our work and our reputation. Anyway, aside from her machinations against me, she was a fine teacher. Maybe a firm warning would salvage the situation.

Leila acceded gracefully. She was "only trying to take an interest," she said. "As long as you're the Superintendent," she continued sweetly, "we'll do it your way."

"*As long as . . .* !"

I had a sinking sensation that cold war had just been declared.

I refused, however, to let one woman stand in the way of my work with two hundred seventy-six youngsters. A good part of my job was paper work, and that day as usual a great stack of mail loaded down my desk. I attacked it from the top and dug my way doggedly down to the last envelope. This final letter proved to be an invitation: a men's civic club wanted me to be its luncheon guest and speaker. They professed great eagerness to hear about my impressions of the school and my future plans for it.

I didn't have time for any outside activities but I determined to get to that luncheon one way or another. Talking with intelligent people would help clarify my own ideas, and might even revise the opinion of a person or two about our inmates. I wanted the citizens of our State to think of them as individuals who were trying to rebuild good lives instead of as lost souls, eternally damned.

What were my impressions anyway? They were still jumbled, subject to amendment as each new experience unfolded. Public opinion seemed to be split into two factions. One side asserted that there were no bad girls. That sanctimonious statement always stopped the conversation cold. If you agreed, there was no argument. If you didn't, you became an object of suspicion and someone to be avoided.

The other faction snorted in disgust at such a Pollyanna-like approach, and declared that delinquent girls were hopelessly bad from birth, and that there was nothing you or anyone else could do about it. I remembered the probation officer, a churchman and civic leader, who said blandly, "Why worry? The world has to have so many Magdalens and somebody's got to be 'em." My own opinion lay somewhere between these extremes.

I agreed with the Pollyannas that all girls are born innocent and that their delinquency is due to an unwholesome environment during the formative years. But however they got that way, ours certainly were imperfect apples now, and it would take much skillful paring to trim away the soft spots before they spread. If drunkenness, prostitution, robbery, arson and, yes, even murder were bad, our girls were bad because they were guilty of all of those crimes . . . aided and abetted, for the most part, by society. Their rehabilitation would require every ounce of heart, soul, skill, and insight we could muster. Simple condemnation and imprisonment, while easier, would turn them back to the world worse than they came.

For the first time in years, I thought of Madame Loubèque, a delightful and wise old friend of mine, who approached great matters with the unerring simplicity of a soul at peace with itself and the universe. One day, with a Gallic fluttering of hands, she announced her latest finding.

"Zat Jesus! 'Ow I luf Him! You know somesing? He is so firm wiz ze men; oui, like a rock." She thrust a small fist in my face, and then her face grew tender. "He gave zose men ze vairy dickens, but He nevair, nevair scolded a woman!"

So far as I was able to learn, it's true. Jesus never did scold a woman, not even the adultress. But he did try to lift her up. I accepted His precedent as my guiding policy.

This was part of what I wanted to get across to the civic club and to as much of the public as would listen. I wanted, if possible, to talk myself out of a job—to prevent our young people from being wrecked in the first place, so that we wouldn't have to worry about rehabilitation at all in some future utopia.

I'd try to explain that *every* adult, consciously or not, holds down a job much like mine. Somewhere among friends or family, there's a child whose life he will undoubtedly influence for good or evil. This, of course, apart from his public responsibility.

The longer I thought about spreading these ideas around, the more enthusiastic I became. If enough "outsiders" were told even a little of what I'd already learned, I felt sure some good would eventually result.

And while on the subject of influencing others, I wondered, too, if I couldn't beat Mrs. Leila Wiles at her own game. The best part of the idea I was hatching was that it held promise of doing some real good among my older girls. That's how the K.Y. Club came into being. K.Y. for "Know yourself."

A handful of girls came to that first meeting but the crowd grew, week by week, until the chairs and couches in my big sun room overflowed and youngsters sat cross-legged on pillows all over the floor. Everything the girls were thinking, everything that troubled them, was brought out, dissected, examined, and discussed at these meetings. I tried all sorts of gimmicks to loosen tongues. Songs sometimes, toasted marshmallows always. An article in a national magazine sometimes provided a springboard.

My girls were learning, among other things, to debate a question instead of arbitrarily picking a side and defending it with a switch-blade knife. The girls were earnestly attempting to understand themselves and their problems, and complete trust in me was of primary importance. I assured them that any incriminating facts they might reveal about themselves would be inviolate; the information would never be used unless, of course, it came to me some day from another source.

If nothing else, our conversations covered a lot of territory, and the kids came up with some pretty provocative questions.

"Is it ever right to fight?" a scrappy little thirteen-year-old asked.

"What's the difference between love and lust?" it was Florrie's question that time—big, sweet, placid Florrie, who knew very little about the first subject and a great deal about the second.

They talked about their ambitions. Gertrude, a little gamin from the city, said her ambition was to be a lady.

"You don't even know what a lady is," Beth hooted.

"Do you?" I challenged. "Does anyone here?"

"Why—a lady is—a lady—is—like—well, I guess I pass." Gertrude floundered and gave up. Everybody else immediately started to contribute opinions. After much discussion and a few heated scraps, they boiled it down to a decision that a lady is a woman who is neat, clean, well mannered, courteous, kind, honest, friendly, not over-friendly with strange men, dependable, and more thoughtful of others than of herself. They listed these attributes on a rather dog-eared sheet of paper for my approval.

"Good definition, girls," I nodded. "When do you all expect to become that kind of a lady?"

There was a thoughtful hush, broken at last by pudgy, and slightly obnoxious young Doris, who labored under the impression that she had us all buffaloed.

"When I'm big and have my own home," Doris stated and waited smugly for my commendation.

"That'll be nice," I agreed. "But tell me, do you expect to be lazy and untidy, to quarrel with everyone in your cottage, be rude to your matron, and impudent to all your teachers . . ." Doris looked daggers at me, ". . . and wake up some day when you're thirty years old and say, 'Well, here I am. A lady at last, just as I've always intended to be'?"

Anna broke in eagerly. "You mean we oughtta begin right now?"

"Sure, dope! Whadya think she means?" Lil got into the act but eased out again when she caught my eye. "Sorry," she mumbled, "I guess ladies don't call each other dopes, huh?"

I sat back most of the time and allowed the girls to work out their own rules for living—rules that should have been a part of their lives from earliest infancy. Whenever possible, I avoided direct dogmatic statements and led them where I wanted them to go via questions and casual asides.

Patty popped up with a social problem. "Why do I hafta be nice to someone who's not nice to me, 'specially when I don't like 'em anyway?" she wanted to know.

"Why don't you like this person?" I answered Patty's question with a question. "Because she is less courteous, less pleasant than you?"

"Well—yeah—I suppose that's about it." Patty was flattered.

"If you saw someone who was ragged and hungry and you had plenty of clothes and lots of food, what would you do?" I wanted to set Patty thinking. "Would you throw away your own good things and go ragged and hungry just because the other person was?"

"Of course not," Patty was scornful. "I'd give the poor drip some of what I had."

"Well then, what about someone who's poor in character?" I asked, and was delighted to see understanding dawn. "Would you throw away your own kindness and good manners to be as mean as she is?"

"I get it!—I get it!" Patty bounced excitedly. "If she's a goon, that's no reason for me to be one. Right?"

"Right!" I nodded vigorously.

Linda spoke for the first time. "And the funny thing is, when you give away something like kindness or love, you always wind up with more than you had." She sank back into silence for the rest of the evening, but I considered it an evening well spent.

These were adolescent, delinquent girls. They'd broken every rule of conventional behavior, but through their own reasoning powers, they were now attaining heights of understanding which they could never have been forced to scale any other way; they were making practical application of their new ideas too.

Gertrude waved her hand frantically for attention. "I'm goin' to try it," she was very emphatic. "I'm goin' to try out some of this here kindness an' courtesy on Grouch Puss."

"Grouch Puss?" I tried to sound as if I didn't know whom she meant.

"Oh, Mrs. Burnham, don't kid around. Old Lady Trent. I'm goin' to try it on her. It may kill me, but I'll go down fightin'," she said flippantly. "I'll let you know what happens."

Two days later, Gertrude came running toward me as I walked around the loop. "It worked, Mrs. Burnham, it worked," Gertrude yelled as she waved her hand for me to wait for her. "I had the most courtesy, and it worked!" The girl was panting from her run. "Grouch Puss let me have it this evenin'. 'Gertrude, you're the noisiest girl in this cottage, and the frowsiest. Look! You're so messy you spoil the looks of the whole bunch!' " Gertrude's mimicry of the matron was too perfect. I almost broke up.

" 'If you don't quiet down,' " Gertrude assumed the pose of an overweight and exasperated woman, " 'and if you don't get cleaned up before supper, I won't let you have any.' "

"I started to answer back, but golly, I was hungry," Gertrude grinned. "So I sez to myse'f, 'This is it, Gertrude. This is your chance to see if this courtesy stuff works.' " She tilted an eye up at me to see how her recital was being received.

" 'Okay, Mis' Trent,' I sez, just as sweet as I could," Gertrude's eyes twinkled, " 'thank you very much for remindin' me. I'd sure like to have you feel proud of me.' "

"And what did Mrs. Trent say to that?" I really wanted to know!

"Well, her mouth came open but she never said nothin'." Gertrude chuckled as she clung to my arm. "She just went back to her chair and looked at me like she didn't know whether I was sick or just bein' sassy. But it worked, Mrs. Burnham, it worked! I got my supper. Boy, what a system!"

K.Y. Club provided a wonderful emotional outlet for the girls; but it couldn't solve every problem immediately, nor could it prevent occasional backsliding. One spring morning this fact was made strikingly clear.

Vicky jumped the fence and ran away!

Telephone lines to all the villages in the area crackled with urgent requests to keep an eye out for a slim brown-haired girl in a pink dress. In spite of our asking, we had little hope of help from the surrounding townships. In our neighborhood, as in the rest of the United States, most people believed that "reform schools" were still medieval establishments, dedicated to starvation, torture, and other amusements of a bygone era. Actually, most of our inmates had comfortable beds, nourishing food, plenty of clothes, recreation, schooling, peace, and security for the first time in their lives.

The only thing the school had ever withheld from Vicky was the right to come and go at will—a restriction only slightly more stringent than that binding the daughter of a fairly strict family. Vicky was a lovable child, and I shied away from thoughts of the unspeakable things that can happen to a scared kid, alone and without resources.

Every car on the campus turned out to patrol the highways. Officers with trusty girls scoured the ravines, but dusk fell and the searching parties returned for a belated supper without anyone having glimpsed the pink-clad figure.

Several days passed without a sign of Vicky. The youngster had been a general favorite, and her continued absence cast a pall over the whole place.

On the fourth afternoon the farm girls came running back from the pasture, leaving the cows still mooing for their evening milking. The whole crew tried to talk at the same time. I shushed them and picked the calmest one to speak.

"We think we know what happened to Vicky." Essie's voice trembled. "We were down in the far pasture. There was an awful smell—somethin' dead." She began to bawl.

"We couldn't find out what it was," a tall, thin redhead took up the recital, "because it was outside the fence and we couldn't go see."

Essie had control of herself again. "We thought Vicky could a' fell and broke a leg or something. Nobody coulda heard her holler for help way off down there!"

My heart skipped a beat. It *was* possible. That was rough terrain. An injured girl would have had little chance of attracting attention. I sent out a search party at once, wanting desperately to go myself but deciding at the final moment that a firm hand might be needed at the school if the news leaked out.

It was probably less than an hour before the hunters returned, but it seemed at least a week. They came up the lane with an air of jaunty relief and I knew, with a sharp stab of joy, that it hadn't been Vicky in the ravine. The moldering carcass was that of a neighbor's sheep which had broken its leg trying to jump a ditch and died there. The frightening experience sent me right out to get some bloodhounds. It *could* have been Vicky in that isolated ditch.

Many people have visions of savage beasts baying at terrified children when they hear "bloodhound." Actually, the sad-eyed, long-eared, high-smelling hounds we finally got from the penitentiary kennels were the girls' dearest pets. Of course, we kept them securely penned, apart from the girls, but nevertheless they soon became the most spoiled and overfed animals I've ever seen.

The dogs tracked many a runaway for us. It was a grand game from their point of view. Even the girl who was eventually run down took it in good grace. The dogs always got scratched behind their floppy ears or chucked under their wrinkled muzzles when they caught up. The same girls would throw rocks at human chasers.

A few days after the dead sheep episode, we received an anonymous call saying that a girl in a pink dress had been seen in a cabin back in the woods. We followed the tip. Sure enough, it was Vicky—a filthy, very defiant Vicky. Her resistance didn't break down for days, but then it went in a great tide: she wept on my shoulder until she simply didn't have the strength for another sob. She said the people who had sheltered her were dreadful, and gave details. She was right. She only stayed, she said, because she was afraid to go on and ashamed to come back to us. That was the last time she ever attempted to run. School was a haven now, not a prison.

Vicky had the highest I.Q. of anyone ever committed to Tecumseh. She finished our grade school and studied in our commercial class. As an assistant secretary in my office, Vicky was a wonder to visitors and court officers, who found it hard to believe that she was an inmate.

As often happened, one flare-up was almost immediately followed by another. Maybe the barometer's dropping had something to do with it—abrupt weather changes always caused trouble—or perhaps trouble in the air breeds trouble. Whatever the reason, Vella picked that time to act up. The fault was probably mine for putting too much responsibility on her shoulders too soon.

The State Fair was in progress. Our school had a booth in a corner of the main display building to show the public what its tax dollars were accomplishing in our department. We'd laid out a handsome display of quilts and bedspreads and fancy work and canned goods, but the tide of sightseers wasn't rounding the corner to look at them. In a flash of inspiration, I rented a piano for our booth and put Vella at the keyboard. She did a fine job of drumming up an audience.

I thought I'd provided for every contingency. Two ladies in an adjoining booth agreed to chaperone Vella on the Fair grounds and she was to room with a personal friend of mine whose daughter would drive her back and forth to work. For two days all went well, but on the third day Vella wasn't at the booth when the young lady called to take her home.

Several hours later, Vella drove up to my friend's house in a taxi. Evidently she and the driver had discovered they were soul-mates. They sat together on the front seat and indulged in rambunctious but innocent horseplay punctuated by peals of laughter. Vella's hostess arrived on the scene just as the girl kissed the young man a hearty good-by and waved him off . . . with a kewpie doll in one hand and a china dog in the other.

Vella smelled like a distillation of Coney Island. Hot dogs . . . onions . . . assertive perfume . . . popcorn. She still held a huge cone of spun sugar and nibbled at it as she walked up the path. She and the taxi driver had had a wonderful time.

Vella's hostess reported this performance to me over the long-distance phone, and, as fast as possible, I hauled my good-natured but weak-willed girl back home. Our display went unnoticed during the rest of Fair week. It was a necessary gesture, but useless, I knew.

I'd only be able to keep an eye on Vella for another few months, till she turned eighteen, and then this blithe spirit was on her own. The Fair would be over but she'd find something else. If not, she'd *start* something else. What had I been able to accomplish for Vella? What would the future hold for her, or she for the future?

The natal day arrived and Vella collected her meager belongings with a bright gleam in her eye and a bounce in her walk. I knew that she'd think of me often, but I wondered where and when.

I waved to her as long as I could see the car.

10

At Tecumseh, an interesting visitor was as welcome as a bonus check. A new face made us feel that we were still a part of society instead of an isolated and expendable segment. Often our guests brought practical ideas for improvement. If they happened to be State officials, I latched on and clung to them like the most tenacious of all turtles. Before I turned them loose, I talked them full to the brim about a new building program.

Many of our buildings, while sound enough structurally, were poorly adapted to the service expected of them. The administration office was a small, three-room, single-built frame, bitterly cold in the winter and unbearably hot in the summer. It had no sanitary facilities, not even a water faucet, and the nearest "convenience" was clear across the campus.

The inadequacies of other buildings made all our jobs a good deal more difficult. Since no provision had been made for recreation, except for an outdoor swimming pool usable only in warm weather, there was no safe outlet for the pent-up energy of two hundred seventy-six lively and inventive delinquents. In desperation, we tried to solve the problem with an outdoor period of vigorous calisthenics.

We had an auditorium of sorts. It, too, was a long frame building, located at the back of the campus between the hog pens and the chicken runs. In summer, the grunting and the cackling and the unmistakable odors added little solemnity to the Sunday school hymns. It was so cold in winter that our Sunday school teachers complained; their fiery flames of Hell sounded like Heaven on earth to blue-nosed girls with frozen feet.

The original planners presented us with our worst, and almost insuperable, problem in the six residence cottages. Every sleeping room contained twenty-five beds within arm's reach of one another. No privacy was afforded anywhere at all. How could we teach modesty, fastidiousness, good taste, where every physical function drew free and easy comment from all sides? Nothing belonged solely to one individual—not her tears, her triumphs, not even her own stomach-ache.

The officers were as badly off as the inmates. No provision had been made to relieve employees from constant contact with their charges. Many of them occupied rooms just a few feet from the same girls they'd worked with for weeks, months, sometimes years, on end. Being cooped up with the same problems, day and night, in an explosive atmosphere, made for frazzled nerves and spastic digestive tracts.

I reached the point myself where I felt an acute need for physical exercise to drain off the pounding pressure. My hours were too long and irregular to permit of planning a pleasant evening in town. The few times I tried, we had riots or runners or other crises to contend with, and my friends were left with a lopsided dinner table or an extra ticket. All else failed, so I ran foot races with Big George.

We had two Georges on the campus, both of them excellent men. George was the farmer, Big George the engineer. Big George weighed nearly three hundred pounds, but despite his bulk, he ran with the easy-breathing agility of a trained athlete. I had a weak ankle that occasionally threw me, so I was afraid to traipse off alone in the night.

On those evenings when I felt more than usually tense, Big George, his wife Minnie, and I would wander our separate ways down to the power house. Having been on her feet in the kitchen all day, Minnie would drop down on the steps to rest while Big George and I sailed off in a sprint. We'd leave the loop, race down the lane to the pasture gate, around the playground and back to the power house, where, exhausted but relaxed, I'd sit with Minnie to rest a while.

I've often wondered what the girls would have said had they seen their dignified Superintendent streaking around the grounds—especially in tandem with bashful Big George. Anyway, those races kept my circulation stirred up and the turbulence tamped down. I've often thought of incorporating it as the "C.B.B. System for Soothing Strained Nerves." Supply your own engineer!

Much of the strain on staff members could have been eliminated by a better architect. Even now, our buildings could probably be adapted or modified in some manner. I kept mentioning this to visiting legislators as they gorged themselves on our home-grown pork chops and fabulous foot-high cream pies. When they staggered off—after a series of "seconds"—it was with solemn vows to come to our assistance.

Newspaper men wrote propaganda in our behalf. One of our ablest editors dined with us on a day so bitterly cold that he had to wear his overcoat to the table. The girls warmed their hands in their armpits before they were able to manipulate the knives and forks. He wrote an impassioned appeal, stressing the need for an adequate dining room with steam heat, a cafeteria service, and a modern kitchen.

I sat back, expecting results. Still a tyro, I failed to realize how many other hands were stretched out in the direction of Mecca—in this case the State treasury. Politics has always been a game of give-and-take and we had nothing to give. New lives aren't tangible assets.

I put our need for new and remodeled buildings at the top of every requisition. Those requisitions were scourge, curse, plague, and pestilence—all rolled into one big gob. Every two years I had to take inventory of everything in every department, from a pound of salt to a commercial-size laundry mangle, and from a fifteen-cent dress pattern to a Jersey bull.

I was supposed to estimate our needs for the next two years including toothpaste, toilet tissue, and everything in between for an unknown number of girls. Then, in some mystic fashion I was to figure out future gas and electricity bills . . . which roofs would require repair, and what it would cost . . . the amount of farm machinery that would fold . . . the assorted spare parts required all over the place . . . books, clothing, canned goods . . . and far on into the dark, dark night.

I had to memorize those figures and build up logical arguments in support of each and every one of them. Of course, the Budget Officer felt honor bound to make a drastic cut in any estimate presented to him, but I soon learned to allow for *that!* The mutilated requisition went next to the Budget Committee, which usually felt that further amputation was indicated. They tossed questions at me two at a time and demanded specific answers on such items as competitive prices of a thousand feet of gas at my school, at other schools, in other towns. They wanted to know—names and dates—what range of estimates we'd had on a square of roofing, a carton of soap, or a gross of coats. Some gimlet-eyed son of the soil was forever trying to impress the folks back home with his stern guardianship of the State's purse strings.

I felt that my appearance, as well as my information, had to please the committee. Somewhere I'd picked up the odd idea that committee resistance weakens in direct proportion to a Superintendent's eye appeal. I tried to make up for nature's omissions by wearing clothes as chic and daring as my purse and my husband would permit. On one occasion, I nearly overstepped the mark.

The hat was a pancake of tucked, black chiffon, up-ended at the back in a huge satin bow and sliding down in front to obscure my right eye. It made me feel like Madame Du Barry, but I had nothing more in mind than a modern dining room for my girls.

A friend reported back that, in a private session, one outspoken solon delivered this statement, "Nossir, no, I will not! I will not add one thin dime to an appropriation to be managed by a woman who wears a hat like that!"

My undying gratitude goes to those few seasoned committee members who always came to my rescue when the going was rough. They did their best, but the desiccated appropriations that finally dribbled down to us had few decimal points of similarity to the budgets we'd slaved over so long.

However, what I needed most of all was something that couldn't be requisitioned in triplicate . . . and that was a whole new approach to one of our problems on the part of the general public and our elected officials.

Instead of forcing young delinquents to putter away much of their time, I wanted to put them to work producing tangible objects of some intrinsic value. A girl who could create something useful and honestly say, "I did it!" would have taken a seven-league stride toward a richer life.

The happiest face I've ever seen belonged to some young

girls marching proudly down the aisle of our dining room to present their first perfect loaves of bread for our inspection. I saw the identical expression on a fourteen-year-old hovering over an intricately tucked skirt. One of my girls evolved a unique Christmas tree ornament out of plain glazed paper and a clever pair of shears. When a national magazine awarded her a twenty-five-dollar prize for "originality and fine craftsmanship," I could see her literally straighten up and out before my eyes.

I wanted to incorporate these skills in addition to, not instead of, our regular vocational courses. Why shouldn't a typist also know the joy of making something of beauty or practical use with her own two hands? I thought, too, that the girls should be paid for their work, which might be graded and accredited by the vocational training department of the public schools.

I soon found, however, that handwork has fallen into sad repute in a mechanized America. But even if I forgot the commercial aspects entirely, I still felt that the knowledge of accomplishment would give our girls an added sense of security in the world.

I never abandoned that daydream, but I had to set it aside for a time. My years of effort in another direction were finally being rewarded by one new building. It was a hospital which we had thought less imperative than a new fireproof dining room and kitchen. It was a beginning, however, and we accepted it gratefully. In conferences with the contractor, the doctor and the nurse planned hopefully for treatment and operating rooms with maximum lighting and ventilating facilities, and for a diet kitchen with a dumb-waiter that would get hot food to both floors.

My great concern was for the four rooms used to house incoming girls. I'd learned the hard way that new girls go through a period of frenzied unrest when they're likely to do anything at all that comes to mind. Extroverts either try to escape or start fights or destroy property. Introverts are apt to try self-mutilation or suicide. I wanted the detention rooms to have recessed lights, smooth walls, and ornamental grilles at the windows that would assure maximum security without making the place look like a prison.

When finished, the new hospital was a beautiful building, whose custodial provisions positively solicited disaster. The floral grilles at the windows were made of such soft lead that they could be pried apart by strong hands. Hissing steam from the boiler room ran through big pipes hung from the ceiling by iron braces. It was the work of a moment for a girl to pull her bed under those pipes, climb up, and unscrew the braces with a bobby pin or spoon handle. They did it out of sheer deviltry, never realizing that a loosened pipe might break and scald them all to death. Supervision became harder than ever.

If the hospital was a sharp new disappointment, the dairy held the record for long-range, deep-down disillusionment. Of all our departments, it seemed to me to be the most expendable. Only one girl out of all the fifteen hundred I knew ever expressed even a passing interest in keeping cows as a career. But one of the men on our governing board was a dairy enthusiast and that settled our destiny.

Our sleek cows made an enviable butter-fat record and took blue ribbons at every fair, but each morning at half-past five, thirty girls had to slog through the rain or the mud or the snow to pitch hay and curry rough hides, or to wash udders and milk the animals. Then they weighed the milk, marked the production and butter-fat charts, turned the cows out to pasture, cleaned the milk shed, measured the feed—and looked forward to repeating the whole process again in the evening.

A political turnover brought in officers who discontinued the dairy but oddly enough proceeded with plans to build a large hay barn. It made a very nice and expensive storage place.

In all sincerity, though, I always felt the lawmakers were to be congratulated on all the good they managed to achieve in the face of constant political push-and-shove. With every passing year, I realized anew how herculean a task it is to keep a legislature influx informed, enthusiastic, and cooperative on behalf of a small school.

We had no glory to reflect. A benefactor would never make the newsreels while receiving an ovation. He couldn't even look forward to an honorary degree and acclaim by a cheering audience of correctional school alumnae.

In spite of the certainty of no presonal reward, some of the senators were keenly sympathetic and cooperative. I remember with gratitude Senator Mead Norton. He was the senator from our district and was also a big business man, yet at any of my numerous S.O.S.'s he dropped his own affairs to drive out from Shawnee and give me wise and well-considered advice. His seasoned counsel was of real value to the State and saved me a good many boners.

Of course there were still areas in which we could use plenty of help. Our school situation for instance. Most of our girls had to be completely self-supporting as soon as they left us, and for that reason, grade school was followed by industrial training that would fit them for jobs. Our courses included business, cosmetology, commercial art, professional catering, and dressmaking.

But some of our girls had potentialities that demanded more than an eighth-grade education. On their behalf, I asked the local board to let them attend the village school. An atom bomb couldn't have caused more commotion. The board split up over the matter and so did the city council. It looked as if I'd started a small civil war.

Frankly, the fuss and fury would have amused me if my girls hadn't had so much at stake. These same youngsters had been attending public schools when they were committed to Tecumseh, yet none of their schoolmates had felt the need for decontamination. The former delinquents were now healthy, well behaved, and ambitious and suddenly they were untouchables. The arguments grew so loud and ludicrous that I finally withdrew my request to the school board.

At the beginning of the next term, I learned that a child who resided in the community could not be refused admittance to a public school. I promptly rented a room from a neighbor in town and moved three of our best girls into it. They continued to eat their meals with us, but as they had a legitimate street address, it was legally possible for them to attend the local high school.

The three girls were good students, hand picked, but the gibes thrown at them by both pupils and adults often sent them home in tears. They persevered until the day Mrs. Yates addressed the entire student body and urged them all to join a certain youth club she was sponsoring.

"You'll love it," she gushed. "There'll be dances and parties —we want you all to join . . ." Mrs. Yates trailed off as she eyed my girls, frankly aglow with anticipation.

"Yes, we want you all to join," she amended pointedly, "if you're eligible. You're only eligible if your parents live in this community."

My three guinea pigs came home grimly determined to get an education in spite of such "youth sponsors." Fortunately they were well enough balanced to bear up under the blow, but other girls might have been thrown back into apathy or pushed ahead into some violence against society. My head was whirling again. What could my youngsters do against the Yates women of the world?

At least one of my girls, however, had no fears for the future. I found out that Leta had her whole life neatly laid out, whether I liked it or not.

She was a strange changeable sort of girl, romantic one moment and intensely practical the next. I'd once promised to read poetry with her and she held me to my word, wheedling me easily out of my few precious hours alone.

One evening she turned to me abruptly and asked, "Mrs. Burnham, why do you give me so much of your time?"

I didn't have to hunt for words. "You're an exceptionally bright girl, Leta. And I'm not telling you anything you don't know," I added. "You have a fine mind and I want to help you put it to work."

"That isn't all, though, is it?" Leta deliberately egged me on.

"Not exactly," I acknowledged. "I also think you're a pretty mixed-up person. Maybe I can help you unscramble yourself."

She nodded her head but said nothing. I spoke again, "You can have such a wonderful future, if you'll just . . ."

Leta interrupted. "That's what I thought you were trying to do. You're after me to reform, aren't you?" She was the tolerant woman of the world, talking down to a naïve innocent. "But you might as well give up, Mrs. Burnham. I don't intend to change one bit."

For one of the few times in my life, I was speechless. When I began to gurgle, Leta cut in again. "Don't worry. I intend to behave myself while I'm here. You folks have treated me okay, and I don't want to get you into any trouble. But you can't change me." She was definite rather than defiant. "When I go home, I intend to go right back to what I was doing. I like it."

"You can't mean it!"

She nodded calmly.

"You can't enjoy the mauling . . . the strange men . . ."

She never stopped nodding. "I like it," she repeated. "And I like the pretty clothes and the money and the drinks and the fun that go with it, too."

"I just won't believe it, Leta." I was dogged if ineffectual. "What about your future, the danger of disease, no home life, no children, nothing in your old age?"

She listened to my catalogue of disaster with a patient smile. "I don't know about the future," she paused, "but I know it's a hell of a lot of fun while it lasts." Then, in a final burst of candor, she delivered the blow supreme.

"Besides, dear lady, I wouldn't live the kind of life you do for anything in the whole wide world. It would simply *bore* me to death."

I was too stunned to move, so Leta bent toward me like an elder approaching a hurt child. "Don't let it make you feel bad, Mrs. Burnham. I appreciate your trying so hard, honestly I do." With that, she patted my hand and lightly skipped off.

When the numbness wore off, I began plotting and scheming. We still had a year before Leta left our jurisdiction. Maybe she'd change her mind if she learned some other, some honest way of making a living. Without consulting her in the matter, I marked her down for the cosmetology class.

Leta did everything we asked of her. In all respects she was an A-1 pupil, a credit to Tecumseh. But every once in a while, I'd catch a sidewise glance in my direction—a slightly mocking smile. We never spoke of her future again. We both knew it was useless.

But often my responsibility continued long after the girls turned eighteen and left Tecumseh. Vicky would soon celebrate her last birthday at the school. No one awaited her.

"Please, Mrs. Burnham, put me with someone who'll send me to high school," she pleaded. "I'll have to have an education to get by in my business."

I was curious, "Business, Vicky?"

"I'm going to be a banker." She said it with absolute assurance.

My own reply was pretty feeble, but then I'd just had a severe shock. "You really will need high school, won't you?" was about the gist of my counseling service.

At least I was able to place her in a good home with a woman of sterling worth. In spite of a poor background and limited schooling, Mrs. Tibbets had nevertheless become a kind of minor business tycoon. She seemed Heaven-sent for Vicky.

Vicky eyed Mrs. Tibbets appraisingly. The lady was voluble but the girl was strangely silent. Her only question was, "Will you let me go to high school?" With that agreed upon, the deal was made.

I watched Vicky walk through the gate with Mrs. Tibbets' arm around her shoulders. From now on, Mrs. Tibbets would be Vicky's confidante, not I.

That twinge was jealousy; I'd felt it before when one of my girls exchanged allegiance. But it only lasted until I remembered the hundreds I had left. There were so many girls and each needed help—desperately and immediately. I couldn't follow them all out into the world. All I could do was to train their wings and toss them out of the nest.

11

LINDA INTRIGUED MY INTEREST AS MUCH AS ANY OTHER GIRL I'VE ever known. Perhaps it was her obvious pride in her mother—a beautiful tribute that few of our inmates could pay their parents.

"Her clothes aren't very elegant and she doesn't use nail polish or anything," Linda was explaining, not apologizing, ". . . she's just a plain ordinary person, I guess, but when you get to know her . . ." the girl searched helplessly for adequate words. "Anyway, you'll see when you meet her this Sunday."

To please the child, and because I was curious, I stayed on duty in the visiting rooms that Sunday afternoon. The gates opened at half-past one and a motley assortment of friends and relatives surged in.

Once again, I noticed that the blowzy, overdressed women made the most noise. And today, as usual, we had a few sight-seers, with letters of introduction from legislators, and, as usual, they were the most nuisance. We simply didn't have time enough to give them the Grand Tour and all the gory details they demanded.

I saw a prim middle-aged couple sitting disdainfully erect in a row full of silent, grimy men and slatternly women, most of whom were poking snuff sticks around their abscessed and aching gums. A wan baby clung like a limpet to the heavy-veined breast of his vacant-eyed mother.

The small brothers and sisters of inmates wriggled and squealed until slaps from impatient parents either shut them up or set them to a nice steady scream. A solemn little boy in one of our new and highly polished chairs was too shy or bewildered to make his needs known, and a small puddle grew, drop by drop, on the floor under the woven slat seat.

Over all hung an ever-strengthening stench of unwashed bodies, decayed teeth, stale beer, old sweat, wet diapers, and the inevitable overripe bananas in somebody's gift box.

Linda hovered around, but her mother hadn't arrived in the first influx. Carol's parents had come, however. Mr. and Mrs. Holzer knew that she was near the end of her cosmetology course and hoped to take her home with them. I knew that a local beauty parlor had offered the girl a job and now I overheard them planning to have a new T.V. set out of her first earnings.

Everything about the Holzers was heavy. Garments stiff with grease covered square shapeless bodies which sat as lifelessly inert as run-down robots. Their dull faces had a doughy look and vertical lines of sullen hopelessness were engraved with ground-in dirt. Even the air around them was soggy-heavy with the odor of clogged pores and accummulated filth.

"We come to git Carol," Mr. Holzer announced.

"—Git Carol," echoed Mrs. Holzer.

"We aim to take the girl home today," her husband repeated, in case I hadn't understood.

"She's not quite ready to go," I sparred for time, wondering if I could condemn anyone, even their own daughter, to the tender care of this grotesque couple. "I'll send for her . . . we'll talk it over."

While we waited for Carol to come, they simply went into a state of open-eyed hibernation. Yes, I could see a resemblance to the girl who'd come to Tecumseh two years before. She was just recovering from a drunken spree, still a little silly and thick of tongue. A tight blouse had popped its most strategic button and the cheap wool skirt bagged around her body. From the aura around her—about 160 proof—she'd been sitting it out of shape on bar stools. One shoe had been lost in transit and toes showed through what was left of the exposed sock. A good while later, when the alcohol had been sweated out and the make-up of months scrubbed off, she was revealed as a wholesome-looking girl with hair the color of heavy honey and the kind of complexion that would make a cold-cream ad jealous. In a short time, she was one of our star boarders and spiritually no kin at all to the sodden drunk I'd first seen.

Now she came dashing across the lawn, full of the eagerness that was her most endearing trait. Even at this distance, I could see that her whole body radiated joy at the prospect of going home. She'd forgotten so much in such a short time. I couldn't bear to see what sudden remembrance would do to her, so—mistakenly perhaps—I sent her in to revisit the squalid past alone. Since Linda's mother still hadn't arrived, I left word that I could be found at my office and retired from the scene.

A half-hour later, the door opened slowly and Carol approached my desk. She looked shrunken, less vivid, as if a giant hand had squeezed out all the happiness and left just the bare essential structure.

"They want me to go back with them." Her voice was so

low I could barely hear it, and I noticed that she hadn't said "home."

"Do you want to go?"

"No— Oh— No—!" a quiver passed along the length of her body. "I'd forgotten—"

"You don't have to leave unless you want to," I assured her. "It's your decision, not theirs."

"But they're my parents—" she stopped and bit her lip. "I suppose I ought to go, but I can't. I just can't go back—not to that—." She pressed the heels of her hands tight against her temples. "If it's money they want, I'll send them some as soon as I can make it. But I just—can't—go back—." She was beginning to shake uncontrollably.

"All right," I was brusque and matter of fact about it. "That's settled then. You don't have to go in there again if you'd rather not. I'll see them and explain."

"Thank you." Before I could stop her, Carol caught my hand and kissed it. "Thank you—all of you—I didn't realize all you've done." Two tears welled and in a moment she was sobbing as if the world had come to an end. A part of hers had.

I left her to cry the wound clean and returned to the impossible parents. "I'm sorry to have to tell you that Carol can't go home with you today." I stated it baldly but in as kind a voice as I could summon up. Not a flicker crossed either face.

Mr. Holzer shifted slightly in his chair. Mrs. Holzer gazed at him woodenly. Neither of them moved. I couldn't imagine what they might be waiting for, and then it occurred to me that I hadn't mentioned the magic word "money." I decided to try it out.

"As far as the money goes . . ." They both sat up straighter and looked really interested for the first time. ". . . I'm planning to send Carol to a job in a larger town than yours . . ." I neglected to mention that it would take her clear across the

State, as far as possible from them. ". . . She can earn more there than at home, and she'll send you some money as soon as she gets started."

The clock ticked noisily in the silence that followed. They exchanged glances again—in Morse code for all I know. They must have had some form of communication because both rose from their seats simultaneously. Mr. Holzer stood for a long moment fingering his shapeless hat. "I guess that's all then. We better git goin'."

Carol's mother started out the door after him, then turned to utter her only wholly independent series of words. "You'll see she sends the money?" I must have nodded, because they left without further comment.

Someone tapped me on the shoulder, and I found Mr. Hines twinkling up at me. He was a wizened little man with an oddly charming though toothless smile, and today he was dressed for an occasion in spotless blue overalls and a tie straight out of a surrealist's D.T.'s. I took Mr. Hines back to my office. Carol was gone.

As soon as I shut the door behind us, Mr. Hines began to twist nervous fingers together. "I'd like to take Ory home with me today—if it's all right with you, that is."

Another one! "I'm afraid I can't let Ora go today, Mr. Hines." But this time I had no trouble keeping my voice kind. He was quite another case.

"She ain't done nothin' wrong?" His face was genuinely anxious. "You wrote me she was a'doin' all right."

"She is," I nodded, "but we never dismiss a girl into a home unless there's an older woman there to act as her adviser. Her mother or an older sister, even a cousin or an aunt. You don't have a wife now, do you?"

"No'm, I ain't." Mr. Hines' fingers were now drumming on the arm of his chair. " 'Course you know I was married once—

Ory's legal, you know," he assured me proudly. "But the old woman got so she et two potatoes at one meal and I had to get rid o' her."

"Oh," was all I could manage. Somehow his statement just didn't lend itself to a snappy comeback. "Do you have a mother or a sister, or any woman?" I added desperately. "Can you think of anyone to look after Ora?"

"I got a housekeeper," he announced, but his flash of triumph faded even in the telling. "Howsomever, I'm tellin' you the truth—I think I'm a'goin' to fire her. She's costin' me three dollars ever' week of my life. I might just as well git married agin'."

Mr. Hines looked glum and agreed that Ora should stay with us until his domestic situation had been satisfactorily solved. He thanked me politely for my time and creaked toward the door in his neatly polished work shoes.

Sunday afternoons always seemed endless, especially when we had the "honor" of entertaining the assorted friends and relatives of political nabobs. Visitors—especially wide-eyed inhabitants of the upper crust—always asked a good many questions, and then looked shocked or reproachful when we gave them true and uncensored answers.

Our final chore, when the last visitors were saying their farewells, was to examine the gifts left behind for the girls.

Most of the packages were harmless enough. They abounded in soft bananas, mashed chocolate cake, and cheap candy. However, we found switch knives or other weapons often enough to keep us alert. And it was always necessary to remove quantities of pornographic post cards, trashy magazines, pep-up pills, and a certain type of nauseating perfume that permanently impregnated anything it touched.

Whenever anyone objected vehemently to having a package checked, we knew we'd better dig deep in it. One Sunday,

Kim's mother kicked up a fuss. "What's the use of goin' through that?" she whined. "Tain't nothin' but a little old box o' tissue. Aintcha got nothin' better ta do?" While she was still talking I came up with a box of contraceptives. Mother dear was looking out for her daughter in the only way she knew.

Visiting hours left school officers hanging on the ropes, but the day wasn't over even after the last guest had gone. To keep them from feeling completely left out, the girls without visitors were always divided into "Treasure Teams." With their supervisors, they scoured the fields around the school for specimens of nature. After the evening meal, a contest was held and the group which had collected the greatest number of oddities won an enormous cake which they were allowed to gobble up immediately.

Birds' nests, snake skins, horned toads, odd rocks, twisted roots, and terrapins usually turned up. In fact, each cottage soon had a "stable" of terrapins which the girls groomed with great care. They caught flies and wheedled bits of food from the kitchen to feed the clumsy creatures. Every day they took the turtles out of their tubs and timed them as seriously as if they were really race horses. The terrapin races became a regular feature of our yearly Halloween program.

One memorable year Halloween fell on a visitors' day—and that occasion was known ever after as "Double Trouble." Triple trouble, so far as I was concerned.

To my dismay, one of our political wheels chose this same All Hallow's Eve to send out a job applicant. A lavender-and-old-lace little lady appeared on my doorstep just as I was confiscating a copy of *Spicy Stories* left by the last visitor. I wouldn't dream of denying the girls their anticipated frolic, but I tried to warn my visitor ahead of time of the hullabaloo she might expect. Obviously, my explanation hadn't sunk in at all.

She censured my costume with one quick glance. I was masked and had on a green linen dress like those worn by the girls in one of the cottages. My toothbrush and comb were stuck in the neckline of my dress in imitation of the inmates who found this to be the only way they could keep these intimate articles sacred to their own use. I'd intended to sit, incognito, with the green-dress girls, but in deference to my guest, I removed my mask and presided at the head table as usual.

There was a period of quiet just long enough for the prayer which preceded every meal, and then bedlam broke loose. All noise restrictions were off that night. The lady chose that moment to ask, "How many girls do you have here?"

"Two hundred and seventy-six," I replied, but my answer was lost in a loud rendition of "Old MacDonald Had a Farm, Ee-i-ee-I-oh—"

"How many did you say?" The lady leaned a little nearer.

"Two hundred and seventy-six," I yelled over the din. Another table had taken up the song and the girls were beating out the rhythm with their tableware.

"Oh, seventy-six. It looks like more." The lady's lips formed the figures but her words were completely drowned out.

"No, not seventy-six. TWO-HUNDRED-SEVENTY-SIX," I shouted the correction at the top of my voice.

"That's what I thought you said—seventy-six," she stared at me disapprovingly.

I gave up. If the lady joined us, she'd soon find out how many girls we had. If she didn't join us, it didn't matter whether or not she knew our number, I thought grimly.

The high jinks started with a costumed grand march around the campus, in which we all participated. Thoughtful ladies of the Lieutenant Governor's family used to send their discarded finery for our fancy dress, and our daydreamers became fairy princesses or queens of the silver screen. Others, less elegant but more earthy, stuffed pillows under their dresses and wheeled doll buggies containing unhappy terrapins or toy pandas.

After the traditional supper of wieners, baked beans, gingerbread, and apples, the girls were allowed, on this one night, to whoop up as much noise as they wished, so long as they steered clear of quarrels. Needless to say, they took full advantage of the opportunity provided.

When the revelers had worn themselves down to a nubbin, they dragged wearily home to bed—the only night of the year they went willingly. They were too exhausted to plan any important mischief, we figured, and for a change we all anticipated a real night's rest. I had a relaxing hot bath in mind, and I'd been saving a magazine to read in bed—but I should have known better. Just as I was kicking off my shoes, an S.O.S. came from the kitchen. Like all the rest, it started, "Come quick."

Mrs. Jaynes stood in the center of the room with her hands on her hips and an expression of dismayed outrage on her face. Her kitchen had been desecrated and she didn't know what to do. Looking at the three glassy-eyed girls twined together, laocoön-like, for support, I could understand her dilemma. It looked as if they'd all collapse if you set finger to one. A fourth girl sat at the kitchen table with her head resting on arms bedded down in a litter of dirty soup spoons.

Drunk? Definitely. But how? Not even the instructors were permitted to keep intoxicants anywhere on campus.

Mrs. Jaynes came to life before I figured it out. "Maybell, come here," she ordered.

A stocky, freckled-faced girl quivered in recognition of her name, and the two others in the clump lurched.

"Maybell!"

She unwove herself, limb by limb, and sidled unsteadily in the general direction of Mrs. Jaynes.

"Where did you get the liquor, Maybell?"

She giggled foolishly and fell over her own foot. Mrs. Jaynes hauled her up, and I took a crack at the questioning, taking one word at a time and enunciating like an elocutionist. About the fourth time, it began to penetrate.

"No—o—o. No liquor." Maybell shook her head, and it continued to wobble alarmingly. "Never shaw any liquor."

"I know," Dortha burped happily as she tried to focus her eyes on me. "I know ev'ythin'," she patted her chest. "Jush ashk me somepin'."

"All right, Dortha," I challenged. "Show me where it is."

Dortha thrust her arm chummily through mine. "C'm on, Supe. Wan' a li'l drinkie? I'm jush the girl what knowsh." She careened across the kitchen, with me in tow, and stopped abruptly in front of a supply cupboard. Before I had any idea what she was about, she jerked one arm up and swept a whole stack of canned goods off the shelf.

Mrs. Jaynes lifted down the gallon jug which now stood revealed and handed it to me with a shudder. Just an inch of the nauseous stuff was left. The jar had been filled with fruit juices, doctored with sugar and yeast, and allowed to ferment especially for tonight's spree.

The drink must have possessed a powerful wallop. Irma, the girl at the table, had passed out completely. Maybell and Dortha weren't coordinating very well, and Jimmye was beginning to be violently sick at her stomach.

In the rush of getting supper, Mrs. Jaynes had noticed that the girls made more trips to the pantry than seemed absolutely necessary, but she was too busy to investigate. Not until they began staggering and fencing with the bread knives did she realize that this was more than normal Halloween high spirits.

There was nothing we could do now but rouse the nurse and try to get our amateur carousers sobered up. Our girls sometimes had difficulty learning to fry an egg, but over the years I was amazed to learn how many were adept at making home brew of various exotic varieties.

The hectic day finally ended. At midnight, the Halloween revelers were well into their night's sleep. Employees' windows were all dark, and the night watchman was in the kitchen enjoying his snack of sandwiches and coffee. Even the drunken girls were already sleeping it off at the hospital. I plodded home, feeling very alone in the world, and too tired to care about the haggard reflection that met me head-on as I approached the mirrored doors of my apartment.

But then I was startled wide-awake. The mirrors were throwing back another image in addition to my own . . . that of Leila Wiles, watching me furtively through her window. So she was still keeping me under surveillance. It was too far and too dark to see her face, but I could imagine the expression it wore. "If looks could kill," I thought with a shudder. Exhausted as I was, I knew sleep would be a long time coming. I'd consciously put the latest "Leila-ism" out of my mind, but now it forced itself back and demanded attention.

As I undressed, I thought back just two days. Minetta was leaving in the custody of an aunt. She'd thrown her arms around me, kissed her favorite matron, said polite "good-bys" to the rest of the staff, and scooted hastily by Leila without looking up. In that moment, Leila had looked murderous . . . and puzzled too. Her plan, put into operation a month ago, hadn't worked, and she didn't know why. Curiosity was consuming her, but she couldn't ask questions without connecting herself with the crime. For it was a crime.

I looked in the mirror again and saw the curtains move at her window. She must be in a real twitch, I thought with great satisfaction. How much did I know? Did I know anything? Not knowing what *I* knew was probably driving her out of that cold, calculating mind.

I recalled that day, almost a month ago, when the plot began to unravel at the edges. A note, hastily scrawled on toilet tissue, had been shoved under my door. It read simply, "I got to see you tonight in your apartment. P.S. Dont tell nobody." Signed, "Myra Mae." Myra was a tall girl, terribly thin, a twitchy hyperthyroid type who couldn't sit still a second. My first thought was that she was feeling the urge to run and wanted to be talked out of it. The postscript, however, puzzled me. A reluctant "runner" was always intense but not secretive.

Myra Mae studiously avoided my eyes during dinner but I was ready for the nervous tattoo on my door a bit later. She slid in before I had the door half-open and started to pace even before she began to talk.

"Missus Burnham, whatever I do, it's wrong." Her voice was always both shrill and breathless. "What I mean is, what I gotta do now, it's wrong if I do and wrong if I don't. I'm all mixed up."

That made two of us. I suggested that she start at the beginning and settled back to listen. Knowing Myra Mae, I was prepared for a non-stop story. It boiled down to this:

Myra Mae had been one of Leila's special pets until I put a stop to the bribery. "She was awful nice to me, Missus Burnham. Sometimes she'd say something kinda funny about you—nothin' bad—just kinda funny," Myra Mae added hastily, "but that was just her way."

That was Leila's way, all right. Nothing definite that could be defended or disproved, just "kinda funny" things the girls could wonder and whisper about.

Myra Mae continued, ". . . so when she gave me this to put in the mail, I didn't think nothin' of it."

The envelope she handed me was addressed to one of our State senators, a "crusader" who loved to see his name in the newspapers. Then I saw that the envelope was open. I looked at Myra Mae.

"Yes, Ma'am. I opened it." I had my mouth shaped for a lecture when she rushed on, "Look at it first, Missus Burnham, then you can jump on me." She was positively jittering.

The letter was on plain, cheap paper, and my eye was first caught by the large childish signature sprawled clear across the bottom . . . "Minetta Doorken." Minetta? The child was a pretty but almost moronic eleven-year-old, who automatically answered "yes" to every question in an effort to please.

When I started to read the erratic typescript above the signature, my heart gave one big bounce and then settled down to a steady racing beat. "Whipped me bloody . . . all by myself two days with nothin' to eat . . . pulled my hair and cut it all off . . ." The page was black with accusations

Myra Mae broke in. "See what I meant. I mail it, it's wrong . . . I give it to you, you're mad I opened it." She looked at me hopelessly.

I tried to control myself until I could send her away and study the incredible words alone. But I couldn't be too abrupt. I had her to think of too.

"It was wrong of you to open it, you know that; but it was very brave of you to bring it to me and face the punishment. It would have been easier to mail the letter and forget it. I'm very proud of you, Myra Mae. Don't talk about this please. We'll discuss it later."

When she'd gone, I dropped the letter as if it had suddenly writhed in my hands. Minetta hadn't written it, I knew, but if questioned, she'd nod her head to anything. I picked up the sheet and forced myself to look at it again. Anyone could have typed it—even Minetta, I realized—but it must contain a clue somewhere. The whipping and starving made my blood boil, but "hair" rang a bell. I'd come upon Minetta in my office one day, happily chopping her hair off with the office shears. I'd had to finish the job and even it off to keep her from looking a freak. I remembered that I'd been scolding and she'd been laughing when we walked down the corridor—and past Leila Wiles.

Because I recognized my prejudice, I tried to hold back the growing suspicion. Suddenly the big clue—the incontestable clue—leaped up at me from the letter. The hunt-and-peck typing could have been done by anyone at all, but the type itself—a dainty elite—was to be found on only one machine at the school. Leila's new portable. She'd shown it around so proudly.

A half-hour remained before "Lights Out," and I made an instant decision. I turned on the bathroom lights and switched off the living room lights before leaving my apartment so that Leila would think I was safely showering. I'd known for some time that she kept an eye on me. Then I ducked out and took the back way around to the cottage in which Minetta slept.

When we were alone together, the sweet but vacant-faced child slipped her hand into mine and waited cheerfully for something—anything to happen. What it was didn't matter to Minetta. I talked with her about her new dress, admired her panda, and then asked about her schoolwork. "Can you write your name now?" I took a pen and paper from my pocket. She nodded happily. "I write *good*." The pen pressed into the paper, engraving rather than writing her unsteady signature, which she then presented proudly to me. I held my breath before asking the next question. "Did you write your name for anyone else?"

She nodded again, but I knew that didn't mean too much. "Who?" I pressed gently. Minetta smiled shyly. "My uncle—when he came . . ." Not her uncle, I thought. He appreciates what we're trying to do for her. But Minetta wasn't finished ". . . Miss Wiles said I wrote so pretty she gave me a piece of candy," she finished triumphantly. I was feeling shaky, but we weren't quite finished yet.

"Did you write your name for Miss Leila on a little piece of yellow paper . . . like this?"

"Oh, no, Ma'am." She giggled with delight. "It was a great *big* piece of paper. White paper. And I writ clear across the bottom."

She was still giggling when I tucked her in.

It was only a two-minute walk back to my apartment, but I felt ten years older than when I'd left. I could understand jealousy and thwarted ambition, but Leila had now gone far beyond anything I'd ever encountered. Obviously she'd typed the false charges above Minetta's name, and was now waiting for the senator and the newspapers to descend upon me. Ruining a life or two didn't bother her a bit. I felt cold, right through to the bone.

I could fire her—but not without a messy scandal. I could confront her—but nothing pierced that enameled exterior. She'd slide out somehow, without a scratch. Suddenly I knew what I would do. Nothing at all. Just leave Leila waiting for the blow that would never fall. The suspense and then—eventually—the knowledge of failure would, I knew, gnaw away at her composure as no words of mine ever could. I was discovering that I could be vindictive too.

She's not really so smart, I remember thinking. She slipped up on the typing, and she slipped up on Myra Mae. Of course Leila didn't have access to Myra's case history, so she couldn't know that one of the girl's main troubles was a compulsion to pry into other people's belongings. Myra Mae could sooner fly than resist the temptation to open a sealed envelope.

All that had happened a month before, and Leila was still doing sentry duty at her window. She'd never know, I thought with satisfaction. Myra Mae had been released three weeks ago and now Minetta was gone. The lights in Leila's room snapped out, but somehow I doubted that she would get much sleep.

12

MUCH OF THE GIRLS' MISCHIEF COULD BE LAID TO EXCESS ENERGY and imagination allowed to run rampant. Their creative ability had never been channeled into productive outlets. I wanted training in music, art, drama, and dancing for our inmates; but, of course, self-expression had to play second fiddle to the necessities of institutional life. As it was, our budget was barely holding its own.

Quite by accident, I discovered that the seventh-grade teacher was an exceptionally fine artist. She'd concealed her talent because my predecessor felt art was a frippery that "put ideas into people's heads" and that, of course, was bad. When I asked Mrs. Lyndheim if she'd volunteer to teach an art class, she acted as if I'd just awarded her a paid-up plot in Paradise.

I intended to kill more than a couple of birds with one stone. First, harness the effervescence of our girls to keep it from running hog-wild; second, turn up and develop any latent talent; and—a penny-pinching third—paint murals on the soiled panels of our main reception room! There was no money with which to clean them up otherwise.

I was nervous about broaching this last to Mrs. Lyndheim, but she couldn't have been more enthusiastic. Before I could catch my breath, she'd recruited the first art class, presented the problem, and started the project. Out of a welter of odd ideas, ranging from science-fiction to Fairyland, the girls finally chose to do a succession of scenes from American history. The first dirty panel was treated to the Pilgrims landing at Plymouth Rock. We got clear through the Revolution, the Civil War, Reconstruction, and up to Boulder Dam before we ran out of wall space.

The murals brought us fame. Too much, as it turned out. A calendar company sent a representative to see them, and he was impressed enough to offer our Mrs. Lyndheim a three-year contract at a spectacular salary.

However, other good teachers kept cropping up and eventually our girls were painting on *clean* panels. On the walls of the resident cottages you could see Ruth and Naomi across the room from a Pandora, who'd just opened her box of evil. Epimetheus watched from the back wall while Joan of Arc listened to the angels' voices. Aladdin rubbed his magic lamp and gathered up jewels to the astonishment of Snow White and the Seven Dwarfs.

Since music was my particular passion, I investigated its status in the school as soon as I was settled in. Besides being just plain enjoyable, I'd always felt that this art form has therapeutic and cultural value beyond that of any other.

A little white-haired lady assured me that Tecumseh was well supplied with all sorts of music. "I direct an orchestra," she said with visible pride, "and sometimes we sing in the dining room."

That night the orchestra—composed of piano, drum, trombone, banjo, and three violins—demonstrated for my benefit. The trombonist was tone-deaf but she made up in volume all that she lacked in accuracy. The horsehair had frayed out of the violin bows and the conductor—a matron in her more prosaic hours—had restrung them with Number 40 white Boilfast. The resulting wheeze sounded like an acute case of catarrh. The snare drum gave off a dead "clunk" because someone had stolen the key and the tension rods couldn't be tightened. The banjo wasn't bad—if you happen to like banjos.

The tiny white-haired conductor teetered up and down in waltz time as she waved her ruler-baton for a rousing Sousa march. It was rather disconcerting.

In rapid sequence, we suffered through "Juanita," "Tenting on the Old Camp Ground," and "My Little Gray Home in the West." The tempo slowed a bit more with every bar of each selection. By the time we arrived at the last long-drawn woeful "We-e-e-est," the atmosphere was fit for an old-fashioned wake. A few more mopish notes and I'd have supplied the lifeless body. As an ex-music teacher, I felt that I'd just endured a fate *worse* than death. I may be exaggerating a little, but not much. To anyone with an acutely sensitive and trained ear, certain sounds, stresses, accents can be sheer agony.

At the close of the concert, the little conductor bustled up to me, as anxious for a pat on the head as a pet poodle. Well, she'd done her best, so I could honestly say "Thank You"—which I did with as much warmth as I could muster. She looked straight into my eyes, smiled quizzically as she read the condescension there, and said gently, "You'll be happy to know you've just heard my farewell performance."

I flushed and started to protest, but she smiled again and held up her hand. "Don't feel you have to be polite, dear. I don't know any songs that came out after the First World War and all I know about conducting is that you need a stick . . ." she waved the ruler ". . . but I figured *some* music was better than no music."

I could have kissed her. As a matter of fact, I did.

I found that a new staff member had a trained and beautiful contralto. In a short time, Miss Dunning had us beginning each breakfast with a hymn. Simple classics and popular songs provided an extra dessert after the other meals. The shiest girls would harmonize when we sang "God Bless America," and the latest cowboy number was always good for an impromptu solo from somewhere in the room. The tongue twisters full of gobble-de-gook set them laughing so hard they came in hungrier for the next meal. But one song brought a hot, hard lump to my throat.

> "Highways are happy ways, when they lead the way back home,
> Highways are happy ways, to the lonely hearts that roam."

What could "way back home" mean to these kids—these forsaken and unloved youngsters? After the second rendition, Miss Dunning—without a word from me—dropped it from her repertoire.

From among our community singers, we chose forty girls and taught them four-part harmony. In time, they learned an amazing number of anthems which they then presented in churches all over the State. Eventually, they even staged some charming operettas. The pseudo-music teacher and I coached their singing and acting, and another instructor exhibited a rare talent for choreography.

Operettas became a project in which the entire school could participate. Girl cooks and housekeepers voluntarily assumed extra duties in order to give the singers added time for practice. Art students painted curtains and back drops. Sewing room girls made all the costumes which were faithful to the country and period portrayed. In one dance of the fairies, diaphanous white silk floated around the dancers while colored lights wove enchantment that reached out and enveloped the very last row.

People who admired that act criticized us because of the expensive costumes. Actually, the material used was casket cloth which we bought for twenty-five cents a yard. Thoughts of commerce probably shouldn't sully art, but we made a nice profit on that show with which we bought more casket cloth and treats for the girls.

During World War II our operettas were responsible for the purchase of many a government bond. In one small town, the bond salesman raised three thousand dollars from the crowd which came to see our play. The players profited in improved carriage, poise, and grace. One of our girls finally landed in a famous dance organization in New York, and another young actress was seen by a talent scout who advised her to lose five pounds and get to Hollywood as soon as she could. Some day I expect to see her in Cinemascope.

The musical Miss Dunning was a wholesome young woman, full of vitality and "bounce"; the girls adored her. One wisp of a child was completely obsessed. Sarah trailed Miss Dunning with worshipful eyes, watching for a chance to pick up her handkerchief or carry her books.

"I wish she weren't so devoted," Miss Dunning confided to me. "Aside from being embarrassing, it's bad for her. She's terribly jealous, you know. When I'm nice to the other girls, she sulks or else she makes a regular spectacle of herself."

One day Sarah's cottage-mates heard an alarming commotion in the bathroom. They took one quick look and ran for the matron.

"Come on," they urged. "Something awful is happening. Sarah's trying to commit suicide."

Sarah had thrust her head deep into the toilet bowl and was

sputtering and choking as she kept her finger pressed on the flush button. The exasperated matron pulled the sodden girl to her feet. "Why on earth are you doing such a fool thing?"

Tearful and bedraggled, Sarah sank back to her knees. Her hair hung in dripping wisps, her eyes were swollen, and her long thin nose looked redder than ever.

"I want to die! I want to die!" the thin voice wailed. "Whyn't you all let me alone so I could have drowned myse'f?"

"For goodness sake, Sarah, why?" The matron yanked her up again and enveloped her in a big bath towel.

"Because Miss Dunning was so nice to Julia today." The rest of her words jerked out as she was ungently toweled dry. "I just know—she don't—like me—well as she does—that—that ole Julia—OUCH!"

The matron dried her back and spanked her lightly. "Now, Sarah, shame on you! You know Miss Dunning likes one girl just as much as another. That means you too. She likes you all just the same."

Sarah wailed, "I don't *want* her to like us all the same. I want her to love me best."

I was forced to move the child to another schedule until she learned to control her infatuation for the teacher. These child-teacher attachments were common and—Dr. Hathcart assured me—a normal part of growing up. However, he did caution me to take nothing for granted—not even his own assurances. If anything looked excessive to my eye, he warned me to throttle it down one way or another.

The real trouble lay in the coupling-off of inmates. By now it was clear that Dr. Hathcart had been a true prophet when he warned me that I'd have plenty of Matties and Pinkies on my hands before I was through. Eternal vigilance was the only answer. I'd cautioned every employee to watch for any signs of unnatural attachment. When it occurred, I found that it was generally evidenced by an over-intensity, a certain high shrillness, much touching, if only the clothes, of the other girl involved, and a rash of lame excuses to avoid set schedules and duties that might separate one from another.

Ellen was an acute and awful example. A genuinely attractive girl herself, she felt a strong and, to me, incomprehensible craving for Jewel, a nondescript person whose only distinction lay in the fact that she lived in a cottage set aside for venereally diseased inmates. Knowing that they couldn't be together while only one was diseased, Ellen decided to acquire syphilis herself. Since the conventional method of acquisition wasn't open to her, she tried everything else, including housebreaking, bribing, and attempting to smuggle out Jewel's infected underclothes. As long as the passion lasted, matrons and supervisors were on the jump every minute to prevent Ellen from achieving her unholy ambition.

It was cold comfort at the time, but at least life was never dull. Something happened just about every hour on the hour. One morning Lizzie happened. I knew she was an event out of the ordinary because the transportation officer stayed as far away from her as possible. Generally, he was clutching the arm of anyone he brought to Tecumseh to keep her from hauling off and hitting him and running away.

At first glance, all I could see was that Lizzie had pasty features, a long nose which was probably always red, and hair the color of old paper left lying in the sun. Obviously, too, the child was starved for everything—food, care, love—and soap and water. She did look a little mangy.

Lizzie followed her guide to the hospital for the routine clean-up. In a few minutes I received a "Come quick" message from the nurse. When I opened the door, she had her mouth already shaped to speak and her wiry hair looked more than ever like an indignant, red aurora borealis.

"That new girl has the worst case of pediculosis I ever saw. It's terrible! Come see."

"Pediculosis" was less offensive to sensitive ears than "lice," but the bugs bit just as hard. And anyway, the ones Lizzie harbored were flourishing enough to warrant the full five syllables. Some clung to strands of hair, while the older members of the colony burrowed visibly into her scalp.

Nurse Allen seated the awed girl in the middle of a big cloth spread out on the floor. After tying her own hair in a tight turban and wrapping a coverall apron around herself, the nurse combed out as much as she could, and then burned the floor cloth and the apron.

Poor Lizzie was next subjected to a scouring which fell short of flaying alive by a microscopic amount. A potent lotion of some sort was applied to her scalp by rubber-gloved hands, and the child's head was then tied up tight. Every day for a week the process was repeated and every day the nurse shook her head as she reported grimly, "She's still got some, but I'm running 'em down."

At last a day dawned on which Nurse Allen marched triumphantly into my office with a beaming, red-nosed Lizzie in tow. Her hair had been bobbed short and between the wisps I could see a scalp as fiery as a desert sunset. Too ecstatic for speech, Lizzie just beamed.

"Well, we got 'em all." From her triumphant tone, the nurse might have been talking about man-eating tigers. "Not a one left. Head's as clean as a baby's."

"Lizzie, I'm so glad," I smiled at the peeled onion of a girl. "Now you can move into a cottage like all the others. And I know you're much more comfortable."

So much attention was a new experience for Lizzie; her shyness finally faded and her voice was rapturous. "Oh, Mrs. Burnham, it's just swell, honest. My head feels so good. An' Mrs.

Burnham, ma'am, please send for my daddy—he's got 'em too!"

Washing lice out of Lizzie's hair, trying to solve the problems of our Matties and Lindas and Letas . . . were we really fulfilling the purposes of a correctional institution? More and more often, I asked myself this question—and each time I had to give myself a qualified answer. In one area, we were doing an excellent job, or at least making an honest effort. Our girls were learning skills which would enable them to earn wages after parole, and we were also attempting to teach them to conform to an acceptable social pattern.

Unfortunately, this positive part of the picture was overbalanced by two negatives. First, reports on paroled girls revealed that too many of them were drifting back to old gangs and old habits. The school, of course, couldn't be blamed in any way for the large majority of "relapsees." Most of the time, the drift back was due to our returning the girls to the same unsavory surroundings from which they had come. Their new, unfamiliar virtues were no match for the old, established vices.

The second negative, however, *was* the fault of the institution. Some of our girls were fortunate in getting a good fresh start on the "outside"—and still failed to adjust. Why was that? I thought I knew. We were conditioning girls for life, it's true, but life as it's lived in a correctional school—and nowhere else in the world. Certainly we didn't offer a normal setting in which to practice normal social relations.

Normal families don't consist of one mother by day, another by night, and fifty sisters all about the same age. Our groups had no father to lay down the law firmly but lovingly, and so earn their respect for law. There were no grandparents to spoil them and spin them stories of the old days, giving them a feeling of family continuity. There were no babies to cuddle and care for, to instill a sense of responsibility. There weren't any brothers or kid cousins to give a girl an occasional roughing-up—and a rough, wonderful kind of watching over. And there weren't any dates under a protective maternal eye. Yet our girls were expected to go forth and adjust smoothly to all such relationships.

Even the equality of treatment in the school, while necessary and excellent in theory, was contrary to the actual disparities of "outside" life. Every girl at Tecumseh had precisely the same food, the same number and quality of garments, the same privileges and restrictions as every other girl. In an institution, such an arrangement prevents envy and bitterness, but it isn't a sample of normal living.

This abnormal equality doesn't contribute to the mature acceptance of an imperfect society in which hungry men and millionaires rub elbows, and a bank balance may occasionally be achieved at the cost of an ethic or two. Accepting the fact of economic discrepancies without resentment is an important part of adult adjustment. We couldn't do much about that.

It wasn't even possible to teach our girls simple, everyday housekeeping. Instead of a well-rounded day of cleaning, cooking, shopping, sewing, and taking care of the kids which confronts the average housewife, our girls worked on the production line system required to keep an ever-changing group of approximately three hundred persons housed, clothed, and fed.

Some of our girls peeled off enough potato parings to girdle the earth. A few of them learned to bake pies with mountainous peaks of meringue. Others hemmed sheets or worked buttonholes. A normal family can't exist on pie alone, no matter how good it is. And a rich, full life requires more than beautiful buttonholes. We tried to rotate training schedules, but too much shifting around meant that the entire institution ground slowly to a halt. Home was never like this.

For girls who had had plenty of masculine companionship and, in most cases, a good deal of sex experience, the psychological jolt of arriving in an entirely feminine world was severe. Even the daily appearance of the acne-eaten delivery boy created an uproar among the kitchen girls.

We knew the importance of teaching our girls to exhibit a proper blend of friendliness and reserve in their meetings with men. They thought of the male sex in terms of sex only; the concept of men as individuals, to be evaluated and accepted as friends, was completely foreign to them. We knew all this, but abstract ideas are hard to drive into stubborn young heads. What we needed were young men in the flesh . . . under our jurisdiction, of course, but around.

Our newly released girls were so starved for attention that they fell for the first male to indicate any degree of interest. They made ridiculous or degrading alliances, through marriage or otherwise, with undesirable—sometimes incredible—characters. The alliances were generally brief and left the girl with nothing but the memory of another mistake. Sometimes, of course, there was more solid evidence in the form of a social disease or an unwanted child.

Knowing that men occupied the foreground of their thoughts, as is natural within any group of teen-age girls, I felt that our greatest service would be to teach them how to establish and maintain respectable friendships with the opposite sex. With some forebodings, I decided that we would have a party and invite young men. Hostesses would include all girls sixteen or over who had achieved a good behavior record for at least three months. They'd decorate their cottages for the event, make their own party dresses, and prepare the refreshments.

The girls screeched with ecstasy when I announced the plan. They followed me around for hours, demanding constant reassurance. Did I mean it? A real party, like on the "outside"? I wouldn't change my mind? And over and over again, "With boys? Honest?"

I nodded so much that my head felt semi-detached for days.

"What kind of boys?" one girl wanted to know. She had good reason to distrust the entire sex.

"The best in the State," I answered. "Hand picked. Good boys."

"Good boys?" Wanda looked up in surprise. "I didn't know there were any. How do you entertain them, for Pete's sake?"

I saw that she was dead serious. Her social arena, to date, had ranged from dance halls to beer parlors, with cheap motels and the back seats of autos in between.

"My dear," I started to explain to her and the rest of the girls crowded around me too. They'd all had the same question in mind. "We'll have dancing. We'll think up some games to play. And you'll find out how much fun it is to *talk* to a boy. All of you had better start thinking up some good topics of conversation. These are pretty bright fellows. They may get on anything from politics to the New York Yankees," I warned.

Happy and busy weeks of preparation preceded the party. The newspapers and magazines were worn ragged with reading. Practice discussions could be heard at the laundry mangle or in the cow barn. We even had a hot political fight going before we were through. A whole new world was opening up to the girls and they loved it.

Places in the receiving line went to those girls having the highest school grades. We had an embarrassment of riches; *everyone* was good for the months preceding the party so the final selection had to be made on the basis of marks. When that decision was announced, all the marks improved too! The art teacher helped the hostesses design a wooden badge enameled in blue and bearing the word OFFICIAL in gold. The youngsters were filled with a wonderful sense of achievement and importance.

No Paris salon ever radiated more happiness than our sewing room as yards of crepe and Shantung gradually became party dresses. Girls with a few dollars of their own were taken downtown to select fabric. Those with no money contented themselves with what the school had to offer. To my surprise and delight, there was no grumbling.

Leta was one of the girls who made a trip to town for material. She lingered lovingly over every bolt in the store until the clerk became exasperated.

"Please be as patient as you can," I whispered. "This is her first chance to shop in nearly three years. She's having the time of her life."

The clerk caught the spirit of the thing and started pulling yardage from high shelves and special hidey-holes. Five minutes before closing time, Leta finally chose a dusty pink crepe which had been one of her very first selections. Delinquent or not, she shopped like any other young woman!

News of the party leaked beyond the campus. Well beyond. Suddenly the eyes of the world were focused on our little country school. I hadn't thought of the party as propaganda for an idea. Even if I'd known anything about publicity, I'd never have dreamed that millions of people would be intrigued by the same sort of affair that goes on every Friday night all over America. The fact that ours was being held in a correctional school seemed to excite even the most blasé editors.

The press was extremely friendly and more than cooperative. State papers ran streamer headlines. Paramount sent newsreel photographers. The national wire services arranged to have newsmen on the scene. *Life* magazine scheduled a picture story of the event.

Our girls, movie-struck like most kids, discovered how hard it is to be natural in front of a camera while broiling lights pour down and perspiration washed furrows through careful make-up. The kibitzers coaching from the side lines didn't help either.

The Fire Chief of Oklahoma City called and offered the services of his excellent band for the gala evening. Heads of psychology departments in our three largest universities brought boys from their classes as guests. For them, it may have been research in sociology and extra classroom credits. For our girls, however, it was a glamorous date.

Non-college boys were obliged to furnish letters of recommendation from a county judge and from an accredited local minister, and we required that applications be in our possession a week ahead of time for checking.

Some mothers broke into print with their objections; respectable boys, they said, shouldn't be exposed to contamination at a "reform school" party. We overrode objections. The boys were old enough to do their own thinking. If they were susceptible to temptation, they were in greater danger in the back streets of their own home towns than they'd be with us.

As for permitting boys and girls to mingle, I was following an unimpeachable precedent. God had made boys and girls in almost equal numbers and had even put them in the same families. Evidently He expected them to mingle, so how could anyone else logically object?

The party day was typical of Oklahoma . . . a turquoise set in sunlight. The sound of egg beating drifted out of the kitchen as cakes were whipped to tender lightness. Girls emerged from the beauty parlor, heads bristling with knobs that would become waves and curls later on. Bright party dresses sailed down to the laundry on hangers for last-minute pressing. The air seemed to crackle like an electrical display.

By seven o'clock, refreshment and game tables had been set up in the big screened porches of the honor cottage, and all the furniture had been scooped out of one dormitory to make room for dancing. The musicians were tuning up their instruments and the reception line was in place when a professor arrived with the first young men. Happiness rippled under the prim decorum with which the girls acknowledged the introductions. Two of the young men had brought corsages for their dancing partners. Neither of the girls had ever had a corsage before, and they radiated so much ecstasy it was almost visible.

The music started, and the dance began with a grand march. A country club might have been slightly more elegant but certainly not as much fun. A commentator reported the progress of the party to an interested public.

One girl furnished a comedy note by holding up her pet pig to squeal into the microphone. She thought she'd been raising that little porker on a bottle to save its life; actually the pig had been given to her, contrary to general school policy, because she'd felt so unwanted and unneeded. The responsibility of caring for something more helpless than herself had restored her self-confidence.

I could tell that our young teachers, acting as chaperones, were enjoying themselves as much as any of the girls. For me, of course, the evening was unalloyed joy. Not one incident marred the occasion. But at eleven-thirty, the band drifted into "Home, Sweet Home," and our party was over. The boys left in a body and tired girls tumbled into bed. I knew that many of them would fight sleep for hours in order to review, again and again, the happy time.

Wanda, the only inmate who had scoffed at the whole idea of the party, came to see me the next morning. "I was wrong, Mrs. Burnham. I just had to tell you," she confessed. "I had the best time last night that I ever had in my whole life. And there wasn't even any liquor . . . and no dark corners!" She looked at me shyly to see if I understood before adding, "And I didn't have a single thing to be ashamed of this morning."

I felt rewarded for every moment of doubt and fear. There had been one or two along the way.

Every newspaper in the State commended the party as a "means of conditioning girls for social integration." Out-of-State papers lauded the experiment, and we received congratulatory letters and telegrams from as far away as Brazil and the Philippines.

Every State official but one expressed his approval of the affair. That one, however, broke into print with a heated condemnation of the whole procedure. Without offering any documentation at all, he stated that the girls had experienced a most unwholesome reaction. Nothing could have been further from the truth. However, since he was searching for personal publicity rather than the facts, he had no compunction about issuing several more inflammatory statements.

Psychologists and well-wishers came to our defense and the battle raged for a surprisingly long time. A few mothers evidently thought that there must be *some* fire to create so much smoke, and they were seized upon by the publicity-hungry politician. The affair was rapidly evolving into a full-scale war.

Eventually, since we'd stirred up so much dissension, our Board decided it might be the better part of valor to discontinue the experiment.

There was much wailing on the part of the girls and a notable sliding back in all areas of training and deportment. I tried to bury my disapointment, but it never would stay decently beneath the surface.

13

As soon as we judged them to be reliable and trustworthy, our girls were placed in homes or jobs. That left us with a mixed crop of the new arrivals, the unprepared, the incompetent, and the incorrigible. Many of these had participated in crimes against both people and property. They knew no law but their own. We maintained a perpetual alert to protect the school, the staff, and the girls themselves from the misdeeds of any inmate.

Mrs. Jaynes was our chef and she drew her share of the unruly girls for the kitchen work squad. I suspected her of possessing a sixth sense—and she needed it to maintain any kind of discipline in a K.P. crew. Keeping track of the cutlery was one of her most tedious chores. After each meal, everything from "Big Butch" down to the smallest paring knife was lined up on the table for inventory. If a single blade was out of place, everyone remained until the missing tool turned up. No knife was ever stolen except for some deviltry, and any weapon, whatever its size, could be deadly dangerous in uninhibited hands.

Mrs. Jaynes missed the knife after the noon meal. After searching for it in every available place, she lined up the girls at arm's length from each other and at a safe distance from any place of concealment.

Three matrons examined every seam and shoe sole. They stripped the girls down to their underwear and then checked that. Rolled stockings were pulled up and investigated. Even mouths and throats were probed in the event that someone had mastered sword-swallowing. Mrs. Jaynes was tempted to give up and report that the knife had been carried out in the garbage. However, intuition and a healthy fear of the possible consequences kept her hunting.

Baffled, but stubborn, she stood off and eyed the girls speculatively. Seven of the girls had short bobs, but eight others had hair long enough to pin up and offer a place of concealment.

One by one, the long-haired girls stepped forward; removed all combs, bobby pins, and ribbons; and then slowly revolved for front-, side-, and rear-view inspection. The fourth girl in line was Pansy . . . and the tight roll around the back of her head hid the short, sharp knife.

Our most treacherous inmate was a sweet-faced killer, incongruously called Pansy. Poison cactus would be closer to her character, but Pansy did describe her face. Her big, violet eyes always looked expectant—as if incredible wonders were about to occur. Childishly soft brown hair framed pleasant features, free of make-up. She was about five feet four, with a graceful figure just beginning to emerge from baby fat. All in all, you'd say she was the girl most likely to win hearts and a happy home.

The facts were grimmer than the façade. Although Pansy was only fifteen years old, she was the wife of a notorious young thug. With him and two other companions, she'd taken part in several hold-ups, the last of which had resulted in the fatal shooting of two respectable citizens. It scared me to think of a weapon in her possession.

Pansy was promptly marched over to my office. She entered wearing her usual mask of sweet innocence. Now, if ever, I had a chance to crack that shell of composure and get to the festering core. The knife was my weapon—my opening wedge.

I dismissed everyone else from the office.

"All right, Pansy," I laid it right on the line, "stop grinning at me and tell me why you took it."

"The knife? Oh, I don't know." She shrugged carelessly. "I just thought I might need it some time."

"Need it?" My eyebrows climbed. "What for? What did you intend to do with it?"

"Oh, there are lots of things you can do—with a knife." The hint of menace in her voice didn't fit the baby face.

I tried another approach. "Pansy, why don't we forget everything that's happened so far and start from scratch? I'm here to help. Let's see if we can't work together . . ."

She cut me off. "Save the soft soap, Mrs. B. I don't like you and I never will." Pansy delivered the line without even rearranging her bland smile.

"Why don't you like me?" I challenged.

"You're law, and I hate 'law.' " For the first time there was real venom in her voice. "And you're small time. Tecumseh!" She spat the word. "A kindergarten. I belong in Chicago! I could do myself some good up there. No more two-bit stuff like with Bennie." She spoke of Chicago as I imagine crusaders spoke of the Holy Grail. The plans I had to offer Pansy would be about as alluring as a saucer of milk to a man-eating tiger. But I had to keep trying.

"You're married to Bennie!" I reminded her, and watched for some sign of softening. "You'll be waiting when his term is up, won't you?"

"Bennie'll never get out. They'll give him life, or else he'll fry. Don't you think I know?" She was completely cold and callous about it.

Further attempts were useless. Pansy's exterior was hard enough to nick a diamond drill. As long as we were to have the honor of her company, I cast about for something to keep her busy—and well away from any instrument with a sharp edge. She sewed beautifully, so I put her with a crew of expert seamstresses who were quilting a coverlet for the Governor's Christmas gift. As they needed nothing but plain short needles, it seemed like an ideal solution.

For a few days all went smoothly. Dainty stitches outlined the pattern and Pansy's were the smallest and neatest of the lot. Then the quilting groups became morose and sullen. Only Pansy retained her smile. The supervisor sensed an ominous undercurrent and asked me to investigate.

I sent for a girl, less surly than the rest, who might be persuaded to talk. She turned her face away and resisted my probing for a while. I was about to give up when she blurted out the whole story, non-stop.

"It's that Pansy, Mrs. Burnham. She's all the time talkin' about Chicago an' guys she calls 'Slick' and 'Swede.' Other guys too. She tells us a lotta things they do. Pulling off big jobs, shooting cops—that kind of thing.

"She says they dress swell an' have lotsa money and don't never get caught," her cheeks blazed with excitement. "An' she says we're pantywaists to hang around down here when we could go up there and bust into the big time.

"An' Mrs. Burnham, that ain't all. She hates you bad. She says we oughtta set fire to the whole place an' make a run for it." She was wound up and I couldn't have stopped her if I'd wanted to. "An' you know that quilt we're makin' for the Governor?"

I nodded.

"Well, she keeps jabbing her needle down into it like she was stabbin' somebody. An' she says, 'This is for the Governor, damn him!' An' then she does it again an' says, 'This is for Mrs. B., damn her!' She goes on like that for all the teachers . . . everybody! An' it's awful when she pokes the needle real hard and says, 'Through the eyeballs' . . . An' then she talks about black magic.

"It makes me sick to my stumick, Mrs. Burnham."

Apparently Pansy was beyond help, but I couldn't permit the poison to spread. I'd simply have to segregate her before she had everybody in a state of hysteria or insurrection. When I left her in Meditation, I promised to restore her privileges as soon as she decided to be a cooperative member of the group instead of a menace. She made no comment but I could feel her baleful blue stare—like needles—as I walked away.

The next morning the service girls who had carried Pansy's breakfast to her came rushing back with blanched faces and frightened eyes. "Something's the matter with Pansy," one of them panted. "She's laying on her bed with her eyes wide open but she don't move any."

"I think she's dead," the second girl said huskily.

We rushed to Meditation. Pansy's pulse was slightly lower than normal but otherwise we found no evidence of any physical illness. Her chest moved so slightly, we could barely see her breathe. When we lifted a foot or an arm, it fell back inertly as soon as it was released. Sudden stabs at her eyes produced no flinching or blinking. Cold water dashed in her face caused a slight shiver to run through her, but her eyes never closed for an instant.

"Better get her to the hospital," I ordered, and two of the larger girls propped her up between them and propelled her through the door while I followed, completely baffled.

Although Pansy seemed oblivious to everything, I noticed that she avoided a pile of sand left on the sidewalk by some workmen. That proved some degree of awareness, but for twenty-four hours the doctor and the nurse worked over her without result. Tests for nervous reaction failed. Pansy didn't flinch even when an experimental needle was thrust under her fingernail. When she was lifted to her feet, she moved like a robot.

My self-taught psychology indicated that Pansy had induced a kind of trance, a sort of self-hypnosis. The doctor put in a call for a State psychiatrist, who arrived forty-eight hours later with a little vial of sodium pentothal—"truth serum."

The drug melted her rigidity as fast as a flame-thrower might dissolve a snow man. She yawned and stretched as if awaking from a deep sleep. Before full consciousness returned, the psychiatrist plied her with questions. The first answers were a halting jumble of gibberish that soon became names, dates, and details of past misdeeds. She spit them out in the rapid-fire staccato of a machine gun. Pansy told who'd planned the recent hold-up, who'd shot the bank officials, and how much loot they'd "lifted." She described the landmarks on the river bank where they'd once tossed a packet of narcotics when pursuit grew too hot.

A stenographer got most of the confession. When the pentothal wore off and Pansy realized that she'd told all her secrets, her rage rattled the windows. Even the psychiatrist winced at the foulness spouting from sick depths he hadn't suspected.

Proving the truth of Pansy's confession wasn't my business. At Tecumseh, our task was to break down her resistance to any improvement. Pansy, however, erected new barriers before we could clear off the old debris. And she was no "loner." At every opportunity she'd try to recruit new insurgents, indoctrinate them in her special brand of hate. Other girls still had some chance for rehabilitation, but Pansy was a malignant growth in their midst.

I phoned Pansy's judge and implored him to take her away. He'd been expecting the request. Since several other charges hung over her head, the judge assumed responsibility until the day she turned sixteen—then employed one of the pending sentences to put her in the State penitentiary. It was the same penitentiary that housed her husband, Bennie. Prison authorities reported that she was one of the most insubordinate inmates they'd ever had, and that she spent most of her time in solitary confinement.

Shortly thereafter, Bennie was sentenced to be executed in the electric chair. On the Sunday prior to this event, a big city paper ran a full-page story of the affair. There were pictures of a beautiful, heartbroken girl, gazing wistfully through the bars of her cell toward the building which sheltered her doomed husband. Paragraphs of tear-jerking sentiment featured Pansy's youth and helplessness and sorrowing love for the man who'd led her astray.

Pansy had obviously spoon-fed the reporter, and he'd swallowed it all. The story was written with a sob in every line, but evident sincerity . . . and it told exactly what Pansy wanted people to think. I never checked again on Pansy's progress. I think I was just plain afraid to find out.

Even when Pansy's problem loomed most like the Matterhorn, we had hundreds of little mole-hills to contend with daily. Stumbling ceaselessly over the small crises took more out of me than the occasional hard climb. Mental muscles never had a chance to ease out and nerve endings seemed to be in a constant quiver.

Frayed carpets and leaky faucets fought for attention with

efforts at escape, stomach-aches, spite fights, abnormal acts, and far on into the etceteras. Weevils in the cereal were as much my concern as attempts at suicide.

My dearest wish was that I might, just one night, wipe my mind clean of all anxieties and start fresh the following morning. nstead, each decision spawned a dozen new issues to be faced the following day. Plans, questions, protests, budgets . . . everything hinged on something else, and they all swirled murkily together as sleep closed in. Our problems were the kind that resisted clean-cut quick endings. They were tangled skeins to be unraveled slowly and with infinite care, rather than Gordian knots to be severed with a single stroke.

A thousand bits and pieces, large and small, seemed to be sharing the front half of my skull, immediately above and behind the eyes. There were nights when they grated against each other uneasily.

In time, of course, I became habituated to the constant jabbing of anxiety and the unrest always in the air. Occasionally, though, I felt something stronger—an almost tangible tension. In time I learned that this usually presaged a "run" or major rebellion of some sort among the girls. Once the fog of unease warned us, we could generally smoke out and stop the plotting.

Now, however, I was encountering something new which I didn't want to admit even to myself . . . but it was becoming impossible to ignore. Several of my staff members were watching me too closely, and too furtively, for my liking. When I caught them at it and turned to inquire, they beat hasty retreats. Direct questions brought forth evasive answers. Not denials, precisely. And some of my best people were among those acting oddly; they were the ones who molded opinion in the school. Relays began clicking in the back of my mind. When I noticed that Leila Wiles was being as nice as she knew how, the warning bells went off!

One night, when the air was particularly thick, I decided to do a little observing of my own, with Leila Wile's window the subject of my scrutiny. During the first half-hour of my vigil, I saw only her stick-thin shadow; and then a billowy silhouette moved into the scene. There was only one bosom like that in Tecumseh, and it belonged to the matron who presided over the cottage closest to Leila's. Probably dropped in to borrow something, I thought to myself. But within fifteen minutes, four others joined the group—and stayed. Even from a distance, I could tell that Leila was leading the conversation like a conductor.

In the following weeks, I caught glimpses of almost nightly gatherings, and every day I felt a little more authority slip out from under me. Finally, without even bothering to think up elaborate excuses, I made a point of identifying all the women who attended the pow-wows. Plain old-fashioned prying and none of my business, I told myself sternly, except that everything that went on at the institution *was* my business, whether I liked it or not. Anyway, where Leila Wiles was concerned, I was a scorched child with a healthy fear of the flame.

When I found out who constituted her new following, my curiosity increased a thousandfold. So far as I could tell, the women had absolutely nothing in common, aside from the fact that they were all officers of the school. It seemed more than odd that Leila—chic and shrewd Leila would voluntarily subject herself, and her fragile pastel furnishings, to the dull and rather frowsy night matron. And two of the others weren't anywhere near her type either; in fact they'd always been on the frigid side because of some imagined slight in the past. But more than anything else, Jen Hurtevelt's presence jangled the warning bells to a frenzy.

Jen, while always polite and completely the lady, had never made any secret of the fact that she preferred to be left alone.

I'd tried to bring her out of her shell a little, but when it became increasingly obvious that she extracted more pleasure from her books and records and puttering in private, made no further attempt. Still, she'd turned up at Leila's three nights running.

Daily now, I could feel the change in the staff attitude toward me. Whatever Leila had evolved was spreading through the school like a virus. Simple established procedures were questioned. There was grumbling, the under-the-breath kind of complaint that's almost impossible to cope with. No one volunteered for special assignments, and when I was forced to parcel them out, I felt rather than heard the discontent. The over-all pace became slightly slower—imperceptibly so except to the more acute inmates. The word went around. "Something's wrong in 'Staff.' "

The girls grew intractable, and I knew that any breach among us would be the signal for a real outbreak. The girls were as sensitive as barometers to our ups and downs. But until something definite happened—some single actionable anything—there was nothing I could do but wait. Or was there? Suddenly a phrase I'd heard flashed into my mind, "If you can't lick 'em, join 'em."

That night, I knocked on Leila's door about ten minutes after the regulars, now eight in strength, were settled in. When I showed up, the buzz of conversation diminished to dead silence. Leila was more self-possessed than the rest.

"Come in, Mrs. Burnham. We don't often have the pleasure of your company."

Somebody gasped and somebody else shushed her. I said, "It's lack of time, I assure you, not lack of interest. I'd like to know you all better. At any rate, it's nice to see my people getting on so well together."

Leila retaliated with, "Yes, we find we have a great deal to discuss."

No one picked up the cue. With so much to discuss no one uttered a word for a full minute. Then three started to talk together and all three stopped. After another lame attempt or two, every one of the eight women thought up an urgent errand to do elsewhere. Leila and I were left alone.

"I'll drop by again one night soon," I promised. My promise didn't appear to fill her with unalloyed joy. She smiled but I heard a small sound behind the façade—rather like a gnashing of teeth, I thought happily.

The following day, I made a point of greeting Leila and "the tribe of eight" with my cheeriest smile. It seemed to embarrass all but the Wiles woman. Then, with a great effort of will, I dismissed the matter from mind—temporarily at least—and got down to the day's cases.

Vicky was on the agenda. Mrs. Tibbets was returning her to us. She sat in eloquent silence while Mrs. Tibbets reported that she was impudent, disobedient, and ungrateful. The lady washed her hands of our erring child with great thoroughness and vigor.

Mrs. Tibbets, securely wrapped in a mantle of indignation, climbed back into her shiny new station wagon; and I sat looking at Vicky, wondering where to begin.

She started us off. "I don't like her! She can't even spell . . . not even simple things."

"Is *that* the reason?" my voice rang with dismay. "You could have learned so much about business from her. Why didn't you try?"

"I did—but she's so crude I forgot about everything else." Vicky jumped up and started to pace the floor. I'd never seen her so jittery. "I just couldn't stand it," she continued. "She makes noise when she eats and she leaves her false teeth all over the place. Why, she can't even write decent English. I had to do all her business letters for her."

"That was good training for you," I tried to sound stern.

"I suppose—" she agreed unhappily, "—but I thought *you'd* understand. I want to be a business woman, but I want to be a lady too."

I did understand, that was the worst of it. I remembered how bad grammar had almost driven me crazy during my first months at Tecumseh. But we had a major problem here. Vicky was almost eighteen. I patted her hand absently while I tried to think of another place I could send her. She understood that she was forgiven and relaxed.

"Don't worry, Mrs. Burnham." Vicky had read my mind and was grinning impishly. "Right now, I'd rather be here than anywhere else. Polish me up a little bit more, and maybe I can go farther next time. Something will turn up. You'll see."

It was wishful thinking but it worked. An excellent family applied as foster parents just as Vicky was rounding into her eighteenth birthday. She accepted the little miracle as a quite natural part of her program.

Vicky fitted happily into her new home, began high school again, and at the close of the spring semester found a sales job with a very reputable firm. I thought she was well settled, but Vicky was barely getting started.

During lunch hours and rest periods, when the other girls loafed and smoked, or repaired their make-up in the employees' lounge, she'd spread the society page of the metropolitan newspaper on the floor and pore over it, as if she were cramming for an exam.

The girls kidded her unmercifully. "Miss Top Hat!" they jeered. "You don't know any of those people and you never will. Why make yourself miserable? Read the funnies like the rest of us peasants."

"But I will know them," Vicky defended herself good-humoredly. "One of these days I'll be up there with them. Just watch me."

No amount of teasing could shake Vicky's self-confidence. Neither advice nor sarcasm disturbed her serenity or caused her to deviate from her goal for a single instant. She became a walking *Who's Who*. She knew the names of all the young socialites, their schools, love affairs, past and current marriages, and even bothered to look up a particularly promising few in Dun and Bradstreet.

She stared at the newspaper pictures until she felt she'd recognize the features in the flesh. Vicky existed as a salesgirl, but she lived in a dream world peopled by her chosen ones. At the same time, however, she memorized Emily Post and started to study French.

Vicky's employer told me she treated customers with the charm and courtesy of a well-bred deb. They loved it and came back for more. Her co-workers began to have a wholesome respect for her determination. Gradually the kidding died off entirely.

Most of the young men who met her tried to make dates. Some of them were among the socially eligible, but Vicky refused them in such a way that they went off vaguely flattered instead of offended. One day the good-looking son of a prominent family walked in to buy a piece of jewelry—a pin, he thought. Vicky sold him a necklace and earrings. When the transaction was completed, he started off, hesitated, turned halfway back to her, then propelled himself violently out of the store.

Vicky sauntered back to join two other salesgirls who'd been casually watching. "That's it!" she announced. "That's the one."

"The one *what?*" they asked.

"My future husband." Vicky spoke with the bland confidence of a queen.

"You're crazy!" The admirers turned scoffers again. "You're good, honey," one of the girls admitted, "but not that good. Don't you know who he is? They call him Foxy Freddie. That boy's dizzy from dodging dames. And they chase on polo ponies in his crowd."

"Okay, girls," Vicky broke in. "Lay your bets. Within a year I'll be Mrs. Foxy Freddie. Any takers?" She sounded flip but she was deadly serious. The others grinned sheepishly and shook their heads. As they moved away, Vicky called blithely after them. "See, that's the trouble. You don't have the courage of your convictions."

She remained blithe through the beginning of an odd courtship. The kibitzers watched closely as the young man started his campaign. He was in the store every day, but left every day with the same puzzled, somewhat stunned expression.

"Doesn't he ever ask you to go for a ride or anything?" one of the girls probed.

"Sure, he does," Vicky said airily. "I always tell him I just can't get away that particular time."

After weeks of wheedling, the young man dropped the gay banter and demanded an explanation.

"What's the matter with me?" he asked heatedly. "I'm rich and I'm not repulsive. Other girls give me dates."

"I'm not 'other girls,' " Vicky blazed back at him. He turned brick-red and she put her hand out quickly. "I'm sorry." He took her hand and the watching girls gasped. The two of them didn't notice.

She continued in a new soft voice. "I don't know just what kind of a date you want. I'm down on my luck now, but it hasn't always been this way. I'm not cheap. I'm just as proud of my family as you are of yours." She flicked an appraising glance from under long lashes and continued, "If you want to take me to a private dance or party and introduce me to your personal friends, I'll be glad to go. But if you just want to ride out in the country and park—no, that's not for me."

From there on, Vicky held the whole deck. Her scheme may have included a cold-blooded element or two, but as the courtship moved inevitably toward marriage, I could tell how head-over-heels, wholeheartedly she loved the boy. The wedding was secret. Vicky, even in the throes of love, was shrewd enough to know that the parents wouldn't succumb to her charm as readily as the son.

My first inkling of trouble arrived in a letter about three weeks later. "Fred's parents found out about the wedding when they walked into our apartment unexpectedly last week," Vicky wrote from the college town where her husband was studying for his master's degree. "They were terribly upset but they were sweet to us. His mother will be in touch with you any day now to find out all about me. Fred knows, of course.

"Please, Mrs. Burnham, stand by me. For the first time in my life I have happiness and security. I'm crazy about Fred and I've worked so hard for all this. I couldn't bear to lose it now. I'll make them proud of me if they'll only give me a chance."

The letter lay open on my desk as I pondered Vicky's problem. She certainly *had* worked hard—right from the moment of her commitment. I remembered when she'd been curious about the *id* and vowed to make it her slave instead of her master. She'd sternly developed what she called "fundamental life tendencies" which could advance her and obliterated all "negative attitudes" as relentlessly as a surgeon cuts away gangrenous flesh. Certainly her discipline was worthy of all the support I could give.

Fred's mother contacted me and, even loving Vicky as I did, I felt sympathy for the woman. Her distress over an "unsuitable" marriage for her only son warred with her instant response to Vicky's charm. She wanted to end the battle within herself—and she wanted Vicky to be the victor. But she felt she had to know *all* the facts. Sometimes all the facts don't add up to a true picture. I thought I would help everyone most by side-stepping some of her most searching questions. After all, a mature woman ought to know that judges don't send girls to correctional schools for saying "ain't." If she didn't know it, there was no use telling her now.

I mentioned all the good things I could think of about Vicky and predicted that she'd be a wonderful wife for Fred. Her unswerving determination, I said, was just the quality a young businessman needed in a mate. The mother may not have been entirely convinced, but she was a plucky person herself and I could tell, when she left, that she meant to help the marriage work.

The whole family grew to love Vicky and she adores them all in return, soaking in and sending out love like a thirsty sponge. She lives in a beautiful house in an exclusive residential district and belongs to the best clubs. She's a successful wife, daughter, mother, and home maker; and she moves in precisely the social set she admired. At the same time, she tells everyone about Tecumseh and constantly beats the drum for bigger budgets and better teachers. With Vicky in there pushing, something's *got* to give!

I find myself recalling the individual steps of her progress. In the beginning her chances had just about paralleled Pansy's. Their ages, mentalities, and backgrounds were similar; yet one girl left us to climb steadily without a slip, while the other one immediately sank back into the morass. At a quick appraisal, it would seem that my environmental theory took a beating this time. Perhaps there is such a thing as a bad seed, but I still believe it only sprouts in a climate of evil—and that the unhealthy growth can almost always be pruned away.

I marked Vicky's file, "Closed," and wished my own

problems were working out to as satisfactory a solution. Leila was still presiding over her "at homes," and almost every staffer had joined "the tribe of eight" at one time or another. The atmosphere on campus was no worse, but no better either. About all I could do was continue my policy of "passive intervention."

Once or twice a week, without warning, I'd drop by to pay my respects. The first few times my presence put a stop to all talk about as effectively as an anesthetic, and my staff members would shamefacedly melt away. Gradually, however, the atmosphere grew more normal until, finally, we'd all sit around in a cozy kind of kaffeeklatsch. I couldn't afford the time but it was really a rather pleasant period of the day—especially with Leila scurrying around, waiting on us like a proper hostess, and having to dig deeper each day into her precious hoard of delicacies. Superficially, at least, she was too well bred to withhold any of the courtesies—but I could see it nearly killed her!

Then, just as slowly as the deterioration had set in, it disappeared. I no longer felt "watched," and necessary orders were complied with without argument. Leila—with an exquisite sense of timing—requested a short leave of absence on a fairly flimsy excuse; though she returned in a week, her "at homes" were never revived. The entire episode had had an unreal air and I wanted to forget it. My kind of mind, however, requires definite beginnings, middles, and ends; so I knew I'd never really be at rest until I was able to put a period on Leila's wiles.

Several months later, Jen Hurtevelt supplied the missing segments of the story. An emergency at home had forced her resignation, and she was packing to leave Tecumseh for the last time, when suddenly she straightened up and spoke. Just four words.

"Look out for Leila."

It was so unexpected, I could only stare. Jen apparently had been storing the words for a long time, because once the break was made in her wall of reticence, the words poured out without a pause.

"She's slick and she's smooth, and she's just as twisty as a snake. She points one way but all the time she's heading in another direction. And she uses people to get where she's going, only this flea steers the dog! I had to tell you before I left."

The whole story spilled out. The "at homes" started when Leila offered to help some of the other staffers with their Christmas presents. Our acknowledged expert on all forms of handiwork, she was always in great demand to unsnarl argyle socks or work out a new embroidery stitch for somebody's tea towels. All the women she approached accepted her invitation gratefully.

Leila had selected her guests carefully. Each was an "old-timer" at Tecumseh and she figured that for that reason alone, they'd be inclined to resent a newcomer. Just a grain of resentment was all she needed to start swatting at "The Busy Bee." That, I discovered, was Leila's slyly malicious name for me, derived from my initials, C. B. B. Jen said, "Leila used to kind of sing out 'See the busy bee.' She'd laugh and say you were trying to take the place apart and put it together again in your own image. You do sort of scurry around," she pointed out, "and maybe we'd gotten 'some lazy' as my mother used to say. Anyway, she'd start us all going on some little thing and I guess women just naturally enjoy a little gripe session once in a while," Jen ended up out of breath.

I could just imagine Leila's subtle leads . . . the way she'd play on the fears of mostly middle-aged women, dependent on their jobs for a livelihood . . . the sly insinuations . . . the careful workman-like building up of a barricade of suspicion behind which she could maneuver at will.

Jen went on again, "But time worked against her. We could

see you were doing your best and working harder than any of us. Then when you started sitting down and talking to us instead of picking on us for being at Leila's, well—I guess we were just plain shamed. But not Leila!" she added vehemently. "Look out for that woman. She wants your job and she means to get it!"

14

VISITORS INSISTED ON TRYING TO REFORM OUR GIRLS IN LONG after-dinner speeches when one good laugh would have been far more effective. Their daily training was, of necessity, filled with preachment; any more added insult to resentment. For some reason, however, they made an exception of the Budget Officer and received his little sermons graciously.

As a servant of the people, the Budget Officer maintained a coldly efficient façade—and protected the public funds with close to fanatic zeal. In contrast with his tight-fisted control of the State's purse strings, his heart opened warm and wide to its helpless children. Having no child of his own, he lavished on these youngsters all the love of a starved paternal heart and more money from his own slim funds than he could truly afford.

The Budget Officer loved to make speeches, and the girls had long since resigned themselves to kind, fatherly discourses from a man who didn't even know the names of some of the sins they'd committed at the age of eight.

This dear man's knowledge of the feminine sex was based solely on the shining examples in his own family. In his mind, all women—especially all mothers—came out of the same mold which made his own mother, his sisters, and his wife. Starting with that premise, he made a speech one day which appeared perfectly logical to him but which appalled me to the point of shock.

"Girls, I want to leave this thought with you." His voice shook with the intensity and sincerity of his convictions. "Honor your mothers. If you had listened to the words of that dear old mother of yours when she tried to advise you, you wouldn't have to be in a correctional school today."

By now I could read the seemingly impassive faces of my girls. Fortunately the good man couldn't.

"When you go home, girls," he pleaded earnestly, "listen to that dear old mother. Don't break her heart again. Remember that Mother is your best friend."

I studied his audience. Patricia, still bearing signs of debauchery, was staring up at him from the first row. Only two weeks ago, officers had raided a bordello where she and her mother were practicing their profession in adjoining rooms. And there was Berta, a straight "A" student, whose parents literally made her sick at her stomach. They were practicing nudists with a twenty-four hour emphasis on sex. So far she'd managed to get away from them three times by deliberately committing offenses she knew would land her in the Tecumseh school.

Without searching too far or too long, I could have compiled a list of dozens of evil, stupid, or scared mothers who had contributed to the downfall of their daughters. My eyes fell on Debby. Would the Budget Officer enjoy *her* dissertation on "Mother Dear"?

Debby was a run-of-the-mill child with ordinary intelligence and no special looks. But she had a friendly disposition. For reasons of his own, an old man in the neighborhood coveted the thirteen-year-old girl. He made a contract with Debby's mother and took the child off to live with him. In consideration of this arrangement and the privileges it afforded him, he agreed to pay Mrs. Frazer a weekly sum. It was a cold-blooded business transaction. Debby resisted the plan with unexpected fierceness, but Mrs. Frazer had no intention of letting such easy money escape her. She unearthed her own marriage license from an old trunk and proceeded to erase her own name and that of her former husband. With great care, she then inserted the names of Debby and the old man.

"Y'see, Debby, I know what's best for you," Mom wheedled. "I been down to the courthouse an' got y'all married."

"How could I get married when I wasn't even there?" Debby objected doubtfully.

"Well, I'm yer mamma, see? An' yer a minor. That's what the law says—a minor." The words were impressive to a thirteen-year-old. "When yer a minor, y'ain't old enough to do law things by yerself so us old folks has to do them for you." The woman watched Debby's spirit wilt. "So I done got you married. Now you gotta go live with Mr. Humboldt 'cause yer his wife an' the law makes you."

The plot was too deep for Debby and no amount of argument would stand up against the evidence of that "law" license. She went to live with Mr. Humboldt, and Mrs. Frazer blossomed out in bargain-basement frills and finery.

But when Debby started sneaking off to Sunday school, it gradually dawned on her that her life was different from that of the other girls. One day she screwed up enough courage to tell her story to her Sunday school teacher. Debby was sent to us and her mother began to serve out a stiff sentence in the penitentiary. Mr. Humboldt was fined—and turned loose to pick himself another playmate.

As Debby listened to the Budget Officer's eulogy, I wondered if she was remembering the Sunday a few weeks before when her mother, newly released, had paid her a visit. Mrs. Frazer had proudly displayed snap shots of herself in prison surroundings, and my hackles rose at her lurid tales of crime and degeneracy.

"Stop those stories and put up those pictures," I ordered. "We hope that Debby will forget that her mother was in jail. And if I can help it, she'll never return to you. You've forfeited your rights to her."

"Oh, Debby'll come back to me," the woman grinned loosely. "Won't you, hon? You want to come back to Mamma, don't you?"

"No. Never." Debby's kind little face turned granite hard. "I won't ever go back to you. I won't ever see you again."

She turned on her heel and walked out of the room without a backward glance. Mrs. Frazer fumbled her pictures back into her handbag and tearlessly ambled away. Watching her go, I wondered what sort of creature could be so unmoved at the loss of its own flesh and blood. The separation was as final as death, yet a cat would have shown more concern. I believe that moment aged me at least a year.

Somehow the word "cannibal" stuck in my mind. Mrs. Frazer had been a moral cannibal, devouring the soul of her own child. Where would she turn for her next victim? Thank God, Debby was safe now. A sympathetic cousin was waiting to welcome her, and the mother would never be told where the girl had gone. I was willing to wager that she'd never even ask.

I looked at the audience again as the Budget Officer began a new paean of praise. It was liberally strewn with victims—some despoiled at an unbelievably early age. Margaret's story had been told to me by a transportation officer, a big, burly man who'd grown a comfortable callous over his emotions. But tough as he was, his mouth worked and his hands knotted as he talked. Margaret was eight.

Her mother, for a small payment, had promised the services of her child to a notorious ex-convict. Since the hoodlum had enough decency left to make him balk at being the cause of any girl's original downfall, Mom had assured him that her daughter was fully experienced. A rendezvous was arranged down by the river bank. The mother carried a whip with which to beat Margaret into submission in case of rebellion.

In spite of her fear of the lash, Margaret screamed in terror at the intimate approach of the man. Her innocence and the sincerity of her fright roused a dormant streak of manhood in the scoundrel. He turned on the mother with her own whip. "I may be low," he blazed, "but I'm a hell of a lot better than you." Though still on parole, he was incensed enough to drag her to the nearest police station.

Local officers sent Margaret to us. She was a gentle, sunny child and my blood boiled at the thought of the indignities she'd been forced to endure. I was trying to make up for the mothering she'd never had until we could find a private home for her where she could live like any other little girl.

I located another of the young victims, sitting far back and smiling—as always. Daisy was a cuddly blue-eyed bundle, but she'd been participating so long and so actively in assorted evils that I held less hope for her than for Margaret.

It didn't seem possible that a dainty nine-year-old could have committed all the acts reported by the officers. I suspected that they were embellishing the case to see my expression of horror. Daisy's manner was so winning that I discounted most of the murky details, waived the usual merit procedure, and settled her at once in the honor cottage.

Daisy skipped happily around the place and delighted us all. But soon I had reports of a series of small thefts in the honor cottage. Lipsticks and stockings and cosmetics vanished with astonishing frequency. No one suspected Daisy, if for no other reason than the fact that the missing articles could have been of no use to a nine-year-old.

"What became of my nail polish?" a puzzled girl would inquire of her roommates. "It's gone and nobody's been in here but Daisy."

"I remember laying my compact right on the dresser like I always do but it isn't here now," another girl would say in bewilderment. "Daisy, you were here. Did you see who took it?"

Daisy would smile sweetly and shake her head, but the incidents were too frequent and too much of a pattern to be ignored. Gradually our suspicion crystallized, and a surprise search revealed the loot, carefully stuffed into hollows dug out of Daisy's pillow and mattress. Even her rag doll yielded some treasure.

A cheerful smile wreathed Daisy's face as she accompanied me to the office. She admitted the thefts freely and waited for me to praise her skill. When I attempted to show her the error of her ways instead of commending her for a job well done, she was honestly amazed and her blue eyes filled with tears. Suddenly her world was topsy-turvy. In the past, she'd always been rewarded when she succeeded in stealing something.

A study of Daisy's case revealed that there was no father in the family; nevertheless the number of children increased at regular intervals. At present there were eight brothers and sisters. From infancy their mother had instructed her daughters in her own two professions, one of which was picking pockets. Daisy proved to have an aptitude for both lines of work.

A venereal disease eventually caught up with the youngster, and the mother was scared enough to seek treatment for her. In addition to medication, we were trying to pump the concepts of chastity, honesty, and integrity into the child. She improved—a little—but I knew that the lessons learned at a mother's knee had become almost as much a part of her as the parent's very genes and chromosomes.

The Budget Officer came to the end of his eulogy and the girls filed out of the makeshift auditorium. I turned away, suddenly unable to meet their eyes.

Hundreds of the torn and warped products of weak or evil parents passed before me, and I never ceased to feel a deeply personal guilt. Sometimes I could help—often I was helpless.

What could I have done for Linda . . . Linda who loved her mother so? Mrs. Dawson, a meek, amiable creature represented everything pure and lovely. Each visit left her daughter high-spirited and hopeful, full of plans for the future. Linda led the sopranos in the choir and took the part of Prince Charming in a school operetta. She was a central figure in every creative undertaking and a joy to overworked supervisors. Then Mrs. Dawson's visits ceased without explanation. For several months Linda worried and wondered, growing more dispirited each day. One Sunday the lady came.

In place of the drab wren of previous visits, I was astonished to behold a brassy bird of paradise. The ashen hair now had a metallic wash which added color but not beauty. Heavy pancake and a double handful of cosmetics had built up her face to a parody of prettiness.

Mrs. Dawson wore platform soles and rhinestone ankle straps, a bright silk dress, and a hat with pink and purple plumes. Even her personality had had a face lifting. Now she talked, volubly, about trips she had taken, hit shows she had seen, and dinners at expensive restaurants.

This time Linda didn't sit with her arm around her mother. She huddled in miserable silence clear across the room and tried not to look at her at all. Mrs. Dawson talked herself out and rose to go. As a farewell caress, she twined a braceleted arm around the stiffly resistant shoulders of her daughter. When Linda twisted away, a large "emerald" raked her cheek. She didn't seem to notice.

For several days Linda walked around like the living dead. Her buoyancy was gone—as if it had never been. She avoided the supervisors and couldn't be drawn into more than monosyllabic conversation. At last I was forced to order her in for a talk.

"Linda, what's troubling you?" I began bluntly. Gentler queries had failed completely. "If you'll tell me, maybe I can help."

Linda sat silently, regarding me through lusterless eyes. Obviously something was breaking her heart but she couldn't bring herself to speak of it.

I said, gently but firmly, "We'll both stay here until we get to the bottom of it."

"Where did my mother get the clothes she wore down here?" The words finally burst out of her.

"I don't know, Linda." I tried to soften the bitter facts. "Maybe she can afford more for herself now that your expenses are taken care of here."

"No. That's not it." Linda refused the easy way out. "She talked about trips, too, and shows, and hotels. Those things cost money. We never even had enough to eat when I was home. Where does the money come from now?"

Linda was not to be side-stepped. The issue had to be met.

"No matter what she's done, she's still your mother, Linda." The girl's eyes were stony, but I went on. "We can't ever know all the heartaches and trials of another person, no matter how much we love them. If your mother's done things you condemn, try to remember that she was all alone—tired and discouraged. We have no right to judge. We don't know the circumstances."

The stoniness broke—to be replaced by tragedy. "It's true, then," she said in a flat voice. "Well, it's all over for me now. I just can't take it. No use trying any more."

"What do you mean, child?" But I knew what she meant. "There's all the more need for you to make good."

"No—" Linda spoke with dull finality. "I never had but one thing fine enough to make me hold up my head. Just one reason to be proud. Now that's gone."

The lovely eyes brooded for a long moment. "If my mother could get to be what she is, I might just as well hit bottom too," came the bitter decision. "Guess it was meant to be."

"Don't be foolish, Linda! Nothing's *meant* to be. You can make your own decision in life." I searched for arguments. "You're nearly through your cosmetology course. In a little while you can go to a different town and make your own way. Then you can send for your mother. With your help and understanding, she won't have to do questionable things to make a living. Think! Think how you can help her!"

"Thanks for everything, Mrs. Burnham." Linda's voice was unforgettably forlorn. "You've tried hard on me, but it's no use now. I don't care any more. Just forget about me."

Every employee on the place struggled to restore the old Linda, but it was no use. The mainspring of her spirit was broken and she drifted from apathy into disobedience. She began to team up with the incorrigibles, and then, being a natural leader, she was spearheading really serious offenses. The situation grew so bad that she and some of her accomplices had to be put in Meditation. It was the quickest downhill run I'd ever seen.

For the sake of their physical well-being, Meditation girls

were put on a regular outdoor schedule under close supervision. One day when Linda's group was raking leaves, they managed to get hold of some forbidden matches. Shortly after they were returned to their quarters for lunch and a rest period, a messenger dashed into my office.

"Meditation's on fire!" she gasped. "Come quick! Meditation's on fire."

From all over the campus people were running toward the little building which had smoke billowing from every window. "Get the men and the keys!" I cried as horrible visions of burning girls flashed through my mind. I knew the building was fireproof, but the cotton mattresses and clothing were not.

Someone thrust the keys into my hand and I ran toward the door ahead of the men who had come to help. They'd had sense enough to stop for rakes and hoes.

"Not you, Mrs. Burnham. Not you!" Linda's voice rang out. "Don't you come near that door!"

"I have to, Linda," I shouted above the crackling of the fire. "I have to get you girls out!"

"Not you!" Linda urged excitedly. "Send someone else—but not you! I'm telling you! Listen to me! Don't you come near!"

My shaking fingers managed to turn the key in the padlock. The outer door opened on a service corridor that ran in front of the three rooms. With one glance, I saw why Linda had tried to warn me off. The girls had wrenched their toilet stools out of the floor and beaten them into pieces. Then they'd pushed their mattresses and clothing into the corridor and deliberately set them on fire. Now they stood waiting with the heaviest, sharpest fragments in their hands to hurl at anyone who entered.

In spite of the danger, I felt myself smiling. Linda was still capable of liking and loving. She hadn't wanted me to be hit by one of those death-dealing missiles. Certainly her warning saved all of us from injury or death. Our caution plus the poor aim of the excited miscreants prevented any serious casualties.

Protecting themselves behind the door frame, the men thrust their long-handled tools into the building and pulled out masses of burning material. Screaming obscenities, more fiery than the flames, the girls hurled their weapons, then their shoes, in a last-ditch attempt to hurt someone, somehow. They looked like distorted gnomes behind the billowing wall of smoke.

Mercifully, their clothing didn't ignite, but the smoke soon forced them to surrender. By evening, the building was clean once more and refurnished, and the thwarted girls were back in place. All but Linda. The others would have half-killed her for saving my skin.

That was her last piece of violence. It seemed to subdue an inner torment. Though she was never again the joyous, bubbly Linda we'd all loved, she was docile and industrious enough to earn her release. I made a point of finding her a job in a town far away from her mother. She stayed about a month and then I heard that she'd returned home and was accompanying her mother down the primrose path. The news made me sick at heart.

Many months later, another report reached me and cured the ache. A friend had seen Linda working in a beauty shop in a Southwestern state. She had severed relations with her mother and was a respected member of her new community. She sent me her love. Mixed with my relief was wonder at what had caused Linda's most recent about-face. Each of her reversals had always followed as an aftermath of some great shock. It must have been a terrific one that succeeded in blasting her loose from a whole way of life.

If the problems of a girl whose mother loses her grip on

decency are many and painful, what about the girl whose mother *never* was any good? At least Linda had gained some moral strength from standards set up for her in early childhood. Allie, on the other hand, had a mother without a single redeeming quality, one who had contributed nothing but a doubtful heritage to her daughter.

Allie was already a student at the school when I arrived. Neat, obedient, and industrious, she was an honor girl and a nurse's aide in our hospital. Her excellent if untrained mind was first revealed to me on the day she accompanied me on a trip to Oklahoma City, forty-five miles away.

"Just look at this long highway," Allie ruminated. "It runs for miles and miles right through this rough country. Think how many people had to plan this road and pay for it and level it and make a road bed and spread concrete! They must have worked for months, years maybe, so that folks like us could ride easy. It's something to be thankful for, isn't it?"

Allie's tastes were the more surprising because of her lurid past. She loved music and art, even painted fairly well. I thought, with great satisfaction, that at least one of my lost sheep was safely home. Allie's problems seemed to be all behind her. I felt more than ordinarily sad, therefore, when the school nurse said she was "coming up sick."

Further examination revealed that Allie had syphilis! I refused to believe it. Her tests had been negative when she entered the school. True, she was a hospital assistant who helped work with the venereal patients, but every precaution had been taken to prevent the spread of infection. The doctor verified the diagnosis. She had it all right—but where and how did she get it?

Allie's spirits trailed in the dust at the news. So did mine. I dreaded to break the news to her mother. Mrs. Kelters would be extremely angry at the very least—and hysterical or possibly vengeful at the other extreme. She'd certainly believe we'd been careless about the health of her only child. I wrote and asked her to come at the first possible moment as I had something of the utmost importance to tell her.

"Well! What's she done now?" was Mrs. Kelters' irate question as she arrived a good week later. "It sure didn't suit me to come up here today. I had a chance to go to Detroit with a gen'lman friend o' mine. I passed it up to see what's the matter with the kid. I could a' used that dough, too."

Mrs. Kelters had moved to Fort Worth, where she maintained a housekeeping room which she called headquarters. She was never at home more than a few days since her business consisted of accompanying lonely men who had long, tedious cross-country trips to make. Our letter had reached her just as she was about to set out with a particularly generous customer.

"I hate to have to tell you," I began, thinking that the news wasn't going to help her mood much, "but a recent hospital check shows that Allie has syphilis. I'm so sorry. We have no idea how she contracted it but we're doing everything we can . . ."

"My God! Is that all?" Mrs. Kelters snorted in disgust. "Have you just found that out? Of course she's got syphilis. I've got it too—so has my mother. It don't hurt nobody. Why shouldn't Allie have it?"

"We consider it a very serious matter." My face scorched with anger and I clipped out my words. "We felt it only right to inform her mother."

"Why, she's had it all her life. Had to take her to the doctor twice a week when she was little," Mrs. Kelters curled a scornful lip. "She gets over it but it always comes back. She had a negative when she came out here. Guess it's just wore off again.

Maybe she didn't know what I was havin' her treated for. Where's the phone at? I'll try to catch Butch and have him pick me up here if he ain't gone too far."

"You can't wait for him here." My temper was well in the saddle now. "And you can't use this phone for any such purpose."

"Like hell, I can't," the woman screamed viciously. "Who are you to sit there high and mighty and tell poor folks where to head in! You and that damn Governor! Why don't you give the little fellow a break now and then? You'll be sorry. One of these days we're all a'goin' to club together and show you what we can do. We'll take you apart!"

Mrs. Kelters continued to scream insults while I rang for the watchman. "Please escort this woman outside the gate and lock it behind her," I rose to close the interview.

"I won't go! You can't make me, you she-devil," Mrs. Kelters shrilled as she snatched at the phone. "This is State property and I got as much right to it as you do. I'm a'goin' to put in that call."

"This *is* State property and I'm in charge of it," I slapped the phone back in its cradle. "I'm giving you a chance to walk out quietly with the watchman. If you don't, I shall call the police and have you arrested for disturbing the peace."

Mrs. Kelters snarled at me and curled her fingers to claw. The watchman caught her arm on its upward swing, and twisted it —just a little but enough to get his idea across. She snarled again, whirled around, and dashed out of the room toward the gate.

Allie's fine streak was definitely not inherited from her mother! We kept her beyond the age limit in order to restore her health, then sent her to live with a splendid family who trusted her beyond her capacity. One day she crammed a suitcase full of her benefactress' clothes, gathered up all the loose money and jewelry she could find, and set out to conquer the world for herself. Officers picked her up within a few days and returned the stolen goods but I never learned what disposition was made of Allie.

Linda started out with a good mother. Allie's was bad. Was that why they came through their fiery furnaces with such different results? The crucible finally purified Linda. Allie's good qualities crumbled. Mothers have much to answer for.

15

SOMETIMES I WAS TEMPTED TO BELIEVE THAT A GIRL HAD been born with the character flaws which seemed destined to destroy her. Noreen was one of these. She came to us from a large military center with a record of having furnished considerable entertainment for the soldiers.

Her face was indubitably Irish, except for the oriental cast of heavily fringed, gray-black eyes. Dark hair swept back from a broad low forehead, and she was keenly aware of every curve she owned.

At the time Noreen was sent to us, our doctor was a man—a kind, grandfatherly type, who could never bring himself to believe the damaging facts revealed by his own clinical examinations. To him, Noreen was just an unfortunate kid who didn't have any real comprehension of her acts. Even while she was on his table, cracking wise, he discounted what he heard as sheer bravado and tried to be reassuring.

"Now, young lady," the doctor spoke gently, "just take it easy. This won't take long—and I'm not going to hurt you."

In an effort to put her at ease, he added, "You're a mighty pretty little girl to have to come out here."

Noreen laughed out loud and struck an enticing pose. "You said it, Doc. It's a waste, isn't it?" She wiggled once and looked at him appraisingly. "I'm too damn' good looking to be stuck away off in a joint like this—with no men!"

She waited for a response. Getting none—except well-concealed shock—she slithered back down on the clinic table. The folds of the hospital sheet settled languidly around her body in a sort of reverse strip-tease.

There was no further conversation. The doctor completed his examination in record time, and then washed his hands as if he meant it. My own thoughts were whirling. Somewhere in this little wanton there was bound to be a spark of good. It might take a microscope, I figured grimly, but it was my job to find it. Furthermore, it was my job to fan that spark into a purifying flame. It would take a flame-thrower, I told myself, to burn away the swamp of sensualism in which she was floundering.

Noreen's spark was well hidden . . . I'll say that for it. Just as I was about to give up entirely, she, herself, revealed a clue. The weather had grown bitterly cold and I was still going about the grounds bareheaded. Noreen didn't know that I reveled in the tingling bite of the chill air. She worried for fear I'd catch cold and, without my knowledge, spent some of her scant pocket money for red yarn which she crocheted into a scarf.

With shining eyes, she brought me her handiwork wrapped in crumpled tissue paper and tied with a second-hand ribbon. No gift ever moved me more. The scarf scratched my ears unbearably and mussed my hair abominably, but I wore it with enormous pride. It was the concrete symbol of her "spark." Now I had something to go on.

Noreen's gift was evidence of generosity and thoughtfulness.

Two wedges where I'd only hoped for one! Two wonderful avenues of approach to her regeneration. I used them both for all they were worth. When she was finally ready for parole, I felt that we were graduating together from an important period of our lives. As Noreen's wavering standards stabilized, my own idea took firmer shape and form. Tecumseh was truly my life now and I was learning to cope.

I learned to hide my emotions when necessary, but I never was able to protect myself against waves of shock and outrage when parents proved to be the cause of a daughter's delinquency.

If both parents are weak or evil, a daughter seems doomed. Yet two sisters who came from the same sordid home in a small town—two sisters who had been subjected to identical influences—followed diametrically opposite paths when left to their own devices. Another lesson learned.

Mildred and Edna were red-haired, freckled youngsters whose sturdy bodies survived poverty and neglect without sustaining any permanent damage. Their father was a bootlegger who consumed too much of his own merchandise. During his drunken orgies he was belligerent and bloodthirsty—so much so that he was finally sentenced to a term in the penitentiary. For a while the mother struggled to hold the family together but an easier way soon offered itself.

The man who moved in objected to the presence of the girls while he was consorting with the mother. She solved this problem simply by locking the house door when it was time for the girls to return from school, thus forcing Mildred and Edna out on the street to forage their supper from garbage cans.

As the weather grew chilly and their home remained closed to them, Mildred and Edna sought refuge each night in the rest room of a service station. Huddled together for warmth, they tried to sleep on the bare tile floors.

Station employees discovered the waifs and turned them over to the police. The police, in turn, drove the girls home at two A.M., prepared for tears and cries of joy from frantic parents. A patrolman knocked at the door, and kept knocking for ten minutes. When the mother finally opened it, she cursed him soundly for disturbing her slumber . . . and slammed the door shut again.

At our school, neither of the girls presented any serious problems. They progressed normally in their studies, learned a few housekeeping skills. And in record time Mildred, the older one, was ready for parole. Meanwhile, welfare workers in the girls' home town had assisted the mother and her friend in legalizing their union. They were established in a three-room house on which a welfare visitor kept a watchful eye. The couple agreed to take the girls back into the home and to comply with strict regulations.

Mildred and Edna received the news with monumental indifference, and started home with no show of either enthusiasm or regret. For a few weeks all was serene. But a morning dawned on which Mother dug a ten-dollar bill out of her rolled stocking and turned to Mildred.

"Me an' Jim's goin' away for a while," she said as she held out the crumpled greenback. "This'll keep you an' her in grub till we git back."

"Where you goin', Mamma?" Mildred was wise enough to be suspicious.

"Oh, a lot o' places," the mother turned away. "Goin' to see some o' his folks."

The girls bought groceries as sparingly as they could. At the end of the week, they had three dollars left and the rent was due. Mildred divided the cash with Edna. "They aren't ever coming back," she said with great conviction and no passion.

"They don't want us. I'm going out to get me a job. You'd better get one too."

Mildred became a maid, but Edna was too young for anyone to employ. Anyway, she didn't really believe her mother had meant to abandon them. It was a mistake. It had to be. So she set herself the heart-breaking task of tracking her down. She hitch-hiked to the home of her nearest relative; the mother had been there but had gone on to the home of a cousin. The cousin said she'd headed South. Edna plodded on, always a few days behind her wandering parent.

The trail led to Florida before the girl realized her search was hopeless. The clues had petered out. She began to think of the school as the only refuge open to her. Young as she was, she knew she'd need a judge's commitment; so with incredible fortitude, she turned round and found her way back to her home town. An astonished magistrate listened sympathetically and wrote out a new order for our little redhead.

Somehow, the youngster had made the entire trip without recourse to thievery or prostitution. We kept her until she reached her majority and then found her a home with an excellent family. Maybe she grew lonely in a small domestic group after having had so many young companions. Perhaps her own mother looked even blacker in contrast with her pleasant foster parent. Whatever the reason, she soon drifted away into casual alliances and border-line living . . . and it was too late for us to come to her rescue.

What becomes of such girls? No real home waits to receive them. Their qualifications provide them with the most meager existence. Worst of all, they've lost hope in the future. They see no way but down . . . no alternative to bad but worse. Who can blame them if they finally trade their only commodity for a fling at life? Who knows why an Edna sinks to street-walking, while a Mildred marries and rears a fine family? I don't pretend to.

When natural parents fail, social agencies are inclined to turn automatically toward foster mothers. Unfortunately, they too are far from infallible. While there are shining exceptions, even "board" mothers who do their sincere and conscientious best sometimes lack sufficient understanding and patience. Of all the women I've ever dealt with in connection with delinquent girls, an unpretentious farm wife stands out in my memory as the epitome of everything a foster mother should be.

When she applied for a girl, Mrs. Farmer stated that she wanted someone who would help her raise chickens and take care of the cow. The job seemed tailor-made for Addie, a "runner" without enough intelligence to plan farther than over the fence; we always got her back within an hour or two, but the attempts were frequent enough to be extremely annoying. The dogs had reached the point of leaping and barking with delight whenever they caught a whiff of her; Addie always meant another romp through the ravines.

She was a large, strong girl with a heavy mop of unruly black hair and a burgeoning mustache. With her enormous physical strength and pint-sized mentality, she barged around the place like a Mack truck with a toy steering wheel. Poor Addie was just over the moron mark that would have sent her to an institution for the feeble-minded, and just under the line for adequate school training. She seemed doomed to exist in a never-never land between the two. We tried to help her become self-supporting, but she couldn't be trusted to do more than the dullest and most routine job in any industrial area.

In desperation, I'd assigned Addie to permanent farm detail. Under good direction, she proved to be a strong and generally competent worker. That was the most that could honestly be said of her—and that's what we said to Mrs. Farmer, along with a quick recital of the girl's shortcomings. She looked at me, straight and serious, then smiled. "Maybe she needs me more than a smart girl."

I couldn't leave a woman like that out on a limb with no net spread, so I offered to take Addie back if the arrangement didn't work out. No court order . . . just a gentlewomen's agreement. We shook hands on it, and she chuckled, "It's a pleasure to do business with you." I had a feeling that everything was going to be all right.

For a few weeks Addie was as happy as a kid in a candy store. Then the newness wore off and a stubborn spell struck. When Mrs. Farmer told her to do some small chore, Addie would plant her feet far apart in the middle of the kitchen floor, fold her arms tightly, and refuse to budge. Her black button eyes glittered, and her mouth was as tight as a trap. She wouldn't argue—but she wouldn't move either. Mrs. Farmer pleaded, insisted, cajoled, and along about the tenth time it happened, tried shouting too. Addie didn't move a muscle. At last the woman's patience wore out.

"Get busy, Addie," she gave the girl a little push to help her along. "We don't want to be all day at this work."

The touch—feather-like to someone Addie's size—seemed to galvanize the girl. She whirled and ran up the stairs where she stayed all morning. About noon, Mrs. Farmer found time to climb the steps and investigate. Addie was sitting in the center of the spare room floor with a pair of scissors in her hand. Around her lay a chopped-up litter of ribbon and straw and flowers which had been Mrs. Farmer's brand-new spring hat.

Most women would have blown a fuse and brought Addie straight back to the school. Mrs. Farmer viewed the wreckage calmly and then sat right down in the middle of it and put her arm around the disturbed girl. Somehow she penetrated Addie's fog and made her see that her own self-control and cooperation were far more important than any hat could ever be. When I learned about the incident, I marveled at Mrs. Farmer's success and asked what arguments she'd used.

"Oh, I don't remember what all I said," she stammered in embarrassment. "I just talked to her like I was her mother."

I doubt that Mrs. Farmer had ever heard of child psychology, but she'd worked out a fool-proof procedure, guided only by a good true instinct and a trusting faith in all God's creatures. I shook her hand with true humility when she left. Poor Addie? Lucky Addie!

Connie was another of our problem children whose troubles could be traced back to an unnatural "natural" mother. Reports from her supervisors showed that she was a fair student, a fine piano pupil, and a hopeless liar. Such diversity of talent interested me. I arranged for an interview.

After a shy knock, a small thirteen-year-old entered my office. My first impression was one of warmly smiling brown eyes, a soft voice, and expressive hands. She slipped into the chair I offered, brushed back a dark curl, and murmured, "Hello."

"Hello, yourself," I smiled. "I think it's about time we got better acquainted, don't you?"

"Yes'm," Connie grinned infectiously. "I think so too."

"You're out of breath." I said to start the conversation. "You ran all the way up the walk, didn't you?"

"Oh, no, Ma'am," Connie shook her head. "I walked across the lawn."

I'd seen Connie's approach with my own eyes. Why should she lie about such a trivial matter?

"Tell me about your family." I tried a new angle. "Is your sister older than you, or younger?"

"I don't have a sister," she fibbed unhesitatingly. "I'm an only child."

Shades of Munchausen! Connie had a younger sister and three brothers. Surely she knew I could check on that simple fact? Was she constitutionally incapable of telling the truth? What was behind such deceit? To find out, I planned a simple test.

"Connie, let's play a game." I picked up my paper and pencil. "See this vase of flowers? You describe it and I'll write down your answers." I moved the vase across the desk toward her. "Is the vase tall or short?"

"It's tall—tall and slim," Connie was obviously wondering when we'd get to the game.

"And the color, Connie. What color is it?"

"Why, it's blue," she answered hesitantly.

"That's right, Connie," I nodded. I made her go into detail about the vase while I carefully recorded her statements. She agreed with me that the vase held nine spikes of pink snapdragons.

"Now, here's the game, my dear. I'll set this vase of flowers in the next room and see if you can describe it from memory," I said as I carried the vase out. Plainly, Connie was not thrilled with the game but I ignored her indifference.

"Ready?" I asked as I resumed my seat. "Now, tell me about it. Was the vase tall or short, fat or lean?"

"Short, and kinda fat—and green," Connie misinformed me glibly.

"And the flowers, Connie. What were they like?" I checked her answers.

"Oh, there were lots of them. About two dozen, I guess," Connie's brown eyes smiled straightforwardly into mine. "They were short and bunchy and red. Roses, maybe. Yes, that's it. They were red roses."

"All right, Connie," I said as I brought the flowers back into the room. "Now let's see if your answers match. For goodness sake! They're all wrong, aren't they?"

Connie blandly pretended surprise. She was plainly a psychopathic liar, unable—for some reason—to tell a truth.

"Connie, did you ever try describing something so well that people feel they're really seeing it themselves? It's fun. Let's try it. Want to?" I tried to make it sound inviting but Connie concealed her enthusiasm well. I waited for an answer and at last she acceded with a very small, "Okay."

"Fine," I approved. "Tomorrow morning I want you to bring me a written description of the clock on your living room wall. If you can tell me about it just as it is, you'll win the game and I'll have a nice prize for you. Okay?"

No reputable clock maker would have recognized a time piece from the account Connie turned in next day. The pendulum swung above the dial, the case was square instead of octagonal, the black numerals were gold, and the whole structure hung on the wrong wall. I thanked Connie for her effort and went with her to her cottage to check her report. She hadn't expected that and was a bit embarrassed. We sat facing the clock as Connie corrected her statements. I waited until her description was minutely accurate, even to a chipped place on the frame.

Day after day, we played the game. I chose varied and increasingly complex objects, and for several weeks we went through a painstaking routine of describing and checking until she established a new habit pattern of absolute fidelity to fact.

Meanwhile, I tried to find out what had caused Connie to twist the truth so consistently and completely. As always, I began by checking her personal file. I found that the family lived in a run-down section of a poor mining town, and were addicted to just about every sordid sin on my master list. Connie had only known two types of people: her family and their friends, and the officers and case workers who came out occasionally to arrest somebody or put a stop to whatever they were doing. Naturally she allied herself with the family group. From babyhood she'd seen only deception and heard only untruths. Upon the arrival of "law" she'd learned to hide all physical evidence of wrongdoing and assume the blandly innocent expression of a habitual liar.

Connie had perfected the technique of deceit by the time she could talk. In her world, officers and social workers were strange busybodies who were flustered when they found out the true facts of life in a squalid small town. Therefore you lied and sent them away satisfied. Knowing no other system, Connie had accepted this procedure as the only normal and sensible one. After we succeeded in straightening out this one big twist, Connie became a completely delightful child. We refused to return her to the miserable home we knew would undo the good work and found an aunt who was happy to accept responsibility for a very reliable little girl.

Along with inmate problems, we continued to have our full quota of difficulties in staff circles. Some of them inevitably involved tears. Being a woman, I reserve the right to have an occasional cry of my own, but I always hate myself for it. I'm mortally afraid of looking as ridiculous as did the four-hundred-and-fifty-pound duo of weeping womanhood which I grew accustomed to seeing across the desk from me at regular intervals.

These were two exceptional employees with hearts as big as their ample bodies. Each had a hard job which she did with outstanding ability: one was supervisor of the kitchen and one presided over the dining room. There was no real antipathy between them, but their jobs overlapped just enough to cause clashes. Each woman would fly to her own defense and then the two crews of girls would also choose up sides.

Mrs. A's dining room girls would slip into the kitchen and steal food. Mrs. B's satellites would sneak into the dining room to mess up a couple of neatly laid tables. The ensuing argument would see Mrs. A and Mrs. B. brandishing various kitchen utensils and then bogging down in tears. They weren't physically belligerent by nature, but it sometimes seemed that each tried to outcry the other. The wood of my desk was about to warp.

It was embarrassing to try to arbitrate between two adult, capable women who sat there looking and squalling like horribly bloated babies. Lectures only caused the floods to flow faster, so about all I could do was soothe their ruffled feelings and encourage them to forget their differences and be friends. I felt more like drying their eyes, blowing their noses, brushing down their pinafores, and sending them out to play.

A few such episodes convinced me that we'd better provide some recreation and diversion for employees so they could blow off steam without scalding the whole school. Even as I scolded members of staff for bringing me their intramural arguments, I realized that they had a perfect right to be edgy. Each one was holding down the triple task of working, training, and guarding in an atmosphere which was not always conducive to philosophical calm.

I considered the possibility of having picnics or other outings, but the idea was impractical since most of us had to be on call for emergencies even in our off-duty hours. The next best plan was to import entertainment—bring it right into the school. We all needed mental stimulus to keep our intellects from shrinking to a delinquent girl's level, so I decided to try some lecturers for a start. I visualized our listening to pearls of great wisdom, words which would brighten our days and enlighten our minds. My enthusiasm was inclined to be rather sweeping. My announcement was greeted with all the joy generally associated with a wake. Nevertheless, all who could be spared from school duties attended the first of the cultural evenings, undoubtedly because they thought they had to.

The first speaker was a psychologist who gave us some pointers on handling juvenile delinquency. Perhaps, he'd have have had novice social workers sitting on the edge of their seats, but necessity had shoved us so far ahead of him, it was like a return to kindergarten after college. He shot a few holes in the gloom with some interesting anecdotes and so kept the evening from falling completely flat. Polite to the bitter end, each employee stopped by to say that she'd enjoyed the meeting. The next lecturer was already contracted for, so I could only keep my fingers crossed; one more fiasco and I'd have to frame a public apology to these poor suffering staffers.

Four weeks later, the second speaker arrived from one of our major universities. She had four sets of initials after her name, so I felt that at least we'd learn something even if we didn't enjoy it. Her figure was angular enough to delight a geometrician, and mossy, gray hair topped a painted desert of a face.

The lecturer spoke in little gushes followed by long pauses. Her manner roused my risibilities and I could see that the doctor, sitting next to me, was suppressing laughter too. I decided to move away; her sense of the ridiculous was too much like mine for safety. I left the door near which we were seated and slipped around to one on the opposite side of the room.

The speaker waxed eloquent in fits and starts about an amazing variety of topics. Maybe she didn't have a central theme or perhaps she thought we weren't capable of concentrating on one idea for any length of time. Her mind leaped from one arid crag to another with the agility of a mountain goat who'd lost his directions.

"It's most unwise to use that sort of cooking vessel," she said of a popular household material. "It throws off minute particles of metal which accumulate in the system and eventually—poisons you!" She widened her eyes and held up a warning finger.

"How long does it take to have that effect?" asked an impressed listener.

"Oh—about fifty years. Maybe sixty."

My glance met the doctor's. Her laughter was about to spill over, too. I forced myself to look away in the nick of time and tried to keep my mind busy with other matters. It returned to the lecture in time to hear:

"It's very easy to tell the tall, slender type of man from the short, stocky one. The tall man's intestines are sometimes as much as three feet longer than those of the short, stocky man."

That scientific bombshell was too much. As the lady awaited applause, the doctor and I bolted out of our respective doors and met at the end of the hall for some smothered howls of glee.

We didn't return to the group, but hovered near enough to keep an eye open on the situation. Bewildered matrons sat in respectful silence. The poor farmer, glassy eyed from lack of sleep because he'd been up since 5 A.M. and would be up at that hour again the next day, held himself erect in his chair with visible effort.

The farmer knew exactly how much grain and molasses cake to feed his cows in order to produce the most milk with the highest percentage of butter fat. I knew, too, that he could size up an individual pretty accurately without resorting to drastic surgery. It seemed to me that this brand of information was more cultural than the implied suggestion to disembowel a fellow-creature in order to see how much of a man he was.

Then and there, I determined never again to impose a program on these helpless, loyal people. If they knew their jobs, that was enough for me. From now on they could choose their own recreation without my interference—or blow off steam in my office if they preferred.

Our next entertainment was furnished by one of our own girls. "Entertainment" is the wrong word, but it was something that kept us all interested for weeks. I guess everyone loves a wedding and they're far from frequent in a correctional school. As a matter of fact, we only had two during my ten years as Superintendent.

This bride was a young mother who had previously overlooked the formality of marriage. She adored the father of her baby and apparently the sentiment was mutual. Jimmie hadn't married Laura only because he couldn't make enough to support her. Now he was at home, trying to pick up a few odd jobs, while Laura stayed with us. The baby lived with its grandparents.

We decided that the best solution in this case would be to work on Jimmy's end rather than Laura's. All these youngsters needed to become a real family was steady employment for the new father. I conferred with the probation officer in Jimmie's home town and he responded by unearthing a good job with a reliable firm. With his face wreathed in smiles, Jimmie arrived at the school and formally proposed to the mother of his child.

The wedding was to take place in the living room of Staff Hall. For an altar we had urns of evergreens flanked on each side by tall vases of spring flowers. The carpenter made a *prie dieu* of orange crates which the sewing room girls then covered with white satin and lace.

The grandparents came to the wedding, bringing the baby with them. Laura was a sweet bride in the simple white dress which the sewing girls also contributed. Her little flat round face and shallow blue eyes beamed under the net veil atop her soft light hair. A kindly minister donated his services, someone from town played the wedding march, and the music instructor sang "Oh, Promise Me." The baby gurgled happily in its grandmother's arms—premature fulfillment of that promise.

It isn't every girl who can boast of a parole among her wedding gifts. Laura was proud of hers. She nibbled wedding cake and beamed, threw her bouquet, wept a little . . . in short, acted like any other young bride.

The groom had parked his pick-up just outside the door. Through whirling confetti he lifted his bride to the high seat, settled the baby in her arms, and ran around to the hand starter. Amid much waving and chugging and backfiring, the bride and groom drove away with the baby's bonneted head bobbing over Laura's shoulder and the wedding veil billowing out behind.

The minister's prayer had been beautifully impressive. No girl could have listened to the service without gaining a truer understanding of the wedding vow. Girls who'd never witnessed a wedding ceremony before walked away with thoughtful eyes. All in all, I thought the rite had accomplished a lot—for two hundred seventy-six girls, not just Laura.

16

To a warped intellect, any idea or ideal is capable of distortion. Even as I was rejoicing in the good accomplished by Laura's lovely wedding, one girl was busily trying to twist the same ingredients into a racket.

As soon as she had the scheme worked out to her own satisfaction, Maud ran off. The wedding must have been a powerful stimulant to prod "Mousy Maud" out of her normal lethargy. Mediocre in appearance, intelligence, and manners, we never thought she had ambition or energy enough to jump the fence. Officers and trustees drove off to make a systematic highway search; while another group, guided by the school's farmer-in-residence, ferreted through ravines and beat the underbrush.

Somehow, Maud eluded her pursuers. It was pitch dark before the weary staff members and "honor" girls stumbled home for a belated supper. Not even the bloodhounds had had a sniff of her. Almost before dawn they were all out again, augmented by every adult we could corral. By mid-afternoon, "Mousy" had a new nickname . . . "Slippery" Maud. One of the trustees finally spied her yellow dress as she tried to crawl under a culvert. Maud was dirty beyond belief. Filthy hair straggled into eyes filmed and haggard from the night's experiences. A sickening odor clung to her—an odor I had learned to associate with gonorrhea.

Maud was arrogant and tight-lipped through questioning, bath, and antiseptic shampoo. Her clothing was too foul and tattered to salvage, so I ordered it burned. When the matron picked up a shoe—at arm's length—a half-dollar fell from the lining and rattled on the floor. Maud wilted when I held up the coin and asked where she copped it. I expected her to deny that she'd stolen the money, and I was correct.

"That man gave it to me," she mumbled sullenly as she pretended to be tying her shoe lace.

"What man, Maud?" I insisted, intent on making her admit the lie.

"That old man I stayed with last night." She stood and glared down at me, spitting out the words. "We slept in an empty house. I saw your car lights but nobody could find us."

"Maud! You can't mean it. Not willingly—not with a complete stranger!"

Maud stared at me in level-eyed silence until I added, "I just can't believe it! I can't believe you'd sell yourself for fifty cents!"

"Why not?" Maud was openly contemptuous. "I've done it all my life and I'm going to keep on doing it whenever I feel like it. I miss it here at school."

I was already speechless, but paralysis set in with her next statement.

"Besides," she blurted, "you let Laura go home because she had a baby. Well—I want to go home too."

Several moments ticked off before I could command my voice. I tried for a gentle reasoning tone, but the enormity of Maud's misconception defeated me. I was appalled at the croaking voice that emerged. "Don't you realize that it was the *marriage*—not the baby—that earned Laura's release? Jimmie married Laura to give her a respectable standing and the baby a legitimate name. Did you expect the old man to do that for you?"

Maud mulled over the new thought. "No'm. I guess not," she admitted at last. "I thought it was so she could go take care of the baby." No trace of insolence remained and she sat before me as heavily, as desolately as a worn-out old woman.

I watched the transformation, aghast at her ignorance, horrified now by her hopelessness. Much as I pitied her, however, I knew that a lesson pounded home at this moment would make an everlasting, if painful, impression.

"Can't you see that you gave up your self-respect—your decency—for the price of a couple of candy bars?"

"Yes'm. I see now," Maud's eyes avoided mine.

The reward for that night was a half-dollar and a venereal disease requiring a long course of expensive medication. Our runaways rarely starved or suffered, but a terrifyingly large percentage picked up syphilis or gonorrhea before we could find them. The highways surrounding the school seemed to swarm with drivers who enjoyed their unexpected—and uninhibited—young company.

Maud's experience caused me to stress the advantages of marriage and the sanctity of the wedding vow even more strongly. Few of the girls were stable enough to plan far into their futures insofar as children were concerned, but almost everyone was self-centered and shrewd enough to recognize the advantages of a legal claim on a bone fide bread winner.

Many of our girls appeared to be utterly blank on subjects most of us regard as basic and fundamental. The shock was fresh and new each time I discovered that one of our youngsters had no reverence for God, no regard for honesty, and no concept of chastity for any reason at all. Finding leprosy among the inmates would have repelled me less than seeing them deliberately prostitute whatever sacred impulses they *did* have.

Cynthia's approach was as greedy and fraudulent as any I'd ever seen. "Cyn" (and was ever a contraction so apt!) was much more subtle and much less honest than Maud. And Cyn had so much more to work with. Her pretty little figure was that of a professional dancer and all her mannerisms had been planned with a male audience in mind.

Cyn had often entertained—quite legitimately—at a military encampment near her home. After the performances, however, she offered a more intimate type of entertainment which prompted the M.P.'s to pick her up. In due course, she was passed along to us. Cyn showed no resentment but turned her charm on us, danced beautifully on all our programs, and made herself a general favorite.

In view of her activities, I was astonished to learn that Cynthia was a married woman and seemingly devoted to her soldier husband. She spoke of him affectionately and asked if I would help her conceal the fact that she was in a correctional school. He was, she said, at a post far enough away so that he wouldn't find out for himself. After checking her story, I agreed to let her use our post-office box number instead of the school address in order to spare him any embarrassment.

During the days before Cynthia's commitment, while she had been an involuntary guest at the county jail, her personal mail had piled up at her rooming house. A great stack of it was forwarded to us in one bundle. Although it went against my grain, I had to see to it that all mail was censored. Left to themselves, the girls invariably went to unwholesome love affairs, tales of family sordidness, and plots for escape.

Cyn had aroused my interest to such an extent that I decided to censor her letters myself. All her communiqués were from the military, I noticed. Several soldiers had written of their intention to send money; two of them had included money orders. The forty-eight dollars from a Pfc were accompanied by a letter which read, "Inclosed find the money order for your ticket and expenses. Come as soon as you can. We'll get married the minute you arrive. I can't hardly wait to hold you in my arms again."

I shook eighty-five dollars and a snap shot of a fine-looking young top sergeant out of another envelope. Apparently he was an educated man with a well-developed sense of ethics. He wrote:

> "Dearest Girl:
> I am enclosing the money order for your fare. My aunt and her two daughters live here and they are anxious for you to be their house guest while we arrange for the ceremony. They want our wedding to be in their home. I hope that will please you. I shall wait to choose an apartment for us until you get here. Won't it be wonderful to have a home of our own—just you and me? Hurry! I love you so much.
> Tom"

Cynthia's monthly allotment check from her husband was in the same mail along with a letter from him, addressed to "The sweetest, most adorable wife in the whole world!" I thought the worst was over—but the next note was addressed to "My darling wife" too. She was already a bigamist—and still promising to marry every G.I. she thought due to be transferred. Naturally they were expected to send her the fare with which to follow them. When the money orders arrived, she would cash them and promptly forget about the love-sick swains. She'd carried off this pleasant little scheme with the quiet efficiency of an IBM machine for almost a year.

Money continued to arrive with every mail, and I returned it all with as kind a note of explanation as I could write. The sergeant was the only one who ever replied and thanked me. It was hard to tell which hurt him more, the humiliation of telling his lovingly cooperative family the truth, or the blow to his pride at having been hoodwinked by a scheming little adventuress.

Although censoring the mail was necessary, reading dozens of poorly written letters was a job nobody relished. For the most part, they were filled with minute descriptions of the ruffles and tucks in Aunt Bertha's new house dress, or they told that Uncle Harry or Cousin Joe was out on parole and was going to drive the feed-store truck. And no matter how much you love cats, the tenth time you hear that Old Bet just had a new batch of kittens, you sort of lose interest.

Sometimes a letter yielded a gem like the one in which a mother wrote: "Paw's feeling kindly bad. They taken out all his teeth except the two he holds his pipe with."

I spent hours wondering just which two teeth were indispensable. I even caught myself peering into the mouths of pipe smokers with an intensity that made them squirm. Sometimes my friends must have had serious doubts about my own stability! As a matter of record, I consciously grabbed at any tiny incident which offered "comedy relief" from constant grinding responsibility.

My problem girls required dozens of different and highly specialized analytical techniques, in addition to the basic understanding and care I was equipped to give. Part of the burden belonged on expert shoulders, and I searched ardently for some psychological help. My experience with Celia resulted in a big step in that direction.

Celia was one of the younger girls—not pretty—just a little eleven-year-old. Her round face was pleasant until you saw that her blue eyes were blank windows. Her I.Q. was low enough to justify my transferring her to an institution for the mentally deficient, but her cooperative attitude encouraged me to believe that she might make better progress with children of normal mentality. Besides, she loved some of her matrons so dearly it would have been cruel to separate her from them.

The deeds which had landed Celia in a correctional school were certainly not of her own planning. There wasn't an evil impulse in her whole make-up, but neither was there mentality enough to flash a warning when evil was suggested by others.

School must have been full of heartaches for a little girl who wished so earnestly to "belong"—to be a part of the world around her. In spite of watchful officers, the other girls often managed to exclude her from their games, and Celia was just cognizant enough to be badly hurt.

The girls weren't much to blame. When they played "black man," Celia wandered into the middle of the field and forgot almost immediately which side she was on. If she were tagged and had to be "it," she stood between the two bases and smiled in amiable confusion as husky girls raced past her to safety zones.

Usually, Celia could be seen at the edge of the playground watching others romp through a game she couldn't comprehend. One day I missed seeing her in the accustomed place and quietly started a search; I knew she couldn't be far away. Sure enough, she had headed back to her home cottage which would be deserted at this time of day. Celia was too absorbed to hear me enter.

She stood in a long ray of light sharply drawn by the late afternoon sun. Her small arms dipped in and out of the golden glow, and her bluntly shod toes advanced and retreated in a pathetically awkward pattern all her own. Sometimes she leaped and reached toward something I couldn't see in step with a rhythm I couldn't catch. I watched the scene several minutes before Celia spied me and settled back on small flat heels.

"That looked like dancing, Celia. Am I right?"

"Oh, yes'm." There was a glimmer of light behind the vacant eyes. "Come and I'll show you." Celia caught my hand and drew me toward the shaft of light.

"See?" She pointed up to the sunbeam eagerly. "They dance and I dance with them."

I looked up, but my earth-bound eyes saw nothing but motes in the air. I made a mental note: "The place needs dusting."

"There they are," Celia pointed delightedly to a flurry of dust motes spiraling upward on an eddy of air. "Like fairies! I dance with them." She leaped and whirled in imitation of the swirling particles. Celia had found playmates as free and unfettered as her own soul.

The sinking sun and the returning girls put an end to the dance. "I must go now, Celia," I explained gently. "I promised to ring the supper bell for Miss Rogers tonight so she could leave early. Want to go with me?"

"Oh, yes." Celia accepted the invitation eagerly. Contentedly humming a tuneless song, she skipped along by my side until we reached the hall where the bell rope hung coiled on a peg in the wall. Celia watched as I unwound the rope and jerked it down. At the signal, cottage doors opened and double lines of girls poured out in the direction of the dining room.

"Could I do that? Do you s'pose I could?" Celia turned an imploring face up to me.

"I think so, Celia. Suppose you try." I put the rope in her hand.

Celia gave a mighty tug and shivered with delight as the bell rang out. It was more than childish pleasure at having produced a loud noise. For the first time in her life, others were responding to a summons she had given. For once she was a leader, not a follower. Her joy triggered one of my wiser ideas.

"How would you like to ring the bell every morning, Celia?" I watched the slow wonder spread over her face and spill into her eyes. "You watch your clock and when it says twenty-five minutes past seven, come over here and ring the bell. Nobody can go to breakfast until you give the signal so you mustn't be late."

"Oh, Mrs. Burnham!" She was unable to say anything more.

For the rest of her short stay with us, Celia rang the breakfast bell. Telling time was beyond her capabilities, but she memorized the placement of the hands that meant twenty-five minutes past seven. The moment the hands reached the magic numbers, she dashed out of the cottage and headed for her happy chore.

At last, Celia felt that she had become a person of importance. Now she was a necessary member of the group. The day didn't officially begin until she, Celia, gave the starting signal. Someway it didn't seem to matter any more that the other girls played games she couldn't learn. She had her own game.

Celia's was an exceptional case, but every girl committed to our school required specialized aid of some sort. Approximately fifteen hundred "needy" girls passed through during my tenure in office. Their I.Q.'s ranged from 40 to 124, and their characters and personalities covered an even wider range than that. I was supposed to span these extremes with a program of moral training, education, and recreation; and at the same time, stem interference by officious meddlers, assorted crack-pots, and obnoxious relatives.

Top psychiatrists—the best doctors in the State—came at intervals to examine our border-line cases and to decide whether or not they should be sent to mental institutions. What few taxpayers knew was that these wonderful men contributed their services free of charge. However, many of the girls who fell on the school instead of the asylum side of the line needed guidance oftener than every couple of months.

I issued an S.O.S. to the psychology department of the State University and their response was prompt and practical. Every month several of their finest staffers came to Tecumseh and worked with our most troubled inmates. Their advice was invariably wise and kind—but almost impossible to follow.

In virtually all cases they recommended more privacy for the disturbed girl and urged that she be shielded, for a time at least, from group pressures and irritations. Of course, they were right, but what could be done about it? I'd implored the lawmakers for at least one cottage with private rooms since my first month at the school.

The doctors also advocated that special personalized attention be given each problem girl. They advised me to assign a staff member, preferably one with psychological training, to each troubled inmate—and they stressed the necessity for long daily conferences. Since every professional staff member was already cutting down on sleep in order to crowd advisory service into her schedule, I was forced to ignore these injunctions. Our meager budget barely supported the physical school itself.

I admired those psychologists immensely and their exact and unequivocable diagnoses filled me with awe. But it was like sending an exotic recipe for candied rose petals to a hillbilly cook whose cupboard contains only a slab of salt pork.

To further complicate matters, the girls didn't know the rules of the game and their responses often failed to follow specifications. I worried a good deal until the day a visiting psychologist stepped off his pedestal.

After a prolonged interview with a particularly cantankerous subject, he returned to my office with a flushed face and a wild light in his eye. His fingers fumbled nervously at the simple task of lighting a cigarette.

"Well, what do you think?" I turned my eager trusting face to the great white witch doctor. "What shall we do for her?"

"What I think is strictly unofficial and off the record," he replied bitterly, "but here it is. What that girl needs is a strong arm applying a brisk paddle to the appropriate place. That might take some of the hell out of her."

Apparently the patience of a psychologist sometimes reaches the breaking point, too. Nevertheless, as I was wrestling some warped personality into a safe enclosure, those psychologists were a powerful prop to my sagging strength. It was surprising how often our conclusions coincided even though I reached mine by way of conscience, instinct, intuition, and other unscientific aids. The arrival of my doctor friends was always a welcome interlude in a weary routine. I hope they have happy memories of the excellent meals they ate with such relish. Bless their hearts, second helpings were all they ever got for their good and faithful service.

Naturally our most baffling problems cropped up when there was no psychologist on hand to consult. I wished desperately for one on the day I found a perky, red-haired fifteen-year-old stranger in my office, awaiting my return. Bold, reddish-brown eyes appraised me as I asked, "Are you here to see someone?"

"Sure am," the redhead rose to greet me. "I want to see Mrs. Burnham."

"I'm Mrs. Burnham. Please tell me what I can do for you." I supposed she had come to see a sister or a friend.

"I'm Ginger Caston and I've come to go to school here," she announced with great aplomb.

"You don't want to come to *this* school," I explained. "This is a correctional school for girls who have made mistakes."

"Sure, I know." A smile crinkled the corners of her odd eyes. "I ought to know! Billy and Tom keep telling me they're going to send me here. Just thought I'd come see what it was like. Looks okay. Guess I'll jump the gun on them and stay, now that I'm here."

"Who are Billy and Tom? What do they know about us?" I was a bit irritated by her bland self-assurance.

"Billy's my sister. Tom's her boy friend. It makes me mad because Tom's married and got three children but he runs around with Billy and she helps him bootleg." Ginger related the facts with complete candor, and for some reason I felt myself warming toward the strange child.

"Sometimes I threaten to tell on them and then they get tough with me." Ginger's fist doubled up significantly. "That's when they say they'll send me to a reform school and we usually wind up in a free-for-all. Hah! Dad gets into the act and swears he'll send me himself. But this is a swell place. Think I'd like it better than home."

"What about your mother?" I asked in dismay.

"Who? Mom? She's all right but she doesn't count. She's been paralyzed for years. Can't talk." Ginger wet a finger and re-set a stray bang. "I feel sorry for her. She looks at us and tries to say something but she can't so we just fight it out. Won't they be surprised to know I'm here? Hah!"

"But you can't stay here, Ginger," I said firmly. "Girls have to be sent by their county judges. They don't just drift in."

"How do I get a judge to send me?" Ginger was suddenly all ears, and something cautioned me to go slowly.

"Judges only send girls who are under eighteen years of age and who have committed some moral or legal offense and so are called delinquent," I recited.

"Well, that's easy." She stood up, stretched, and made ready to go. "I'm only fifteen and I'll go home and think up something bad. See you tomorrow, Mrs. B." She headed for the door.

"No, Ginger, wait. You won't like it here," I clutched at her arm in a panic. "Let me show you some of the school. Our girls work. They cook and sew and milk and garden. You've never worked."

"I think I'd like it," Ginger grinned at me mischievously. "You can't talk me out of it, so don't bother. I'm tired of sitting around all day reading murder stories and roller skating every night. I'm a swell skater. Got some prizes."

"We don't roller skate much. The walks are too rough. We've had some broken bones. You'd miss the skating. We don't permit murder stories either." I sensed that I was rapidly becoming incoherent, so I tried to clinch the matter quickly. "Besides, you'd have to obey me and all the supervisors. You wouldn't like that and you know it. Sometimes we're terribly cross."

"It wouldn't be so bad," Ginger commented airily. "I'd be your office girl. I bet you need one. I've taken a liking to you. It would be kind of fun to work for you."

I shuddered at the thought of Ginger as an office girl. Plainly, she would soon be running the office while I ran the errands. My best course was to make the place seem as undesirable to her as possible. I took her wherever the work was hardest—the laundry, the vegetable garden, the kitchen, and the barn.

As luck would have it, everyone was in bubbling good humor that day, and even the worst work looked easy. Girls chatted and laughed and the smell of fresh-baked bread followed us all over the campus. Ginger's enthusiasm mounted higher with every step.

"Thanks a lot," she said. "It's a swell place. I'll be seeing you in a day or two, soon as I can think of something wicked." With those cheery words, she started out.

I grabbed desperately at her retreating form. "Make me one promise, Ginger?" I was practically reduced to jelly by now. "Go to your county probation officer and tell her what you told me. Maybe she can think of a way to let you come."

Ginger promised and blithely started down the highway. I rushed back to the phone to call her probation officer. I told her how dismally I'd failed and that I was now depending on her to discourage Ginger.

"Leave it to me." The officer's voice was sickeningly superior. "I'll calm her down."

Two days later, a triumphant Ginger trotted gaily up the walk, followed by a baffled and apologetic probation officer.

"Don't hate me," the weary lady exclaimed as she dropped into my sofa. "I've done nothing but try to out-talk that girl ever since you phoned me, but I didn't even get to first base."

"What happened?" I had to laugh, but she was too sunk to resent it.

"I've had one continuous session with her. Can't remember talking to anyone else for two whole days. Last night a policeman caught her just as she hauled off to heave a brick through a plate-glass window."

"And then?" I prodded.

"Oh, then?" She put a hand to her aching head. "Why then he asked what was the big idea and she said she had to qualify for reform school or I wouldn't send her!"

Ginger moved in on us. She was as troublesome as a puppy and as jealous as a bridegroom. She had no pastel moods. Everything about her was vivid. She adored some of us and hated others. Either sentiment prompted her to immediate, violent demonstration. She went where she pleased and when she pleased without permission. This free-wheeling drove the supervisors frantic and the other girls were righteously resentful. Most of her excursions wound up in my office. She suggested that since she was there so much anyhow, she might as well serve as my office girl. I remembered that this had been her original intention.

"But you can't be my office girl," I refused bluntly. "I have two now and a waiting list of honor girls if there should ever be a vacancy."

"I'll be your best one," Ginger stood her ground. "I can type better than they can and you can send me on errands without being afraid I'll run off because here's where I want to be." All of us struggled, without too much success, to keep Ginger contained within the basic behavior pattern of the school.

Since she was strictly a non-conformist, I didn't worry when her table monitor reported that she wouldn't eat her meals. However, after a second report—and a look at her greenish complexion—I ordered Ginger to the hospital for a check-up. She agreed to go only if I accompanied her.

The symptoms said appendicitis and the nurse advised sending for the doctor. Ginger rebelled. She sat bolt upright on a straight chair in the hospital reception room and refused to budge. A knitted cap rode rakishly atop her rough red locks and her hands were jammed into the pockets of her plaid blazer jacket.

"I'm not going to bed and I won't let a doctor get near me," she announced. Her eyes were feverish but her lips were firmly set. I'd seen her in this mood before. I pulled every trick I knew: cajolery, anger, even bribery; nothing worked. As a last resort, I tried derision. Ginger couldn't bear to be laughed at. "Fine brave girl *you* turned out to be," I jeered. "Scared to death of a doctor—and before he lays a finger on you!"

That got to her. "I'm not scared," she blurted. "It's just that I didn't come to this school to be a bother to anybody." She twisted her feet around the legs of her chair to keep us from lifting her up bodily and putting her to bed. "I came out here to be a help. If I'd get sick, I'd just be trouble—and I'm not sick," a grimace of pain belied her words.

My patience snapped, "Ginger, you're going to have an examination. You will either cooperate by the time I count ten, or a couple of the huskiest girls in the place will peel you and put you to bed. Of course the story will be all over the school in ten minutes." To emphasize my threat, I sent out a call for two inmates whom Ginger couldn't abide. The girls arrived and stood by.

I counted ten. Ginger glared but she didn't move. I briefed the girls and bedlam broke loose. One took her feet and another caught her under the arms. She thrashed and kicked, but finally lay still, though still rigidly resistant. The nurse and I approached her purposefully. I sat on her legs and began untying her shoe laces. The nurse started to peel off the blazer from the tensed trunk.

"You win," Ginger said admiringly as she relaxed her muscles. "I didn't think you'd do it. No one ever called my bluff before."

Fortunately, it wasn't appendicitis; Ginger had "made up" to the cook and was stuffing herself at odd hours. Her stomach simply couldn't stand the strain. Her arrogance returned with her health and once again Ginger's shenanigans kept the place in an uproar. We chased and chastised and explained until we were too worn out to give the other girls a fair amount of time or attention.

Suddenly I saw that we were playing directly into her hands. She was staging the battles with great cunning to keep our attention focused on—Ginger! I couldn't decide whether her tactics stemmed from jealousy, egotism, or a hunger for love until the evening when Ginger joined me on the playground.

For more than an hour, she managed to edge between me and any other girl who approached. During the games, she insisted on standing by my side . . . picking up my handkerchief . . . tying my shoe lace . . . or otherwise serving me to the point of acute embarrassment.

After an amusing sack-race, I ran down to congratulate some of the contestants. When I returned, Ginger was nowhere in sight. I didn't give it a second thought until a frightened girl slipped up to me and whispered, "Ginger's gone to the cottage. She's inside with the door locked. She won't even let the matron in."

"Round one goes to Ginger," I told myself grimly as I hurried to the cottage. She'd found an unbeatable way to attract my entire interest. No amount of pleading would persuade her to unlock the door. Soon it would be dark, and fifty unpredictable girls would return to find their quarters bolted against them. I had to get that building open. Finally I ordered a screen cut and a glass broken.

"Oh, well, if it's that important to you, I'll save you the trouble," Ginger said condescendingly as she turned the key and swung the door open.

As I entered the cottage, my expression must have indicated extreme disapproval. Without any hesitation whatsoever, she walked over to a pair of heavy, French doors, took a dramatic stance, and slammed a fist through the thick plate glass. Blood gushed from her lacerated hand and wrist. I twisted my handkerchief tightly around her arm and rushed the stoical redhead to the hospital.

"Round two goes to Ginger, too," I admitted bitterly. Now she could count on my personal attention until she was patched up. It was too much. I had to get rid of her. I made long-distance calls and wrote air-mail letters until I located a suitable and willing relative who lived clear at the other end of the U.S.A.

Nobody could corral that lovable maverick. The relative gave up trying in a few weeks. Next, a denominational school undertook the task. Ginger liked both cousin and school, but she couldn't conform to a set schedule of any sort. Her one bright shining virtue was an unswerving loyalty. Some time after everyone had given up and she was too near eighteen for further commitment by a juvenile court, I had proof of that loyalty.

Upon learning that I was to take part in a highly controversial discussion, Ginger materialized at my office door. "I came down here to protect you, Mrs. Burnham," she said as she swaggered in. "I understand some of these boobs don't agree with you and I thought you might need me."

"Some of them don't, Ginger," I answered as calmly as I could, "but that's nothing to worry about. Everyone has a right to his personal opinion."

"No, it's not all right," Ginger's eyes flashed hotly. "Whatever you say goes. I'll be right outside the door listening. If they get tough with you or make you mad, I'll be there to mow 'em down. You can't do anything about it because you're a lady. But I'm not, see? Just let 'em try to bully you and I'll beat hell out o' them right then and there. I'll stomp 'em to death and like it!"

Nothing short of leg-irons would have kept Ginger from that door. I appointed two friends with quick reflexes to stand with her and, if necessary, restrain her. In order to keep my belligerent eavesdropper appeased, I talked so loudly and laughed so loonily that my associates exhibited concern for my "overworked state." But much to Ginger's disgust, not an angry voice was raised in that conference. I was limp with strain but proud to have won one skirmish with my favorite firebrand.

Ginger will never be a conventional success. She'll always leap from crisis to crisis like a mountain goat on a peripatetic pogo stick. She may fall from a great height and break her neck, but she'll never sink in a slough. And she'll never be bored.

17

I'VE OFTEN WONDERED WHAT KIND OF ENVIRONMENT MIGHT HAVE helped Ginger to conquer her personality problems. At eighteen she still needed a great deal of aid—and no aid was available. She had no choice but to slip back to the atmosphere and associations she had tried to escape.

In most cases, readjustment to private life proves by far the weakest point in the process of reformation. Social conformity can be explained, even enforced, in an institution, but as soon as organized support is withdrawn, a weak girl automatically bends to the strongest wind. And temptation is always a gale force.

Success depends upon the way in which a girl is accepted in the "outside" world. Well-meaning foster families often feel they've done their duty when they provide a paroled girl with meat-and-potatoes and a clean-sheet bed. They tend to forget the spiritual and emotional needs of a lonely teen-ager trying to find her way among strangers. She longs for companionship and settles for sufferance. She craves love and is offered the fringes of friendship.

Frequently a family expects a domestic slave, forgetting that the girl paid her debt to society while still in correctional school. They expect her to atone endlessly with a mop rag and a bucket of suds. In such cases the "good" life becomes synonymous with sweat—and the only escape a swift backslide to immorality.

The men of the family present one of the worst problems; males seem to regard a "reform school" graduate as fair prey. Such cases often result in the return of the girl to a correctional institution when it's the man who clearly requires discipline. In this connection, I always think of Coralee.

I'd received a telegram from officers in a western state, saying that Coralee was being sent back to Tecumseh because of gross delinquency. I found it hard to believe, but impossible to dispute—at least without Coralee's own evidence. She'd been with us three years before we recommended parole, and she'd since been out over a year. A girl who adjusts well for twelve months is generally all right from there on in. Rehabilitated in our books.

What could have happened? I wouldn't know until the deportation officer arrived, but I refreshed my memory in the meantime. Coralee's file indicated that she'd come from a fairly respectable middle-class family. One adored young aunt had blazed a scarlet trail which fascinated Coralee far more than the stodgier pathways of her parents. When she'd tried to follow in the aunt's footsteps, however, they led her quickly to correctional school.

I remembered Coralee as a slender, graceful girl with black hair and an olive complexion, set off by startlingly blue eyes. The odd combination had an arresting charm without being exactly beautiful. Her ethics were as mixed up as a three way road sign in a twister, but she had a good mind and a disconcertingly frank approach, which made reasoning with her interesting and profitable. I'd felt that she was unusually well prepared to hold her own in the world.

I waited alone in the office to receive Coralee. The officer ushered in a young lady who might have been the season's outstanding society deb. From her tiny hat to her opera pumps, she was as sleekly groomed and elegantly dressed as anyone I'd ever seen.

Our pleasure at meeting again amazed the deportation officer. She related a long story of clip joints and thefts, but Coralee made no comment. She sat with those wise blue eyes fixed on my face, noting my reaction to every incident. Finally the officer finished and took her leave.

I motioned Coralee to a chair in front of my desk. "This is like old times," I smiled. "We've ironed out lots of your problems right here, haven't we? Want to tell your side of the story now?"

"Boy, do I," Coralee sighed with relief and relaxed the tight grip she'd been keeping on herself. "It's swell to have someone who's willing to listen to me for a change.

"They said they picked me up out of a clip joint. Well—they did." Coralee clasped her hands and faced me squarely. "I worked there, all right, but I didn't roll that guy that had me arrested. Rolling the suckers wasn't my part of the work."

"What *was* your part of the work?" I wasn't up on the duties of clip joint employees.

"I was a floor hostess. We girls dressed up snazzy every night and latched onto the customers who looked like they had the most dough. Funny—some of the lousiest dressers had the biggest rolls. You get so you can kinda size them up."

"What was your job after you—latched on?" I had to ask but I didn't want to know.

"I didn't sleep with them, if that's what you're thinking." Coralee shook her head vehemently. "I got this job especially to keep out of that. No, we goofed the men along and made them buy drinks. We'd ask for stuff that packed a real wallop. The guys got what they ordered but the bartender would send us girls fruit juice or ginger ale doctored up to look like liquor."

"Didn't the men get awfully drunk?" I asked innocently.

"Sure. That was the whole idea," Coralee looked at me in frank amazement—or was it amusement? "Soon as we got them loaded, the bosses took over and started a game going. Craps, roulette, poker—anything the guys wanted. The house used to let them win a little, then they lost their shirts. And they never squawked because they didn't want anyone to know they were such suckers. Besides, they couldn't prove anything. You can't identify money."

"Did you girls take any of the money?" I steeled myself for her answer.

"No, we never touched it. We got a salary and a commission. They paid for our evening dresses, too." Her eyes brightened at the memory of pretty clothes.

"A woman shook us down as soon as we came off duty so we couldn't even hide a tip. But we got paid okay and they wouldn't have anybody but 'straight' girls because they didn't want any trouble with the cops." Coralee's eyes were serious again. "It wasn't such a bad job."

"What about the man who had you arrested?" I probed for the root of the trouble.

"Oh, him!" Coralee flipped a hand in disgust. "I spotted him for a clunk-head the minute he walked in. His old man died and left him a wad. Yachts, horses, things like that. His picture was in all the papers.

"I felt sorry for him." Coralee smiled wryly. "He was just a kid—not more than twenty-one, maybe twenty-two—trying to be a big shot. Like a jerk, I decided to help him out. The size roll he was flashing could have got him killed."

"You're only seventeen yourself, Coralee," I reminded her gently.

"Yeah, I know—but I've been around. Haven't you heard?" I saw a sly twinkle in her eye.

"Well," she continued, with the gleam gone, "I guess I looked good to him. I had on a sparkly dress—what there was of it—all gold lamé. I took him on and ordered just enough drinks to keep the bartender from wising up. The kid began to get high and I backed him off to a table near the coat room where I could put a bug in his ear without anyone hearing.

" 'Listen, baby,' I said to him," Coralee was talking rapidly, reliving the scene. " 'Get out of here, quick, or you won't have carfare. Don't you know what kind of a clip joint this is? Get out that side door and I'll cover up for you!'

" 'My hat!' the goof said. 'How'll I get my hat?'

" 'Forget your hat. Be happy you still have your wallet.'

"I shoved him out the door and grabbed another sucker quick to keep the boss from catching me by myself."

"Did the boss see you? What did you say?" I was caught up in Coralee's story.

"Did he? Wowie, he sure did! I told him the kid went to the men's room," Coralee grinned impishly. "He'd eat me raw if he knew what I pulled."

"But, Coralee, wasn't that the same fellow who turned you over to the police? I should think he'd have been grateful." By now I was completely at sea.

"That louse!" Coralee exclaimed—with feeling. "He came back the next night with a roll like he was Rockefeller. Trying to be a big wheel again. A real jerk type. So when he came over to me and ordered a couple of doubles . . ." Coralee shrugged a shoulder in eloquent contempt, ". . . I figured 'Buster, you're sure asking for it. You want to go to the cleaners?—Go!' So I gave him the smile and the full routine. The works. The big eye—footsies under the table—and enough Scotch to run out of his ears. Then I turned him over to the boss. By the time that guy got out of there, he didn't even have a cuff link left."

"They lifted three thousand bucks and all his jewelry. When he woke up he was fit to be tied. So mad he didn't care about the newspapers or anything. He called the cops, and just because he was too loaded to remember anybody but me, he put the finger on me—after me trying to save him that first night, too." No pillar of society could have been more indignant.

"Didn't you tell the police the whole story?" I was anxious to know why she hadn't even attempted a defense.

"What good would that have done?" Coralee laughed at my naïveté. "His poppa practically built that town. Sonny-boy can make or break anyone in it. Do you think they'd believe me against a deal like that?"

"Wouldn't your boss say something? He knew you didn't do it." My doodling pencil was digging harsh, angular lines into the desk blotter.

"The boss made a deal with me," Coralee explained simply. "If he got stuck, they'd fine him and close up the joint. If I stooged for him, the worst I could get would be deportation back here because I'm under age. He paid me to take the rap for him." With an air of relief, Coralee relaxed. "I didn't mind. I was tired of that rough stuff anyhow, so here I am."

She took off her hat and fluffed up her hair with carefully tended finger tips. From the depths of her purse she dug up some snap shots of herself in the night club and handed them to me. She seemed to think the story was ended, but I wanted to know more.

"How in the world did you happen to land in such a job?" I asked. The snap shots showed—and showed a lot of—a Coralee I'd never seen. She looked like a seventeen-year-old's concept of sophisticated sex. Sequins and bare skin.

She shrugged. "It's a lot more honest than some, I can tell you." Her face flushed hotter than it had in relating the last story. Something *worse*, I wondered. I'd just about decided not to press on when Coralee took the reins in her own hands.

"Can you stand to hear it, Mrs. Burnham? It's pretty rough."

"Of course I can, child," I started a fresh page of doodling. "If you lived it, I guess I can bear to hear it." I never thought I'd feel guilty for lacking background in vice.

"Well, you see, I just had to have a job." Coralee plunged right in. "But I wanted one that would pay all my expenses. I wanted to be independent. Most of the girls I knew were clerks or typists or something like that. They had to dress well to hold their jobs, but they didn't get good enough wages to keep themselves up. Either they had to live at home or get a boy friend on the side. I didn't have a home and I was off this boy friend business—but good." Her voice grew vehement on that last bit.

"Anyway," Coralee continued, "I looked around for something that would pay better. The other girls were ashamed to be maids but I figured that a well-paid maid had it all over a cheap clerk. They get room and board and uniforms on top of a salary. Sounded like a good deal to me."

"To me too," I nodded.

"Yeah, it does, doesn't it? But wait till you hear," Coralee was impatient to get on with her story. "You know, that's a terribly big town where I was and a lot of rich people live on Evergreen Heights. Their houses are like hotels and they hire a raft of maids and butlers and chauffeurs. With their kind of dough, I figured they'd pay top wages. Besides, I thought it'd be fun to live in a swank place for a change.

"Well, I went to the biggest house. I knew it belonged to an awfully important man, an investment broker, I think it was. Every day you'd see his name in the paper. He was always shelling out for charities or libraries or flying his family to Europe or something. I felt so little going up that driveway—sort of like 'here goes nothing.' "

"People like that wouldn't hire a stranger, without references, would they, Coralee?" I frowned doubtfully. "Even I wouldn't do that."

"No'm, not usually," Coralee shook her head. "But it happened that a maid had left without notice and the place was loaded with company, so the housekeeper chanced it. She grabbed me like I was a lifesaver in a storm and the last maid's uniform just fit me. I went right to work."

"Was the job as good as you'd hoped?" I snapped on the desk light against the gathering dusk. "Did it pay better than clerking?"

"I made more money but that was about all. We had to wear the goofiest uniforms. Blue shorts, white blouses, and blue pill box caps. Like car-hops. Had to work in them 'n everything. I felt like all I needed was an organ grinder and a tin cup for pennies, but I was willing to play along as long as the pay was so good. The first day another maid watched me climb into my uniform and she said, 'Take a tip from me and keep out of the boss' way. Old Pussy Foot will be on the prowl.'

"I asked her what she was talking about but she wouldn't say any more—just 'Remember, I warned you. He's a sneaky one.'

"I didn't get it at first and I went to work wondering. I was a personal maid. Waiting on the madam and two daughters and all the women visitors. They sure kept me hopping. I guess I've zipped enough zippers to go clear around the world. And I bet I could press a dress in the dark."

"That doesn't sound like a bad set-up. What went wrong?" I noticed that my doodling was much less strenuous than before.

"It would have been swell if it hadn't been for Old Pussy Foot—that old tom cat." Coralee's face flushed angrily.

"What did he do?" My pencil point went through to the blotter again.

"That old goat! The first time I saw him, he was going upstairs, I was coming down and we met on the landing. I stepped over to one side to let him pass and he cornered me. Boy, was I a dope! The oldest trick in the book! You know the bit. He puts a hand against the wall on each side of you and you're trapped. Then he starts with 'You're the new one, aren't you? Damned good looking, too.' His eyes were all watery and he had a big squashy-looking belly. Ugh! I tried to duck under his arm, polite-like. I said 'Excuse me. I've got to get busy,' but he wasn't having any of that . . . not without a little leaning and pinching first. And when he heard someone coming, he said, 'I'll be seeing you again, Baby,' and I thought, 'Not if I see you first.' I collected an awful lot of black and blue pinches. His wife knew what was going on, all right, but she couldn't do anything about it but act dumb."

My cheeks burned—with anger rather than embarrassment —and the pencil snapped between my fingers. "In his own home? With two daughters in the house? Coralee, are you sure?"

"Sure?" She stared at me disbelievingly. "That's something I *know* about, Mrs. Burnham. He was bound and determined to have me." Her eyes flamed hatred. "Always popping out of a door to grab at me or hanging around the servants' wing when he thought he could catch me there alone. It got so I was afraid to be by myself. I was jumping all the time—twisting around when I heard sounds, any kind of sounds . . ."

Her voice broke. Suddenly Coralee bent her head till it rested on her clenched fists, and her shoulders rocked in tremors of memory. I sat in helpless fury, hating that strange man who could make life so bitter for a helpless girl.

"Honey, why didn't you find another place?" I reached out

to stroke the bowed head, but the brief spasm was over and she raised eyes—defiant now—to mine.

"What was the use? This was supposed to be the best family in town. Wouldn't the others be just like it? Maybe worse. With a couple of sons around, I hear it's really rough. Anyway, I stuck it out and kept out of his way as much as I could.

"Well, one day when he was prowlier than usual, I ran to my room and slammed the door. When I tried to snap the lock, I found out someone had jammed it. I knew what that meant and I wasn't about to take on that fat old slob. I grabbed an armful of clothes and beat it out of there.

"He was turning the corner into our hall just as I hit the last step and headed for the garage. I ducked into the chauffeur's rest room, slid into a street dress, rolled my clothes into a bundle, and climbed out through a back window in about ten seconds flat. I knew then why that other maid left," Coralee wound up with weary wisdom.

"I didn't apply for any more maid jobs. I decided if a man went with the paycheck, I'd go where I could at least control the situation. That's why I took the job in that joint."

She fell silent and I couldn't have spoken if I'd tried. I didn't know there were tears in my eyes until one of them trickled saltily to my lips. I was miserable and mad, all at the same time. How many other seventeen-year-old girls, alone and desperate, were facing the same or similar problems? How could a handful of adults help, when our "best" families were involved in degradation . . . when millions of older and supposedly wiser citizens believed that girls were *born* bad?

I regained enough voice to ask, "But you didn't have any relations with men on that last job, did you?" She'd said 'no' once, but I needed re-affirmation at this point.

"No, sir. They wouldn't let anything sexy—real sexy, that is

—go on out there. They'd have fired us for it. The cops were fixed for gambling—not for hustling."

"I'm so glad you got a job like that, Coralee." Could that be *my* voice, rejoicing because my girl had worked in a clip joint? "I don't mean that, Coralee. I wouldn't want you in a place like that, either. It's not as bad . . . I mean that it's terrible—but it's better than . . ." My confusion sent her into a gale of laughter, and the tension snapped.

"But I still don't understand one thing," I resumed. "We sent you to relatives when you left Tecumseh. Your Aunt Sarah agreed to take care of you until you finished school. Why did you need a job so desperately? Did something happen to her?"

"Oh, she was a nice person, Mrs. Burnham." Coralee's mouth turned gentle. "She and Uncle Frank were both swell, but I found out I was in the way, so I left."

"How did you find that out? Did your aunt tell you so?" I lifted my head in surprise. "She gave you such a warm welcome."

"No, she never told me," Coralee shook her head thoughtfully. "One night at supper she said, 'I saw the nicest dress in the Bon Mode window today. Just my size, too.' Uncle Frank said, 'Well, why didn't you get it?' Aunt Sarah kind of sighed and said, 'Oh, Frank! You know I can't affort it—*now*.'

"She kept her eyes fixed on her plate and nobody said anything for a while. Then one day my cousin Maizie begged for one of those cap and sweater suits all the other girls were wearing. Aunt Sarah looked kind of worried and said, 'I'm afraid you can't have it, honey. Not—*now*.' Maizie started to cry. She looked at me as if she were going to say something and then jumped up and ran out of the room."

Now I thought I was beginning to dig out the roots of Coralee's trouble, but there was more to hear.

"Another day it was my cousin Ralph who wanted something." Coralee controlled her features stonily. "He kept nagging, 'But, Mom, you promised me a bike for my birthday. I don't want any old roller skates. I want a bike! You promised!' Aunt Sarah sighed and said, 'Well, son, you'll just have to be satisfied with the skates. You know I can't get you a bicycle —*now*.'

"Ralph looked at me as if he hated me. All of a sudden I realized that the 'now' tacked on to the things they couldn't have meant me. I was costing them just that little bit extra they used to have for themselves. I watched for a few days to be sure I was right, and I was. I couldn't take it. That's why I had to get out on my own.

"But they were really sweet people," Coralee defended them loyally. "They were good to me and they really didn't want to see me go. They tried to make me stay, honest! I never let them know I'd caught on to how things were. I just made them believe I'd rather work than go to school." Coralee's stricken eyes and trembling mouth proved that this hurt had gone deeper than any of the others.

There it was again—adjustment trouble. Because a well-meaning woman had said "now" too many times, a sensitive girl had almost sunk back into a way of life she hated but couldn't escape. With so little time left to spend with us, how were we going to straighten out the new warp and restore the old hope?

"Come on, Coralee." Her eyes had gone blank from emotional exhaustion. "You're all worn out. Let's put you to bed. It's the hospital, I'm afraid, until your health tests are over. But we're glad to have you back with us, and we'll work out a better placement for you next time."

Coralee smiled gratefully and gathered up her hat and gloves. We strolled across the campus, sharing an odd sense of contentment. How strange a friendship, I thought, between a mature woman, a sheltered wife and mother, and a teen-age girl who'd lived the life I only knew as legend. Perhaps we could learn from each other.

At the hospital I turned Coralee over to the nurse to be checked in. "Good night, my dear," I held out both hands and grasped hers warmly. "Thank you for telling me your story."

"Good night, Mrs. Burnham," she clung to me for a moment. "Thank you for listening. I was glad to get it off my chest and it was the truth—every word of it."

"I know, child," I answered. "I know it was the truth." And I was sincerely sure.

I needed a few minutes alone after leaving Coralee. Her story had shaken me badly, I felt a great weariness. As usual, however, trouble tracked me down.

A matron insisted that I do something about the new bedspreads; they were all eight inches too short. I persuaded her to wait until morning. A few minutes later, four girls in Meditation began to chant original and risqué rhymes in unison, with such volume that they could be heard clearly in every cottage. With the ringleader removed, they quieted down. Next, Tessie, one of our secret smokers, set her pillow afire. The smell of burning feathers still hung in the air when I remembered the mass of paper work I had to plow through before hitting my own pillow. Wearily I dragged back to the office, wondering if it would ever be possible to squeeze in an occasional rest period for a fagged Superintendent.

Still, I'd learned to be grateful for small favors. The plumbing hadn't backed up for weeks and there were no new cracks in the masonry. Best of all, Leila Wiles was off on her vacation and wouldn't be back for another—let's see—seventy-three hours.

Eventually something would have to be done about the woman, but meanwhile I was content to bask in her absence. I wondered idly about her present whereabouts—what she might be doing.

It never occurred to me that she might be forty-five miles away, at the State Capitol, busily digging the biggest pitfall to date!

18

After leaving Coralee at the hospital and signing the last letter at the office, I hurried off in the direction of my apartment. The night watchman flicked on his flashlight, and on seeing who it was, exclaimed, "Where have you been, Mrs. Burnham? That lady's been waiting for you for an hour now."

I'd completely forgotten my guest! Coralee's story must have had a narcotic effect to erase this particular person from mind. Though well into her seventies and frail, Mrs. Seaman was an extraordinarily vivid and intelligent woman, who possessed both great heart and real insight. The rare combination had endeared her to me at our very first meeting.

I made a shamefaced apology, which Mrs. Seaman waved off as unnecessary; her only comment was, "I'm glad you heard the girl out. I know it helped." Since she was leaving in the morning to live with a daughter in a distant state, we talked far into the night, storing up as much of each other as possible before parting. She was going to be busy building a completely new existence for herself, and I thought, with a real feeling of loss, that I'd never see or even hear from her after that night.

Ten days later, I was happily surprised to receive a letter postmarked from her new address. The letter itself was a very real and unexpected gift, but there was more. Fortunately, the envelope missed the wastebasket when I tossed it away. If I hadn't bent to pick it up, and felt a thickness I hadn't noticed before, her check for five hundred dollars certainly would have landed in the day's incinerator load. It was typical of Mrs. Seaman that she didn't mention the check in her letter; she merely said, "I've always wanted to help you get your library started." When I read the letter, I'd regarded this as a casual comment.

The library was merely one of the dreams of my life! In all honesty, I'd never expected that it would materialize, our budget being what it was. Now, with five hundred dollars in my hot little hand, I grew panicky. It was easy enough to select the proper titles for our very special reading audience while the project was far in the future, but now I clamored for help.

"Make way for a plutocrat," I chortled into a long-distance phone. My psychologist friend had volunteered to make up a sound reading list for six- to eighteen-year-olds. At the time, of course, he believed it was a safe promise he'd never be called on to keep. "I have five hundred dollars—yes, I said five hundred dollars—" he seemed to think I'd lost my mind or robbed a bank "—and I'm buying nothing but books, books, BOOKS!" Now he was *sure* I was insane. I convinced him that I wasn't stealing from the bread and butter department to buy my beloved books.

The psychologist, the librarian from the neighboring town of Notman, and I spent some of the happiest hours I can remember selecting a surprisingly large number of volumes. I kept saying, "But surely we've spent the five hundred dollars by now," until I found out that by some sleight of hand we were buying at a substantial discount. I didn't even bother to inquire; for the sake of my library, I was perfectly willing to be a party to all the price cuts allowed.

We received quite a few small donations, but most of them were pretty prosaic. Aside from that five-hundred-dollar windfall, which was the largest single gift ever received by the school, I remember best the pedigreed Angus bull presented to us by a member of the Lieutenant Governor's family. Since the bull was of enormous value, and had a pedigree more distinguished than most of us can boast, we thought it only fitting to receive him at the loading dock in style. Twenty of us admired his noble bearing and gasped at his tremendous proportions when he sauntered slowly down the chute with a haughty dignity befitting his high birth.

My delight was so great, I simply had to share it. One of the members of the Board of Affairs was interested in cattle, so I picked him to call.

"Guess what we have now?" I despise people who start conversations with questions, but somehow it popped out.

"If I know you—trouble," he answered gloomily. I remembered that the last time I'd called, we'd had a riot, a theft, and a runaway all in one week.

I reassured him hastily. "No, it's good news for a change. The school's just been given the most wonderful thing! Mr. Jim Arrington has just presented us with a pedigreed Angus bull from his ranch at Stillwater! An Angus bull with papers practically back to the beginning of bulldom!"

I heard an exclamation of shocked disbelief. "An Angus bull! Did you say Angus?"

"Yes—Angus. Pedigreed! He's a beautiful animal! Isn't it wonderful?" I bragged on happily. "We've just unloaded him."

"Angus!" the man's voice was sputtering like a geyser. "Listen! Don't you let him get near those Jersey cows of yours." There was more frenzied exclamation and then his voice came clear again, ". . . can't mix breeds like that! Pen him up tight until I can figure out what to do with him. Good Lord! Angus!"

Gone were my dreams of raising black-and-tan heifers that could supply us with whichever we wished, thick cream or luscious steaks. We had to send the bull away—and he was a beauty, too. I still don't understand why it is so necessary to keep the breeding strains of animals pure and undefiled when so many of our own kind are throwing away their racial heritage with both hands—with rarely ever a voice raised in warning. I'll wager that in the Southwest, live stock associations are spending more money on research than all the social agencies combined. But if human beings ever do intermingle enough to produce a hybrid race, I wonder if it will be as big a dud as the animal merger that came to a dead end in the lowly mule.

The Angus bull wasn't a total loss. A complicated four-way trade ensued which transferred our black potentate to an Angus harem. In return we received a meeker fellow of unpolluted Jersey lineage. I never could work up much enthusiasm about him.

Repercussions lingered on. I was twitted for weeks about my *gaffe*. Civic club members greeted me facetiously with, "What's the latest Angus anguish?" I'd grin and resist the temptation to retaliate because I was trying to establish as close a rapport as possible between the school and the civic leaders.

The club ladies in the towns surrounding Tecumseh never dreamed of the turmoil incidental to each of their visits. We generally prepared a program for them in which, naturally, our best girls participated. At the same time, many of our ablest employees were needed to supervise the entertainment and the refreshments. That left our least dependable girls to carry on the routine of the school under the direction of a reduced number of supervisors.

I can't count the times I sat with the ladies and pretended to enjoy a solo or sketch while straining my ears for sounds that might mean anything from a small spree to a major uprising. The guests never knew how narrowly they escaped being embroiled in a riot on several occasions.

I wasn't an apprehensive person, but there were moments when I was uncomfortably conscious of the fact that a handful of women, with no protection beyond their personal powers of persuasion, were shepherding a crowd of girls thoroughly grounded in criminal tactics and wholly without inhibitions. The girls were younger and far more able bodied than their supervisors, and they'd come from families or gangs accustomed to living by slyness and violence.

Although many of our wards progressed admirably, and most showed at least a degree of improvement, there were always a few who were beyond salvage. In view of their past records, it would have been worse than foolish to belittle their amorality and capacity for crime. Some of our inmates should properly have been behind bars. We knew it, yet we grasped at even the smallest hope of a fairly large miracle. Turning some of our hellions into human beings would require the active aid of the Lord.

We knew that every day we walked with danger. Employees of other institutions had been attacked by inmates . . . and would be attacked again. A friend of mine, a warden, had met death at the hands of a gangster whose exploits were admired by several of my own incorrigibles. Some day they might decide to emulate him. It could happen, I knew, yet somehow I wasn't really worried. I'm certainly no heroine. I die a thousand deaths in the dentist chair, and crawling things fill me with horror. I can't take credit for courage—just a lack of active apprehension. I felt, for one thing, as if I moved in an aura of—well, *protection* is the closest I can come. And even if I were mistaken about that, I found myself un-aghast at the idea of dying with my boots on. I was so deeply devoted to the job I was trying to do that Heaven seemed nearer and surer than ever before or since.

The tragedy and pathos, the fun and confusion and routine that made up our days were mercifully lightened by visitors from all over the world. People from Denmark and Canada and England and South America and even our own Mrs. Roosevelt paid us visits.

United States Senator Robert S. Kerr, at that time Governor of Oklahoma, was our guest sometimes and his genial smile brightened the spirits of both staff and girls.

On one occasion, Gov. Kerr was the principal speaker at a Christmas celebration in Shawnee where our choir of forty girls had gone to furnish the music. After the regular program, the big, handsome Governor sauntered over to the singers and asked if they knew "White Christmas." Assured that they did, he directed them and joined them in singing a number of songs. He wound up by shaking the hand of each girl and wishing her a merry Christmas.

Those singers didn't know whether they rode home in a bus or on a cloud. Each girl kept her fist doubled up until well into the next day in order to hang on to the Governor's handshake.

Sometimes a guest was unaware of furnishing us entertainment. In this group were three elegant ladies, one of whom was the wife of a very important man. She was young, attractive and supple enough to dress without stays. Her soft silk dress clung to the curves of her enchanting figure with understandable devotion.

The ladies had examined the cow barn, flattered the dairy maids on its spotlessness and turned to leave. I stepped back to latch the barnyard gate. In the adjoining lot was our prize palomino yearling colt, Victory, who nuzzled the girls and romped with them like a puppy. I was just in time to see Victory's long golden neck curving over the fence and his teeth bared for a nip at the delicately curved posterior of the distinguished lady. Dairy girls stood watching in delighted expectation but I managed to shoo Victory away in time to prevent a disaster. Secretly I was rather proud of his discriminating taste. After all, boys will be boys—even though they are only horses.

Not all of the danger that confronts the Superintendent of a semi-penal institution comes from within. Parents or associates of inmates add their quota. One serious threat from the outside came to me from the mother of a fourteen-year-old child-bride named Margie.

Margie's family barely existed on the proceeds of a tiny patch of sour soil, but they were too lazy and ignorant to look elsewhere for a living. Margie was a well-developed girl who attracted the attention of a man twice her age. His intentions were honorable. He wanted to marry the child, but her youth made it necessary for him to have the consent of her parents. They were just shrewd enough to see a chance for personal gain in consenting to such an arrangement. Apparently they negotiated an exchange with the suitor which resulted in his marriage to their daughter.

Margie showed no emotional concern but passively submitted to a wedding ceremony engineered by her parents. Shortly afterward it came to light that, at the time of the marriage, the bridegroom had turned over a sizable sum of money to the father and mother and that the down payment was to be followed by monthly installments.

The deal smacked too much of outright slave sale for the local authorities. A law suit resulted and the newspapers of the State were filled with sensational details. While the controversy raged, Margie was sent to us. I was instructed to hold on to her until a legal decision was reached or the girl turned eighteen —whichever occurred first.

Margie's husband wanted her back and her parents wanted him to have her. No girl, no income. They tried every trick in the book to make me release her. If the parents had devoted that much effort to honest work, they'd have had a substantial bank balance. Her mother even offered me a bribe of fifty dollars made up of a wad of crumpled one- and five-dollar bills. When she saw that my decision was irrevocable, she launched into a tirade that lasted as she lunged out of the office door.

About a week later, my phone rang and the voice of the judge who had committed Margie inquired anxiously: "Mrs. Burnham, are you all right?"

"Why, of course," I answered. "Who said I was sick?"

His next words swept my levity aside. "Margie's mother is on her way to your place and she has a gun," he said grimly. "She's threatening to kill you and take Margie away. She's just crazy enough to do it, too. I should have put her in a mental hospital a long time ago, but I didn't because of her younger children."

"Maybe she's just bluffing, don't you think?" No one could really want to kill *me!*

"No! She's got a gun and it's loaded. She's in dead earnest and she's gone plumb batty!" he warned. "She left town several hours ago but luckily she stopped to see some friends. She raved about what she was up to and they called me as soon as they could. I have some deputies out after her now, but she had a headstart and I don't know what route she took. Be careful!" He hung up without telling me how.

My scalp tingled uneasily as I tried to persuade myself that the whole thing was ridiculous. Me? The victim of gun play? It was just too melodramatic. Like headlines in cheap tabloids. But that was no comfort. There wouldn't be any headlines if this sort of thing didn't happen.

I jumped nervously when the long-distance phone blared

again. It was a member of the Board of Affairs, offering some cheer of his own. "The judge just told me about the crazy woman who's after you," he began, and there was no mistaking the anxiety in his voice. I went cold all over. "Lock your gate and put a watchman on guard. Don't let anyone in. We're sending a couple of police officers to stay with you until she's captured. They'll be there as soon as they can make the trip. You let them handle it now. Don't you try to do it!"

Me try? They either overestimated my spunk, or underestimated my sanity! There was a hollow where my stomach used to be and my head floated queerly as I went about getting the gate locked, the watchman on guard, and everyone else on the look-out. I was later told that I appeared quite calm and unflurried. I wouldn't know. Absolutely the only thing I remember is Miss Lulu's gasp of horror when I asked facetiously if she would witness my will. I guess maybe it wasn't very funny. It seems that I acted quite normal for the forty-five minutes it took two big policemen, reassuring in blue uniforms and brass buttons, to appear on the scene. That's when the world began to make itself felt for me again—like coming out of anesthesia. Their presence was supposed to be comforting, and I appreciated the trouble the State was taking to insure my safety . . . but somehow they gave a substance to the danger it hadn't had before.

Margie's mother wasn't located for two days. Her route had been chosen with a cunning that baffled saner minds. In checking back, we learned that she'd stopped at a number of places along the way to whip up new fury within herself by reciting her grievances.

The judge finally found her officially insane and sent her to a mental hospital. With the danger over, the two genial policemen went home, leaving a bad gap in our bridge games. Margie stayed at the school until she was eighteen and then decided to live with her husband. As far as I know, he never had to pay another installment.

Many of our girls had come to us with a long lurid history of prostitution, but none had either money or goods to show for their years of effort. Out of fifteen hundred inmates, I remember only two who had more than a few cents. One of them had stolen twenty-four dollars from her companion while he slept. The other had acquired forty dollars, probably by some similar sleight of hand.

Our girls never seemed to see this side of the picture. Or, if they did, they dismissed it with the comment that, "A *smart* girl can do all right." It was this conviction we had to attack and destroy. Sex was the means to an end for most of these youngsters, not an end in itself. They were dazzled by the glamorous immorality of cheap movies and third-rate fiction. The wages of sin looked pretty good. Mink coats . . . fast cars . . . swank apartments. They saw themselves glittering with jewels, lounging on leopard skins, sipping champagne. Even the skinniest, dullest mud hen of a girl visualized herself as the heroine of this "success" story.

Fifteen-year-old Nadine was typical of these deluded girls. The police had picked her up in the cheapest brothel on a long bleak street. At our first interview she sat in front of my desk, staring at me unwinkingly out of dull, sullen eyes.

Nadine's mouth was a pouting blob of purple lipstick. Long, greasy brown hair swung against sallow pock-marked skin. A sleazy, violently pink blouse barely met the top of a wrinkled cotton skirt, and soiled saddle Oxfords completed her siren's outfit.

On the desk blotter between us lay Nadine's entire fortune, seventy-nine cents. Though I knew it to be a ridiculous notion, the coins nevertheless seemed to exude an evil vapor that rose like a barrier between us; I couldn't talk through it. I scooped the money into an envelope, wrote her name on it, and tucked it in the farthest corner of a desk drawer.

Nadine watched me in stubborn silence. She hadn't even replied to my initial greeting. The thinned-out bitter features belonged to a middle-aged hopeless drab, but somewhere behind that façade was a fifteen-year-old. I had to reach in with the skill of a surgeon and separate the one from the other. But a surgeon has precision tools and can see his progress. I could only probe with words and pray they were the right ones.

I don't know what I said—and it doesn't matter. Each time the words must be different. All I remember is that she started to lose her unnatural rigidity as soon as she saw that I was sincerely interested. About an hour later, Nadine volunteered some information—blurted it out, in fact, as if she'd been hanging on to it, waiting for the proper time, the proper person.

"I've got a disease—bad. Somethin's got to be done about it."

"How do you know?" I asked. "I was told that you'd just been in that place for a week."

"There are other places," she answered succinctly. "It's been goin' on a year or so," she added.

"What started you off, Nadine?" It was the crucial question. If she answered honestly, there was some hope that we could help.

She glared at me for a moment, then subsided. But her voice was belligerent when she answered. "Don't you suppose I wanted some pretty things too?"

I nodded. "Of course. We all do."

She'd expected a lecture, but there was time for that. First I wanted her story in her own words. She hesitated again, then plunged on.

"Anyway I was crazy about that first guy. He was a swell

fellow, but he turned out to be married and had some kids. He promised to get me a diamon' ring, an' a car, too—like other folks has."

"What other folks, Nadine?" I asked as I marveled at so much gullibility.

"Them girls you see in the movies—an' the ones I read about in the newspapers. Their guys was always buyin' them fur coats an' things like that. So after Ed an' me quit—Ed was his name—I kept tryin' to find someone that'd buy them things for me." Nadine set her jaw obstinately. "I ain't goin' to stop till I get a guy like that, neither."

"Are those some of the clothes you had in mind?" I gestured toward the skimpy junk blouse.

"No'm. I got these at a second-hand store down by the depot." Her voice broke with embarrassment. Then defiance flared again as she declared, "What I want is a fur coat an' a silk dress an' some high-heel shoes. An' I'm a'goin' to get 'em. No ole 'law' cain't stop me."

"Are they any nearer for you now than they were a year ago?" I asked quietly.

She wriggled uncomfortably. "I guess nobody never bought me nothin' much."

"What about the fast car, Nadine?" I turned the knife in the wound, but it was a necessary therapeutic measure. "And the diamond ring and the fur coat? Did you ever get any of them?"

"No'm." Nadine's shamed glance pretended to inspect the chipped red polish on her broken nails.

"Were any of the other girls any luckier than you? What do they have to show for it?" I could see her bravado collapsing, exactly as a tent falls in when the supporting poles are pulled.

"Nothin', I guess." She spoke slowly as realization began to dawn. "They didn't do no better than I did."

"It doesn't seem to pay very well, does it?"

"I guess not." The purple lipstick smeared across her hand when she tried to hide her quivering mouth. "But them other girls got 'em. In the movies, I mean. Why cain't I?" It was a last desperate attempt to keep her illusion alive.

I had to be brutal, "Nadine, do you think you're very beautiful? Very brilliant? Are you a great singer? A dancer perhaps?"

The bewildered girl shook her head to my barrage of questions.

I leaned forward to emphasize what I was about to say. "Nadine, you've made a mistake. A bad mistake. Those girls won the luxuries you saw because of their brains or beauty. Prostitution is the poorest paid profession in the world."

"Prosti—what's that?" Nadine honestly didn't know.

"Prostitution means letting some man use your body for money," I explained. "A girl who does such things is called a prostitute."

"Is that what people call me?" Nadine's face tightened.

"Isn't that what you've been doing?" I countered.

"No! Oh, no!" Nadine's voice rang with anguish. "I've just been trying to get myself some pretty things. I'm not bad!"

Nadine slumped into a miserable heap. "I heard that word before—that 'prostitute'—but I didn't know what it meant. That's what Mom used to call those old girls that lived across the street from us—'dirty prostitutes.' Now I'm one." Nadine cried soundlessly, the tears welling and spilling over seemingly of their own volition. Her eyes were wide open and staring.

"But you don't have to keep on being one, Nadine." I held out my handkerchief, but she made no attempt to take it. I reached over and gently blotted the tears from her face. At my touch, she crumpled, head cradled in her hands, and wracking sobs—soundless, like her tears—tore through the thin, abused body. In a moment, her hand reached out and groped for mine. She held on, as if to a lifeline.

When she'd regained some measure of composure, many minutes later, I hardened my heart and finished the job. "You have a choice now," I told her. "You can gamble—an almost impossible gamble—for all those luxuries and take a chance on winding up a physical and mental wreck, or . . ." I rejoiced as her head shot up to hear the alternative, ". . . or you can forget the past entirely—including those fairy tales about diamonds and furs—and learn to live like a fine, decent woman."

I rested my case.

Nadine, I'm happy to say, was able to face life squarely; not all my girls had the courage to do so. Most of our inmates had been conditioned to false and degrading standards of conduct, and were suspicious of any attempts at change. We were "law," and "law" was always the enemy. The girls resented what they thought was our meddlesome interference in their private affairs and expressed that resentment by cursing, fighting, damaging property, opposing regulations, and running away.

I could understand their rebelliousness. Our standards were as confusing to them as those of the Fiji islanders would be to us. If I were suddenly set down among them and commanded to wear island costume, and conform to tribal custom, I'd run at the first chance, too . . . or start some sort of tribal riot.

That's why sometimes I felt a little numb when I realized that my job was to make *our* tribal customs look interesting enough for a bunch of wild kids to try.

Sometimes I succeeded—as with Nadine; other times I failed—as with Leta.

A good-looking young man, whom I'll call Mr. Jenkins—a member of the County Board—supplied the final chapter of Leta's story. During a business trip to a large southern city, he'd arranged to keep several appointments on the hotel mezzanine. Between callers, he busied himself with reading and reports.

He was seated in a corner, quietly studying an estimate, when an exceedingly attractive young woman swept up to him.

"Hello, Mr. Jenkins!" she cried, holding out her hand.

Our man rose to his feet—desperately trying to remember her name—and then it came to him. "Leta!" he exclaimed. "This *is* a pleasant surprise."

After the usual amenities, he asked, "And what are you doing here?"

He said her eyes opened wide, as if she didn't believe his question. "You mean you don't know?" she asked.

"Of course not. Mrs. Burnham tells me you haven't written, and she's worried."

"She needn't worry about me!" Leta remarked happily.

"You've married well, then?" Mr. Jenkins asked.

Leta laughed. "Not exactly. I'm working the big hotels," she explained airily. "If you're not busy, I'll take care of you tonight." She crinkled her laughing eyes and added, "It'll cost you, but it's worth it."

Mr. Jenkins said that his face must have fallen, for Leta went on quickly, "I've always thought you were sorta cute, Mr. Jenkins, and I'll make you a special price, but I've got a living to make. You understand my point, don't you?"

Mr. Jenkins always ended the story there. More than once I've seen his wife eye him in a speculative silence as he chuckled at the end of the tale. Somehow I failed to find it funny.

19

OUR SCHOOL CHURCH OWED A TREMENDOUS DEBT OF GRATITUDE to the Christian leaders in the community. Without their unflagging interest and aid, our religious program would have been impossible. I like to think that our girls repaid at least a part of the debt incurred; of necessity, the laymen of the churches involved learned a good deal they'd never even suspected before!

Our girls represented every denomination I've ever heard of, except the Jewish. Since I doubt that any group is *immune* to delinquency I suspect that each closely knit family "circle" straightens out its own difficulties. At any rate, no Jewish girls were enrolled at Tecumseh during my ten years, and no one remembers there having been any in a previous administration.

Many of our inmates had no particular church preference, but I encouraged them to attend different services and attempt to settle on one for themselves. Early in my term, a protestant denomination seemed to be sweeping the field. Girls joined that church as if enrollment were about to close. In almost no time, it required six cars instead of the original two to transport them to Sunday night services. Their preacher, I decided, must be a real power to inspire so much spirituality in so short a time. So far as I could see, no new convert ever missed a service. I was full of pride . . . and my fall came to pass as per promise.

Pearl—one of the original joiners—toppled me off my pleasant perch.

"I know something—" she hesitated. "You won't get mad at me if I tell you something, will you?"

I shook my head; she was no tattler.

"Well, you know those girls who go to church every Sunday night . . . ? Well, they don't care anything about the church at all. Maybe one or two," she amended, "but the rest don't."

I stared at her blankly. "Then why do they go? Why do *you* go?"

"I like it—now, anyway. But I started going the same reason they all did." She flushed painfully. "We just went at first for the ride. Then, after we got there, the ladies trusted us too much. They let us kind of scatter out, and there're lots of guys around . . . you know . . ." she finished lamely.

"I'm sure you're mistaken, Pearl." She *had* to be mistaken. Using the church for rendezvous purposes was completely beyond my comprehension.

"No'm, I'm not mistaken. I've done it myself," she declared. "And I wouldn't have said anything except that some night there's going to be a break or a riot or something. Those ladies just don't understand about us girls." Who did, I wondered wildly.

Thanks to Pearl's tip, the Sunday night excursions came to an abrupt end. Religious observances were restricted to the school grounds, and it was disconcerting to see how quickly the ardor cooled.

I prided myself on the ability to keep order within my own bailiwick—and, as usual, had to pick up that pride in little tiny pieces. This time the instruments of my downfall were two youthful pastors who came to conduct a service.

I'd heard that they'd both been dedicated to the church since early childhood, and were now acquiring ministerial experience by serving several small country churches in sequence. On meeting them, I'm sure I beamed; they'd automatically have that effect on any normal American mother. Both were scrubbed-looking, absolutely unworldly young men, straight out of the seminary and full of fervor. So good for the girls, I thought fondly.

With paper work piling up, I stayed at the office instead of attending the service. It was a still, peaceful sort of day and I expected to get a good deal done.

About an hour after the service was scheduled to begin, a teacher burst unceremoniously into my office.

"Quick!" she gasped breathlessly. "The chapel . . . something awful . . . you never *saw* . . . it's just awful . . ."

I couldn't wait for her to become coherent. Her words continued to come in spurts as we dashed down the path. "Hear them? . . . clear up here?" Sure enough, I could. It was a kind of roaring babble—punctured by excited sopranos. I went for a new speed record. As we drew nearer, I could separate more sounds. A man's voice singing a hymn . . . a girl's hysterical laugh . . . loud scuffling noises . . . groans of agony—or was it ecstasy? It didn't make sense.

"What kind of riot is this?" I flung back. The teacher was lagging a few steps behind.

"More like . . . stampede!" She put on an extra burst and caught up, panting harder than ever. "Preacher invited girls . . . mourner's bench. Give testimony . . . confess sins." I thought she'd surely choke to death. "They went . . . swarms . . . for him, each other . . . just awful!"

We were almost there. "Where were the matrons?" I demanded.

"Happened . . . too fast. Besides . . . didn't know . . . not decent . . . interrupt service." With practically her last breath she defended her co-workers. I admired her spirit of loyalty if not her good sense.

As I opened the door, a wave of sobs and groans and psalms and laughter washed over us. A Superintendent's nightmare—extended vision and stereophonic sound. I seemed to see every detail of the scene at the same time. The girls in the end pews, pawing at each other . . . matrons clutching at kids trying to squirm loose . . . one young preacher standing with closed eyes and exalted face . . . "penitents" pressing close to the other . . . holding his hand . . . clawing to touch him.

The two naïve young parsons were aglow with ardor, the joy of the Lord's work well done. Their eloquence had called forth a flood of contrition beyond their fondest expectations! Undoubtedly they already had visions of extending their evangelism to the far corners of the world. It was a shame to puncture their pure young dream, but I did it.

"STOP IT!"

The hubbub stopped as if I'd fired a shot.

"Get back to your seats!"

The two preachers looked at me aghast—but the girls gauged my temper with shrewd feverish eyes. For a long moment, the air was electric. One spark of rebellion would have exploded the whole school. Then the matrons moved in, brisk and competent again, breaking up the groups and couples, drawing the concentrated fury from me into a half-dozen less dangerous channels.

Neither of the embryo ministers had moved a muscle; some explanation was necessary to bring them out of shock, so I went up the aisle in dead thick silence.

"I beg your pardon for this intrusion," I said, "but there are reasons why each girl must remain in her own group with her own matron. You couldn't have known this, and I'm sorry to have had to interfere. Please continue."

Poor fellows! As the full implications filtered through to them, they turned as scarlet as the sins they so earnestly denounced. As a matter of fact, they were still shrimp-pink when they left—a scant five minutes later. The next minister sent by that denomination was a much more mature man. In the neighborhood of eighty, I'd say.

Incidents such as these were few and far between. Our services generally went off as decorously as any attended by the very "best" people, and I'm convinced that they helped a considerable number of our inmates toward real and lasting rehabilitation. Even the haziest conception of spiritual values gave a girl some basis on which to build character. Faith—and its companion, hope—was the best stabilizer I ever discovered.

Occasionally girls came to us devoid of any vestige of understanding. They were always harder to reach than any others . . . even the brightest of them.

Jessie had a better-than-good mentality and no more conception of right and wrong than a cat. "Right" was anything you could get away with, and in her world God was indissolubly bracketed with "damn." Jessie used curses the way other kids said "geewhiz." She was the only purely physical creature I've ever known. If she could feel something, or taste it, she believed in its existence, but I don't think she really trusted her other three senses. Someone else could eat the dinner you saw and smelled, and Jessie's ears, as far as I could tell, were purely decorative. She listened only to an inner voice urging her to "grab while the grabbing is good." That and her oaths constituted almost her entire vocabulary. Oh, she knew lots of words, but why waste them when we gave her food and clothing without requiring conversation in return? The girl gave absolutely nothing away.

Within a short time after Jessie's parole, she was institutionalized again—this time in a maternity home. It didn't ring true to me when she declared great love for the infant that subsequently appeared, and declined to have the agency offer him for adoption. The last time our paths crossed, she was displaying the biggest roll of bills she'd ever owned—seventy-five dollars—suspiciously soon after she'd "changed her mind" and placed her son with a childless couple.

A year after Jessie left us, her two younger sisters arrived at the school. Opal and Shirley were twelve and eight, respectively, and completely unlike their taciturn Jessie. I sent the smiling, friendly little girls to the hospital for their physical checks while I talked with the probation officer who'd brought them. As she unfolded the appalling story, I began to understand Jessie's passion for tangibles. Simple greed was all she'd ever seen.

Jessie had been an accomplished thief, but the younger girls evidently didn't exhibit the same talent. The parents' money hunger finally grew so acute that they sold the services of the two children to a group of itinerant showmen. I was still recoiling from the details of their sexual experiences when a note arrived, asking me to visit the hospital at once.

"I just want you to see for yourself." The tight-lipped nurse ushered me into the examination room where the two little girls were lying on tables. She peeled down the sheets, and her voice was thin and constricted when she said, "Look. I wouldn't have believed it."

Nausea gripped me at the sight, but I stood by in an effort to lend moral support. The girls cringed in terror as the nurse touched them. We calmed them enough so that her strong capable fingers—infinitely gentle now—could repair the worst of the damaged flesh. I wished desperately that I could make the whole population see this outrage so clearly they would rise up in wrath and force such despicable parents into some sort of decency and care for their young.

We were able to make better headway with Opal and Shirley than we had with Jessie. Perhaps they were more cooperative because they were younger, or they may have been grateful for the relief from their almost intolerable suffering.

The girls were released from segregation shortly before Thanksgiving. Turkey and cranberries and pumpkin pie were no more than a pleasant memory. We were about to plunge into excited preparation for Christmas. A really lovely presentation of the story of the Nativity was always a part of our Christmas program. Someone read the moving account of the manger and the star of Bethlehem, and the choir would sing appropriate anthems as the curtains parted to reveal tableaux of biblical scenes.

Clad in homemade versions of oriental splendor, starry-eyed "wise men" knelt in homage for a still, breathless moment. Engagingly girlish faces gazed in adoration . . . a gentle-faced Mary brooded tenderly over a make-believe child in a manger. What matter if this Mary was a misguided youngster? For the moment, her soul was purged of evil, humbly pure and white at the feet of the infant Jesus.

No one could have dreamed that small Shirley would give us the most memorable Christmas we'd ever known. She wasn't even in my thoughts as I sat at my desk phoning for estimates on seven Christmas trees and arranging for Santa Claus to visit us in person. An honor girl knocked at my door.

"Mrs. Burnham," excitement rang in Helen's voice like little

Christmas bells, "you know that little new girl, the one that's been sick—Shirley?"

"Yes, certainly." I set the phone down. "What about her?"

"She believes in Santa Claus—really!" Helen's eyes widened with delight. "We told her he comes here every Christmas and she can hardly wait."

"Are you sure?" It was difficult for me to believe that even a very little girl could have any illusions left after living through Shirley's experiences. "Bring her in, please. I'd like to talk to her myself."

Helen dashed away and returned in a moment with the child clinging to her hand.

"Shirley, it's almost Christmas time and I've heard that a perfectly wonderful person is coming to see us. Have you heard anything about it?"

"Oh, yes!" The little face lit up. "Santa Claus! The girls said he was coming to see us. Is he, Mrs. Burnham? Is he really?"

"He certainly is," I nodded emphatically. "Hasn't missed a single Christmas since I've been here."

Shirley's face broke into an ecstatic smile. "Will he bring me somepin' too?" She left her chair to lean on my desk and her small body wriggled with eagerness.

"I'm sure he will," I routed her last doubt. "But you'd better tell me what you want so he won't make a mistake. He might bring something for a little boy if he didn't know."

"A doll—a doll!" Shirley hugged her arms to her body in anticipation. "Big enough for me to rock! And a real dress for her!"

Shirley jumped and skipped and ran circles around Helen as they went back to the cottage while I watched through the window. "Thank God," I thought, "it still isn't too late to give that little creature a taste of childhood."

The whole school entered into the conspiracy. We bought a

big doll; and the sewing room girls made it a voluminous wardrobe of dresses, underwear, caps, and coats. The doll clothes were carefully packed away in a trunk made for them by the carpenter.

The other girls were to get their main presents on Christmas morning but as all of us wanted to watch Shirley's happiness when she received her doll, we arranged to have Santa Claus present it on Christmas Eve. After handing out the tarlatan socks full of candy and nuts from the big tree, Santa Claus picked up the doll. He shaded his eyes with his hand and peered past the wreaths of holly and down the long aisles festooned with evergreens and strings of colored lights.

"Is there a little girl in the audience named Shirley?" he called out. "I have something here that Mrs. Santa Claus and I made especially for her." Then he told the crowd confidentially, "You know, Mrs. Claus and I think she's a mighty fine little girl. Yes sir—mighty fine."

With arms outspread for balance, Shirley climbed the steps to the platform, as if she were entering Fairyland. Santa Claus handed her an enormous package, and she sat right down on the floor to unwrap it. Santa stepped out of sight behind the tree and in breathless silence every eye focused on the child.

Too transfixed for words, Shirley held the doll against her cheek with one hand while she unfolded and examined the clothes with the other. Then, utterly oblivious of watchers, she held the doll close in her hungry arms and rocked it gently as she crooned a tuneless lullaby.

There wasn't a dry eye in the house. A stifled sob reached me to prove that others were as deeply moved as I. Christmas was the right time to rediscover the fact that innocence lies in the heart of a little child.

But Christmas brought tragedy too. I never learned the

technical name for Earnestine's illness—and I never want to. She was suffering the aftereffects of an amateur operation performed many months before by the relative who should have been guarding her from the need of such surgery. Evidently she'd been internally damaged but not enough to incapacitate her immediately. She dragged around, the condition growing a little worse—a little more malignant—each day, until she collapsed one day in a crowded streetcar. She'd been given emergency treatment and committed to my care.

At first we believed we were making headway. In some manner, her true condition escaped diagnosis for a long time. When the seriousness of the disorder became obvious, we decided to send her to the City Hospital. We knew Earnestine would never come back. I think she knew it, too, but she smiled gamely as her stretcher slid into the ambulance and we stood around making lame jokes about the exciting ride she was about to have.

"Will you do something for me?" Earnestine turned hollow, shining eyes up to me.

"I certainly will," I promised as I forced myself to keep a smile in place. "Anything I'm big enough to do."

"Will you kiss me good-by?" the girlish voice was husky with longing. Her mother had long since disappeared. There was nobody to turn to but me.

My heart was suffocating me as I held Earnestine in my arms and kissed her gently. The ambulance drivers turned away and busily wiped non-existent dust from their eyes. The matrons and girls who were there to say good-by wept openly, and I wept with them.

A few days later, Earnestine had no further need for human love.

My heart was almost too full to bear. Christmas in even the finest institution must depress anyone who has known the richness and close warmth of a family holiday. I ached for each of my girls though most had no idea that anything was missing. Earnestine's death had been like a whip lash to an already bruised and battered body.

Yet, viewed as a whole, dispassionately, the year had averaged out on the profit side of the scale. More and more of our girls were making their way in the "outside" world. I had plenty of letters to prove it. During Christmas week, especially, they seemed to feel a compulsion to write "home"—and Tecumseh was the only real home many of the girls had ever known.

I'd read a few of the new pile of letters on my desk and had rejoiced over some heart-warming messages addressed to "The Best Little Mom a Girl Ever Had," and thrilled at the prospect of seeing again a girl who wrote ecstatically, "I'm coming, Mother!" Tonight I'd try to read the rest of the letters. However, in this Christmasy conglomeration, one letter looked out of place. It was a stark white legal-sized envelope, marked SPECIAL DELIVERY—and somehow ominous today. The Board of Affairs—its name was in the upper left corner—didn't convene during the holidays unless something extraordinary came up. I unfolded the single sheet which contained one terse sentence:

"Please appear before the Board at a Special Session tomorrow at 11 A.M. on a matter of extreme urgency."

Worry over that letter drove all thoughts of Christmas messages from my mind that evening, and cold apprehension gripped my heart as I walked into the conference room the next morning and saw the serious faces of the usually genial members of the Board. What was coming? Had I done something wrong? For years my whole life had been dedicated to the proper care of my girls. Surely they knew that. Then why this appalling gloom?

Tremblingly I seated myself in the chair they indicated at the end of the long table. The minutes dragged on as I waited in lonely anxiety. The three Board members at the other end of the table held a whispered conference before the Chairman cleared his throat and began.

"Mrs. Burnham, some grave charges have been made against you and it has become our unpleasant duty to investigate their truthfulness." His glance dropped to the papers on his desk. "I can inform you that these charges have been drawn up by an employee in your school, Mrs. Leila Wiles."

So that was it! The snake had struck! Leila Wiles! At her name, the whole plot burst open in my mind like a flash bomb. "Mr. Chairman," I tried to say but my tongue was too stiff for speech and my stomach was a cold, sick knot.

"We have supplied you with a copy of Mrs. Wiles' allegations," he went on. "You will find it on the table before you."

With shaking hands I opened the file but my dazed eyes refused to focus on the words until I ran an unsteady finger along the lines.

"Mrs. Burnham has repeatedly used school money to pay for personal purchases such as clothing, furnishings, and household supplies," I read. I gasped and looked up unbelievingly before going on.

". . . squandered State money to curry favor with the girls . . . luxuries for her favorites and not enough food for the others . . . cosmetics, jewelry, and gifts to bribe girls because she is incompetent and unfit to manage them otherwise . . . injustice and cruelty to the inmates . . ." were some of the dreadful things alleged.

Suddenly hot indignation burned out the clammy tension within me. I wanted to burst into vehement denial but I couldn't trust myself to speak. The sudden release of cold strain to anger had me feeling as if I'd fly into a million atoms if I so much as opened my mouth. Besides, I must maintain my dignity and my control at all costs. Maybe the Board believed these damnable lies. Maybe they were going to fire me. All right! Let them! But I'd never lose my self-respect enough to make a scene over it.

I looked up to see all three men watching me intently. I met their gaze with sternly controlled features and hoped my burning cheeks were not betraying my inner turmoil.

"Now we'll begin with the first item," the Chairman said in a dull voice. "Have you ever used school money to pay for private purchases?"

"Never in my life." My voice was a little too ringing but at least it didn't shake, and why should it when I knew I was innocent? "You may check with stores here and in Tecumseh and with my bank. You will find every purchase paid for with a check on my husband's and my joint personal account."

Painstakingly the Chairman waded through the list of accusations and listened to my answers, making occasional notes on his copy. At last he came to the end and closed the folder with an air of finality. All three men settled back in their chairs with visible relief.

"You understand, Mrs. Burnham," the Chairman began as he tapped his arched fingertips together, "when formal charges are made against any employee, it is our obligation to make a thorough investigation—for the protection of the accused as much as anything else. If my own mother had been under fire I would have had to go through the same procedure."

Suddenly he smiled at me and the whole world turned lighter.

"So—when this report came in some time ago," he continued in a friendly voice, "we checked with your bank and the stores you patronize and found everything being handled right and properly. We know your purchases are all paid for from your own funds."

"Thank you," I managed to murmur through a great warm wave of gratitude and relief.

"As for the food," he smiled broadly, "we have to approve your bills so we know you're getting plenty of it and it's of good quality. Besides, we have dropped in on you unexpectedly too often to be fooled about whether the girls are being well fed. We've checked all the accusations and find them equally false."

Suddenly the miserable ordeal was over and we were all smiling and talking at once. The Chairman flipped his folder of accusations over on the table with a contemptuous finger.

"No use giving this stuff any more consideration," he said. "As far as I am concerned it's all bunk and Mrs. Burnham is in the clear. How do you fellows feel?"

"Just like you do," they both agreed heartily.

"Okay, Mrs. Burnham, and congratulations on your poise in a difficult situation."

"Thank you—oh, thank all of you," I babbled with the poise all gone and my eyes full of happy tears.

The three men stood as I left the room and closed the door behind me. They were still standing when I reopened it to say:

"And Mrs. Wiles! What do I do about her? Give her an Oscar for performance or boil her in oil?" I laughed wryly.

"Anything you do will be satisfactory with us," they agreed.

"Then, she goes!" I declared firmly. "But fast!"

I managed to get down the elevator and out to my car without attracting any attention, but inside it my control broke. All the bewilderment and humiliation and indignation and anger and relief and final happiness that I had gone though vented themselves in a deluge of tears that would not be denied. I was limp with spent emotion by the time I reached home but I was calm and controlled enough to write a note to Leila Wiles to say, "Mrs. Wiles, your services are no longer required in this institution. Your dismissal is effective immediately."

I tried to overcome all thought of hatred or revenge in writing that note and to remember only that I was acting for the good of the school. I hope I achieved that bit of self-discipline, but I'm not too sure.

20

Even though Leila's departure restored more staff harmony than we had had for weeks, my spirits never quite regained their buoyancy. Such treachery after so many years of dedication had taken something vital from me. My energy was at a low ebb, and my naïve belief in innate goodness had tarnished around the edges. I'm inclined to think that only sheer, pure stubbornness made me stick it out as long as I did—long after common sense and the doctor said it was time to quit.

But perhaps hope and love were mixed up with the stubbornness as well. In my most pessimistic moments, I would suddenly remember some of my "worst" girls—the ones I'd been warned about—the ones whose records encompassed truly unspeakable actions. While I don't condone their sins, I still remember that when I was tired, kind hands rubbed away the kinks. When I needed a hem fixed or a button replaced, bright young eyes discovered it before I did, and nimble young fingers busied themselves with needle and thread. When some big worry showed itself behind a veneer of cheerfulness, I might find a bouquet of field flowers on my desk with an artless little note. I still have one which says, "We're trying to be awful good because we know something is bothering you pretty bad."

No, perhaps it wasn't all stubbornness after all. I think now that the few things I did—and the many that I tried to do—can be traced back almost to my own beginnings. I used to have to stop and think when people asked, as they always did, "How did you happen to take a job like that?" I'd muse over the question. Why *had* I uprooted my family, sold my comfortable home, forsaken a successful career, left my friends behind, and gone to live in a "reform school" to supervise hundreds of neglected, delinquent, or incorrigible girls?

People still ask, "What possessed you to do such a thing?" and today I can tell them without any complicated cogitation. I've backtracked all the way and found that my consuming pity for the downtrodden . . . the "wrong side of the track-ers" . . . the victims of circumstance . . . the people seemingly destined by fate to be underdogs . . . stemmed from the circumstances of my own birth.

I can't honestly claim any credit for developing a wholesome set of humane instincts; I must confess to inheriting them in my genes and chromosomes. I suppose it's natural for a girl child to think of her mother as saintly—at least during some period of her growth. I saw my mother in this guise as far back as I can remember and never altered my opinion.

Many a forlorn girl climbed back to respectability through my mother's wise counsel and sympathetic guidance. The first such misfit that I recollect clearly came to our house one night when I was about six years old.

Father sat reading the evening paper in a warm circle of light, while Mother—using just a small arc of brilliance—energetically sewed chenille fringe on satin table runners.

"Time for bed, Creighton," Mother said firmly. I was lying on my stomach on the warm floor in front of the big base burner. Firelight flickered through the isinglass panes and across the parchesi board I kept open in the hope that my brother Buddy would finish studying in time to play with me.

I was struggling slowly and reluctantly to my feet when a sudden knock startled us all.

"Now, who's that—out on a miserable night like this?" Mother exclaimed as she laid her sewing down in the circle of light. Father peered over the top of his paper as she went to the door.

"Who is it?" I heard Mother ask.

A half-frozen creature huddled against the door jamb, and I could feel the bitter wind rush in to lap up the heavy warmth.

"Would you," the bedraggled girl faltered miserably, "would you please . . . I haven't had anything to eat."

The sad, shrewd eyes must have fathomed the full depths of my mother's compassion in one glance, for the girl ventured a little further into the room. "An' could I come in—just long enough to get warm?"

"Of course," Mother smiled. "Come sit by the stove while I see what's in the cupboard."

The shivering girl crouched in her chair and held out hands, blue with cold, to the roaring warmth of the stove.

I stared at her curiously while Mother went back to the kitchen and poked the coals in the range to a brisk glow. Hot water was soon bubbling for tea, which was my mother's palliative for most physical ills; and she filled one of her best plates with generous slices of beef and a mound of scrambled eggs. The girl ate with a kind of fury. Mother watched until her pace slowed before she asked, "What shall I call you?"

"Ah—Minnie," the answer came between bites of bread. "Just—Minnie."

"Well, Minnie," Mother sliced some more homemade bread and got out a jar of the best jam, "have you a place to stay tonight?"

Minnie shook her head and Mother, seeing that I was staring with round owl eyes, said a little sternly, "Go back to your father, Creighton. Minnie and I want to have a little talk."

I turned away but I walked slowly and strained my ears trying to catch at least a snatch of the conversation in the kitchen. I couldn't put my finger on it, but Minnie was different from anyone I'd ever seen. Their words escaped me, but I knew when the voices stopped that Mother had put Minnie to bed in the little room off the kitchen. And I heard the sounds that meant she was heating a sad-iron and wrapping it in a blanket to put at Minnie's frozen feet.

"Find out anything about her?" Father looked up as Mother walked back into the sitting room, rolling down her sleeves.

"Not much," Mother shook her head. "Just another streetwalker I'm afraid. Poor thing."

Streetwalker? I pondered the strange new term. It sounded like a funny kind of work. I wanted to ask what it meant exactly but I was afraid that if I drew Mother's attention to me, she'd remember it was well past my bedtime.

"Do you think it's safe to keep her here overnight?" Father inquired with a frown.

"Why, John! I couldn't turn any living thing out into weather like this!" Mother's eyes darkened in protest. "Besides," she said almost to herself, "who knows, maybe we're entertaining an angel unawares." Then, being a practical sort of a saint, she added, "Anyway, we can lock the door between the kitchen and the rest of the house."

Father subsided. He knew when to leave the field. Mother spent several days conferring with our pastor and the city officials, and somewhere they found refuge for their wretched sparrow of a girl.

I never saw Minnie again but I did see many of her successors who came to Mother as if guided by some sort of beam she unconsciously threw into the atmosphere. Her kindnesses to these unfortunates were so much a part of our home life that I naturally expected to carry on in the same fashion. However, by the time I matured, welfare work had slipped out of the hands of private citizens into the many bureaus and agencies which have become big business today.

Supplying potatoes and milk and Bibles and baby clothes to people I never saw, via an impersonal organization, went sore against the grain. My small monetary contributions seemed a poor substitute for the sincere interest and genuine inspiration that had marked my mother's giving.

Of course, I realize that inspiration alone—without the earthy follow-up of food and a warm fire—was not enough. Nevertheless, as I looked around, I wondered why people who were individually humane and warm-hearted could, collectively, become so coldly mechanical. Perhaps "cold" is the wrong word, "impersonal" might be better. But in the shaping of human souls, I felt that emotions and instincts were of at least as much service as dollars and cents.

In my role of Superintendent of a girls' correctional school, I had the opportunity to exercise each concept to the fullest. One moment I might be sitting by the bedside of a scared eight-year-old; and the next, spouting figures like bullets in defense of my budget. I will admit that there were moments when I'd have swapped any empathy or extrasensory perception I might have for a sound, sensible series of school buildings.

Setting all spirituality aside for the moment, I remember how often the physical aspects of our rehabilitation program were hindered by plain bad planning. As examples of practical architecture, our buildings at Tecumseh may well have won prizes; they were strong and sturdy enough, I suppose. However, as proper housing for delinquent girls and as workshops for their most efficient training, they were flops.

All our buildings were low and flat roofed. Supervisors' rooms were about as spacious and inviting as cells, with just enough room for a single bed, a small dresser, a tiny table, and one spindle-shanked chair. No cooling system was provided, and privately-owned fans merely teased the languid air along by inches. Those flat roofs made each room an individual bake-oven beneath an August sun.

If possible, it was even worse for the girls. There were plenty of windows in their dormitories, but they were wide silled and close to the ground. Apparently the trusting souls who planned these inmate quarters never dreamed that delinquent or criminal girls—or even homesick ones—might take it into their heads to swing over the sills and steal off into the night.

Because the windows offered such an irresistible invitation to escape, we were forced to block them off, allowing six inches at the top and bottom for the circulation of air. Consequently, each dormitory resembled the steam room of a Turkish bath; the expanse of closed glass-window panes gathered the sun's rays greedily and the roofs pressed the heat into an almost palpable mass. During the hottest days, we unblocked the windows and threw them wide; it seemed more humane to let the girls escape than to smother them.

All buying for all State institutions was in the hands of a central Board which achieved economy through wholesale purchasing. Such a procedure must lead to a certain amount of regimentation, although the needs of the insane, the senile, the sick, the orphaned, and the delinquent are obviously not the same. I'd always felt that if even a small part of the buying could be done locally, it would allow each institutional head to improve his own operation, and—at Tecumseh at any rate—fulfill a secondary purpose as well. What an opportunity it would afford our girls to learn really useful lessons in taste, economics, and general merchandising!

While each material activity is governed by a State Coordinator, the juvenile institutions stagger along with no adequate over-all supervision of spiritual and moral instruction. I've always been of the opinion that these programs constitute the main purpose, the very soul, of a correctional school. Yet all such matters are left to the discretion of each current chief officer, whose term of service generally ends with the next election.

I had a suspicion—still active—that maybe we didn't have a Coordinator because the State couldn't decide what the juvenile institutions were actually supposed to do. Confusion exists right down the line. Is the institution a *school* for teaching misguided girls how to become worth-while citizens, or a pint-sized *penal institution* for punishing criminals? Until a clear-cut decision is reached, and a set of absolute standards evolved, individual Superintendents will continue to flounder around in an uncharted bog.

The uncertainty plays hob with both inmates and officers. Supervisors and instructors can hardly do their jobs to the best of their ability if they aren't quite sure what their jobs *are*. The girls also suffer because this situation exists; I know for a fact that many areas of employment are closed to them because of their "confinement."

If an institution for delinquents is a school, no stigma should attach to its graduates. If it's a prison, that fact should be made clear. In the latter case, the Warden—not a Superintendent—must be given adequate buildings and personnel to assure restraint. Needless to say, I do not favor the second idea set forth, but it probably would be preferable to the "neither-fish-nor-fowl" system under which I operated.

Seventy-five per cent of my girls finished their training creditably, and should have been eligible for any job within their capabilities. They weren't. I often wondered what the average taxpayer would say to that. There he was, laying out his hard-earned money to recondition these girls—make them productive members of the society in which we all must live—but he hardly ever gave them a chance. Aside from being almost immoral, it isn't even good business!

We buy remodeled homes, reconditioned cars, and restored furniture. Patients return from sick beds or mental hospitals to resume their normal places in the world. Often both people and inanimate objects are improved in the refurbishing process. In the same way, moral rehabilitation can result in wider understanding and deeper insight. It isn't intelligent to cast good "retreads" into the discard.

Rejection embitters a girl who has kept her part of the bargain. How can we expect her to trust a society which reneges on its end? What choice has she but to drift back into the bleak semi-world where we first found her? As a matter of fact, we can consider ourselves fortunate if she succeeds only in ruining herself instead of becoming an actively anti-social firebrand.

If we're to work on the theory that rehabilitation is the primary objective of an institution, I've harbored another good big gripe for a long, long while. It's unreasonable to demand both remarkable business ability and outstanding spiritual guidance from one and the same Superintendent. Each of the two activities is vitally important, but it's like asking for Bernard Baruch's brains in Marilyn Monroe's body. Even when the two skills are present in one person in equal amounts, we still have to contend with the fact that the day is only twenty-four hours long.

Along about midnight, after an eighteen-hour day, my spirit used to rebel at the dual role of business manager and guidance counselor. My spirit might safely rebel, but my body still had to trot itself over to the office for a red-eyed session under the gooseneck desk lamp. With a budget hearing scheduled for half-past nine the next morning, I'd have to shove the riots and runaways and missing knives to the back of my mind and try to memorize rates and figures. Something has to suffer—aside from the Superintendent, that is.

It was hard, too, to keep from crying out in meetings about the lack of recreational facilities. As a matter of fact, I *did* hammer on that constantly—for all the good it did us. Bad weather used to drive us nearly insane. Several hundred disturbed girls, confined in a small area with nothing much to do, can build up the explosive charge of an atom bomb.

My psychologist friend and I had dreamed longingly of a gymnasium. We also yearned to add commercial photography to our program—not just to drain off energy, of course, but as a practical part of our industrial training. While we were building castles in the air, we thought of a candy factory too, and power machines for making and marking uniforms.

We wanted more training which would teach self-supporting skills, but the cost of equipping such projects would have run our per capita expenses above the average of comparable schools. The solution was simple: merely drop less important existing departments. However, good old hidebound precedent—a formless monster—balked at the idea of discontinuing anything already established, even if it was worse than useless. Our hopes never got beyond the dream stage.

Dreams and nightmares. My ten years were full of both. My

living room windows overlooked the three-room detention cottage, you will remember. Well, for a decade I lived with the fear that a girl confined to one of the cells would somehow manage to slash her wrists, hang herself, or find some new and horrible method of self-destruction. As long as the inmates were yelling and screaming, cursing, singing ribald songs, shouting obscenities, I was comparatively unworried. That was their normal mode of expression. But when silence fell . . . when they were less boisterous and obstreperous than usual . . . that's the time I'd take a flashlight, slip into a robe, and—whatever the hour—check every corner of every cubicle.

During my ten years as Superintendent, I saw some indescribably shocking sights. In time I learned to throw up a protective shell to keep my emotions from overwhelming me. Perversion, disease, unbridled violence . . . I was usually able to absorb each single jolt and cushion my mind and heart for the next. If I'd allowed them all to build cumulatively, the resulting pyramid of sin and deceit and brutality eventually and inexorably would have crushed me. When the blows came too thick and fast, I suffered pressures that were like a foretaste of Hell. Nevertheless, I firmly believe I could have taken rape, murder, rebellion, fire, flood, and everything else in my stride for another decade if I had been able to count on some regular relaxing of the terrible strain. Even an hour a week might have been enough margin. But this job comes with no such guarantees. Crisis follows crisis . . . perhaps ten a minute, perhaps two a week. No one can say for sure that "next Thursday at 10 P.M. belongs to you, Mrs. Burnham." Suzie may decide that 10 P.M. Thursday is a perfect time to break both arms.

But as I say, even steady pressure might have been bearable for many more years. It was a sudden sharp blow on top of the constant dead weight that finally did me in.

Odors can recreate whole scenes for me. Whenever I smell

the winy scents of fall, I recall a turning point in my career. The summer heat had been terrible. Tempers grew hotter right along with the weather . . . my weariness had been growing progressively worse . . . some of my best assistants had gone on to better-paying jobs. No, I wasn't really happy. Still, it could have been worse. At least that's the line I was using on myself.

A minute later it *got* worse. Once again I heard, "Come quick," the two words that could mean anything at Tecumseh. This time they called me to the hospital where word had just been received about our Vella. Vella, our gay piano-player. Whenever I thought of her, which was often, I had to laugh. In my mental picture, she always had the kewpie doll in one hand and the spun sugar candy in the other.

She was beyond our jurisdiction now, but an acquaintance of our nurse, knowing our fondness for the girl, had phoned in the news . . . from the beginning to the bitter end.

Vella hadn't done anything more serious than drift after she left us. Her interlude of training had been too brief to make much impression on her, but it had been long enough to endear her to me. I'd been told that she was playing the piano in taverns again, but no one seemed to know exactly where, so I hadn't been able to keep in touch.

A push-over for adventure and excitement, Vella had accepted an invitation several weeks back which promised both. She was to be the jump-seat passenger on a motorcycle bound for Central and South America. I can picture her face, alight with eagerness.

Somewhere near the southern border of the United States—before she saw even one of the romantic places—the motorcycle struck a boulder. It zinged off the road and ploughed through gullies of jagged rocks and skin-peeling pebbles, finally grinding to a hideous stop with my girl underneath.

I walked out of the hospital in the kind of shocked state which sharpens rather than dulls all one's perceptions. The sky was more intensely blue than I'd ever seen it, and my head reeled with the odors of late blooming roses and evergreens drying out in the sun. As I passed by the cottage housing a group of newcomers, their strident voices blasted my ears with a stream of lewd blasphemy. My skin crawled.

I tried to be calm. I reminded myself that such abominations were usual with new inmates. They were the last frenzied expression left open to these incorrigible kids. In the past I'd been able to close my mind to the vileness, knowing it marked a phase that would pass. I couldn't ignore it today. The news of Vella's awful death had left every nerve exposed.

Suddenly I was conscious of the fact that for ten long years I had been listening to the revilings of teen-age delinquents . . . shrill voices blaspheming the Lord . . . girlish lips pouring out scalding venom. Personally, I'd been cursed, insulted, and persecuted. Once I'd been able to endure it all without flinching. Now I felt myself quivering from head to foot, inside and out. My head was pounding and my heart was breaking. Instead of the fruity perfume of fall, the odor became the scent of death. The dying year.

Something within me died too; hope, perhaps. How could this institution ever become the happy harmonious place of my dreams? There would always be girls coming in to pollute our ears and shatter our illusions. When and if their reformation was accomplished, they'd go forward and we'd be left to struggle with their successors. We'd always be in the midst of the unregenerate. A Superintendent never earned a parole.

Within two hours, my resignation lay on the desk of the Chairman of the Board. It was the first day of November, 1944, lacking just three months to make it ten years since I'd first driven through the gates of "The Land of Beginning Again."

Books by Ishi Press made into Movies

Born Innocent	ISBN 4871876136
Peyton Place	ISBN 4871876160
The Treasure of the Sierra Madre	ISBN 4871878961
A Stone for Danny Fisher	ISBN 4871876187
Waltz into Darkness	ISBN 4871876101
Suddenly Last Summer	ISBN 4871876209
Winnie-the-Pooh, the Original Version	ISBN 4871873005
Alice in Wonderland Made Simple for Kids	ISBN 0923891919
Through the Looking-Glass and What Alice Found There, Original Version	ISBN 4871873048
The Story of Doctor Dolittle, Original Version	ISBN 4871873056
Crusade in Europe by Dwight D. Eisenhower	ISBN 4871873137
The Big Player How a Team of Blackjack Players Made a Million Dollars	ISBN 4871876047
A Farewell to Arms, Jonathan Cape Edition	ISBN 4871876152
Flowers in the Attic	ISBN 4871878899
What A Widow!	ISBN 4871878945
Anthony Adverse	ISBN 4871878902
Tales of the South Pacific	ISBN 4871878988
Tobacco Road	ISBN 4871876225
The Circus of Dr. Lao	ISBN 4871876640
Marie Antoinette The Portrait of an Average Woman	ISBN 4871878554
Der Triumph des Willens	ISBN 4871879119
On The Beach	ISBN 4871876284
Phantom Lady	ISBN 4871876128
Elephant Walk	ISBN 4871876217
Ben Hur	ISBN 4871876276
Diary of Anne Frank in Dari Persian or Farsi	ISBN 4871879259

Books by Ishi Press made into Movies

Born Innocent	ISBN 4871876136
Peyton Place	ISBN 4871876160
The Treasure of the Sierra Madre	ISBN 4871878961
A Stone for Danny Fisher	ISBN 4871876187
Waltz into Darkness	ISBN 4871876101
Suddenly Last Summer	ISBN 4871876209
Winnie-the-Pooh, the Original Version	ISBN 4871873005
Alice in Wonderland Made Simple for Kids	ISBN 0923891919
Through the Looking-Glass and What Alice Found There, Original Version	ISBN 4871873048
The Story of Doctor Dolittle, Original Version	ISBN 4871873056
Crusade in Europe by Dwight D. Eisenhower	ISBN 4871873137
The Big Player How a Team of Blackjack Players Made a Million Dollars	ISBN 4871876047
A Farewell to Arms, Jonathan Cape Edition	ISBN 4871876152
Flowers in the Attic	ISBN 4871878899
What A Widow!	ISBN 4871878945
Anthony Adverse	ISBN 4871878902
Tales of the South Pacific	ISBN 4871878988
The Grapes of Wrath	ISBN 4871878996
Tobacco Road	ISBN 4871876225
The Circus of Dr. Lao	ISBN 4871876640
Marie Antoinette The Portrait of an Average Woman	ISBN 4871878554
Der Triumph des Willens	ISBN 4871879119
On The Beach	ISBN 4871876284
Phantom Lady	ISBN 4871876128
Elephant Walk	ISBN 4871876217
Ben Hur	ISBN 4871876276
Diary of Anne Frank in Dari Persian or Farsi	ISBN 4871879259

Printed in Dunstable, United Kingdom

91222511R00178